1-3-20

Cynthia,

All you need is

MORE Of YOU GOD

Love & Blessings

Jackie Dotson

Presented To:

_____

All you need is MORE OF YOU GOD

From:

_____

_____
Date

More of You
God

A Two-Year
Affirming Devotional & Journal

Jackie Dotson

Cover design by:
Elayna Spratley
Leproductionsonline.com

Cover photo by:
Abigail Keenan
@akeenster

Author's photo by:
Thomas Smith
Picturewithasmile

More of You God

Copyright © 2018 by: Jackie Dotson
Published by: God's Divine Journey, LLC
P.O Box 1572, Kennesaw, GA 30156

Godsdivinejourneyllc@gmail.com
Godsdivinejourney.com

ISBN-13: 978-1530434763
ISBN-10: 1530434769 (pbk)

Dedication

I dedicate this book to my dear precious uncle, Benny Hodnett. At 95 years of age, you are, still, a true man of God. Uncle Benny, you are my life's inspiration. A man of valor, strength, humility, faith, purity, love, honesty, integrity, and grace. Daily, you live your life, letting the light of God shine in and through you. I thank God for the favor He has given you, and for the favor He has given me, by putting you in my life. These past several years of getting closer to you and praying with you, has brought me great joy, wisdom, and knowledge. I will never forget how you spoke into my life saying, "If anybody can get it done, you will." We continue to live our lives depending solely on *More of You God*. I love you dearly.

Special Thanks

Thanks to my dear family, Karen, Rose & Cherry for supporting me, by giving me great ideas for creating *More of You God*. Special, special thanks, to my dear sister/friend/and editor, Dorothy. Dorothy, God has brought us together to do great things for His kingdom. I praise God for our unity and love. Let us all continue to strive to have *More of You God*.

Introduction

This book was inspired by God. He was speaking directly to me while I was going through a **seemingly endless storm.** **Have you ever gone through a storm like this, where it just beats you down?** During this season, I was asking God to **"Fix it,"** **"Get rid of it,"** and I was expressing to Him, I was **physically, mentally,** and **spiritually tired.** While weathering this storm, I would practice writing on my tithes and offering envelopes, what I was requesting of God. So, for years while at church, I would write things on my envelopes like, health, finances, debt free, family, Boaz, etc. However, one Sunday, the Lord spoke to me, saying, *"I hear you, dear child, but **all you need is more of me**; I am the answer to every situation in your life. I can **fix it, increase it, and change it.**"* At that exact moment, I started putting on my envelopes, **"More of You God."** God instilled in me, as I seek after Him, He would take care of me, through meeting and exceeding my needs. In His Word He says, He will give us life more abundantly (John 10:10). He instructs us to delight ourselves in Him, and He will give us the desires of our heart (Psalm 37:4-6).

One day, while reading one of my favorite 365 day devotional books, *Jesus Calling* by Sarah Young, God spoke again and said, *"**Jackie, I have a Jesus Calling inside of you, and I want you to call it, More of You God.**"* This really caught me off guard, so I replied, "Really? Are You sure this word is for me? That is a lot of work! Will I be able to accomplish it?" "OK, God, You said it and You know, I can't deny You. So, how do You want me to do this?" At that moment, God started spelling it out and pouring into me, a vision for this book.

Of course, I was obedient; so now, you are blessed with what He has requested of me, *More of You God.* God is truly amazing how and when He speaks. We just have to open up our ears and have them tuned into Him. You never know how God will reveal Himself to you. For example, my first book, *Journey to Praise "A Book of Consecration and Fasting,"* God, first gave me the contents of the book and then revealed the title. We never know what God is going to do through us; but we must be able to distinguish His voice, and make ourselves available to Him. To **hear** Him speaking in our lives, it takes working at having a **relationship** with Him daily.

It was not easy getting this book completed. I was faced with **spiritual warfare**. The enemy came forth like a hungry lion, trying to destroy me; I knew I had to keep pressing and persevering to do as God commanded of me. I heard God loud and clear; this book is definitely needed to help a lot of people through their life's journey. I even started using *More of You God,* before it was completed to help others; as well, as using it during some of my own trials and tribulations.

Prior to finishing the last two months of, *More of You God,* the enemy attacked me in every area of my life. I began to feel hopeless, hurt, and overwhelmed. It was truly a **Job experience**, like in the bible (Job). I knew the enemy was just trying to break me down, distract me, and finally, destroy me. The enemy knew I was very close to my **breakthrough** and to helping others receive their own breakthrough. Fortunately, I know, whose I am and who I am. I trust in God; so while in my storm, I used His tools (**fasting, praying, and praising**), I kept writing, and continued to hold onto His grace. As I used His tools, God spoke to me and said, *"I Got You."* On the third day after a fast, God **completely restored** what the enemy was trying to steal from me. Now, I am on my way to getting double for my trouble, blessings on top of blessings. Hallelujah! Oh, how faithful is our God! God is my help in my time of need. I know, I receive all good things from Him (James 1:17). If He did it for me, He will truly do it for you, because He is no respecter of persons (Acts 10:34).

God has a way of speaking into our lives. He used my dearest cousin and prayer partner, Cherry, who mentioned *More of You God,* reminds her of the intimate relationship David shared with God, as illustrated in the book of Psalms. Cherry's words truly blessed me, as I always wanted to have the kind of praise David had. While he was praising our God, he did not care what people thought of him. You see, God wants to remove every obstacle in your life, as the **answer** is in your **praise** unto Him. Follow David's example: He was known as a man after God's own heart (1 Samuel 13:14). Yes, God is worthy to be praised! His promises are, "Yes" and "Amen" (2 Corinthians 1:20). Thank You, Lord. I'm so grateful! Now, get into His presence and Praise Him! Praise Him! Praise Him! He is worthy to be praised! All you need is *More of You God*!

I pray this devotional is a blessing to you and it helps you, with your intimate time with God. I believe, it will help you build a one-on-one relationship with Him. Every bit of what you read is what God put on my heart. Some messages were inspired from church; others were when I was dealing with the enemy's attacks and when God was re-positioning, transforming, and renewing me. I assure You, I spent many days, meditating, praying, praising, and resting in God's presence, to write this book. God truly hears your cry every day. He wants you to build a relationship with Him and praise Him, no matter what situations you may encounter.

How to Use This Devotional

This book is written as though you are speaking directly to God. Each day *More of You God* will help you start a conversation with your Lord and Savior. Make sure you have access to a bible via phone, or hard copy. God's book is designed for you to read the message for the day, followed by pulling up and reading the scriptures associated with the message.

Also, this book is designed for a two year period, where you can take short notes, journal a few thoughts, or if you are long-winded like me, you may need a notepad to capture your thoughts. This format will allow you to compare the years, so you can confirm what God is doing in your life. Your life is about growing, maturing, living, and thriving, through Christ who strengthens you (Philippians 4:13). Remember, God owns the universe (Psalm 24:1). He has all control in your life and in this world; just trust Him (Proverbs 3:5-6).

I know, this book will help you in your walk with God, as it takes you through the bible, while increasing your knowledge in the Word. The bible is your sword. If you do not know what is in it, you will not know how to put on your armor, using your weapon. **Do you have an intimate relationship with God?** God is asking you for just a little-bit more of your time. You see, there is nothing impossible for God (Luke 1:37). Whatever is occurring, right now, in your life, positive or nega-tive, God wants to be in the **center** of it. He is requesting you, to **seek Him first,** regardless of the situation or condition (Matthew 6:33). Take time daily to submerge yourself into *More of You God*; let it min-ister to your heart and your soul. I'm praying for you to get closer to Him, stronger in His Word, and to increase your discipleship. **God is just <u>waiting</u> on you; He has <u>been here all the time</u>. He wants to en-hance your life and take you to the <u>mountain top</u>.**

January

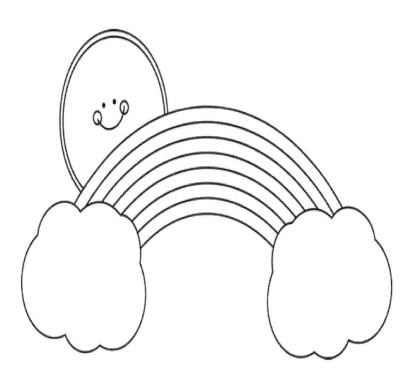

January 1

Lord, God, this year, I will be sensitive to You and Your presence. I know, Lord, I'm only here on this earth to be about My Father's work. God, I do not want to remain the same. I want to get closer to You, every year, month, day, minute, and second. My spirit says, **"Yes" to You, Father! "Yes" to Your ways, Lord! "Yes" to Your will!** I desire to have an intimate relationship with You for the rest of my life. Right now, I'm rebuking my flesh, demanding it to get out of my way. I look back over my past, letting it go, and looking forward to my fantastic future. All of my hope and trust is in You, Lord, God. I want the abundant life You have for me, Father. I'm pressing in for...More of You God.
(Exodus 33:14, Romans 8:8, Galatians 5:16, Philippians 3:13)

Year One:

_____
_____
_____
_____
_____
_____
_____
_____
_____

Year Two:

_____
_____
_____
_____
_____
_____
_____
_____
_____

January 2

Your face, Lord, Jesus, is what I'm seeking after, today. I promise to get into Your Word like never before. I will not just read Your Word; I will **meditate on it**, **speak it**, **teach it,** and **live it**. I know, as I chase after You, You'll wrap me in Your precious arms and keep me. I love to be in this secret place with You, Father. Lord, God, You are my hiding place; I have **no** fear when I'm in Your arms. Holy Spirit, You bring me comfort in all times of need. There isn't any money, fame, fortune, or a person, giving me what you have for me. Your joy is precious. Your peace is indescribable. I thank You for allowing me to experience the **benefits** You speak of in Your Word. Great is my King. I'm desiring...More of You God.
(1 Chronicles 16:11, Psalm 1:2, Psalm 91:4, Philippians 4:7, Psalm 103:2)

Year One:

_____
_____
_____
_____
_____
_____
_____
_____
_____

Year Two:

_____
_____
_____
_____
_____
_____
_____
_____
_____

January 3

I'm approaching this day with You, God; guide me, Lord. I know, You are working everything to my good, Father. I want to sit in Your presence, at Your Holy feet. I do not have time for worrying, today; I'm giving my burdens to You, God. **Even when I cannot see You, Lord, I know You are always here with me**. You tell me, *"I will never leave you or forsake you."* You see, God, I do not want to miss out on the majestic greatness, You are doing for me; Your work is breathtaking, abundant, and overflowing. Your Word says, You will give me life more abundantly; I'm standing on Your Word. Lord, let Your anointing fall down on me like a fresh, cleansing, and renewing rain. Breathe over me, Lord. Consume and overtake me with...More of You God.

(Romans 8:28, Luke 10:38-42, 2 Corinthians 9:8, Exodus 28:41)

Year One:

_____
_____
_____
_____
_____
_____
_____
_____

Year Two:

_____
_____
_____
_____
_____
_____
_____

January 4

My Father in heaven, today, is a day to focus on my temple, where You reside. Holy Spirit, You are welcome here. First, I'm examining my heart; I want to have a pure heart and be more like You, Jesus. Today, I'm preparing to get ready for Your use, Father. I will focus on **eating healthy, exercising**, and **priming my body**. Forgive me, Lord, for misusing this body (Your body) with immoral activity and foolishness. Lord, today, my speech is changing. I am **speaking life and not death**. Because, my tongue is sharper than a knife or sword, I must practice speaking endless positivity. There is life-changing power in my mouth. Right now, I will align my mouth with Your Word, in the Name of Jesus. Let Your Kingdom come down here on earth. I will tap into Your power with...More of You God.
(1 Corinthians 6:19, Psalm 139:23, Proverbs 18:21, Matthew 6:10)

Year One:

_____
_____
_____
_____
_____
_____
_____
_____
_____
_____

Year Two:

_____
_____
_____
_____
_____
_____
_____

January 5

Where You are, Lord, is Holy. God, You are, transcendent, sacred, separate, reverend, totally other, and set apart, from every created thing. Lord, today, I **set myself apart** to live for You. This world is a-gainst me, but as You hold my right hand, I know, I'm victorious. I live in this world, but I must not be of it, Father. Lord, now, impart Your wisdom into me. I want to make the right choices and decisions. With Your power, Lord, I touch and agree, on all of Your promises, You have for my life. God, only You can preserve me. **Miracles, signs,** and **wonders** are following me all the days of my life. Lord, Jesus, You take my wheel. I want to ride with...More of You God.
(Leviticus 11:44, Deuteronomy 14:2, Isaiah 41:13, Mark 16:17-18)

Year One:

_____

_____

_____

_____

_____

_____

_____

_____

Year Two:

_____

_____

_____

_____

_____

_____

_____

_____

January 6

Jesus, today, I want to go on a trip with You; this life You have planned just for me is **beautiful**. I know, You are for me. You will never leave me. Right now, Lord, not every situation in my life is looking favorably. However, You created me in Your own image; therefore, You have a plan and a purpose for me. Lord, I'm available to You. I want to ride with You, Lord. Point me in the right direction. Father, impart Your wisdom and guide me on this adventure. My journey will not be easy. There will be trials and tribulations, I will face; You will be with me; **I shall have the victory**. Victory is mine! Hallelujah, Lord, Jesus! I trust You, Lord. Living with...More of You God.
(Joshua 1:5, Genesis 1:27, Proverbs 15:22, Proverbs 2:6, Deuteronomy 31:8)

Year One:

_____
_____
_____
_____
_____
_____
_____
_____

Year Two:

_____
_____
_____
_____
_____
_____
_____

6

January 7

Jehovah God, You are with me. You know all of my heart's desires; You know what I need. I reverence You and delight myself in You, Lord. I want the life You want me to have. I love You, Jesus! Father, do a **splendid work in me**, today. Lord, You said You are going to do a **new thing** in me. This is **my season,** and I choose to serve You, God. Lord, I want You to use me to Your glory; have Your way with me, Lord, Jesus. I'm putting on Your **armor**, girding up for the **encounter and the calling**, You have on my life. There is no greater calling on my life, than to serve the purpose and plan, You have for me to accomplish. It is an honor to serve in Your Kingdom, Father. Use me, Lord, to Your Glory with...More of You God.
(Hebrews 6:17-19, 2 Corinthians 13:4, Ephesians 6: 10-18)

Year One:

_____
_____
_____
_____
_____
_____
_____
_____
_____

Year Two:

_____
_____
_____
_____
_____
_____
_____
_____

January 8

Dear Precious Savior, I have a **spirit of expectancy**. I know, Father, with You, there is **no limit** to all the great possibilities of prosperity, in my life. Today, Lord, Jesus, I feel Your presence of having **more than enough**. I have **no pain and all gain**, in my finances and my health (mentally and physically). God, I know, **nothing** is impossible for You. I accept this new season in which You have bestowed upon me. My mind and heart, are open to You, Father; I'm now **touched, delivered,** and **set free**. It is all about You, Lord, Jesus, filling my life up with... More of You God.
(Matthew 21:22, Genesis 17:1, Luke 1:37, Matthew 19:26)

Year One:

_____
_____
_____
_____
_____
_____
_____
_____
_____
_____
_____
_____

Year Two:

_____
_____
_____
_____
_____
_____
_____

January 9

Lord, all I do is for You, Jesus. Lord, all I have is Yours, Father. Today, I **sacrifice** unto You, Lord, the Almighty King. I bow down at Your throne, saying, "Holy, Holy, Holy." I give of myself to You, Lord. Right now, I block out my surroundings, **humbling** myself before You. Father, reveal Your **supernatural power** over my life. With You strengthening me, I can do all things through You, Father. You are my King, my Lord, and my Savior; there is **none** above You. Holy is the Lamb! I just want to be near You, having... More of You God.
(John 17:10, Revelation 5:12, Isaiah 45:21-22, Exodus 6:6-7, Revelation 4:8)

Year One:

_____
_____
_____
_____
_____
_____
_____
_____
_____
_____

Year Two:

_____
_____
_____
_____
_____
_____
_____
_____

January 10

Jesus...Jesus...Jesus...what a precious Name. Today, I cry out to the sweet Name of Jesus. Lord, Jesus, do a **180 turn-around** in me. Father, examine me, and let my motives reflect only the purpose and plan, You have designed. I want to be obedient to You, Holy Spirit; I know, it isn't easy, but with Your strength, Lord, I can **conquer** all things. Lord, I'm standing on the **empowerment** of Your grace, You've given me. Your grace doesn't say sin more; it empowers me to **do better** and **sin less**. Thank You, Lord, for Your grace and mercy. You are the only judge, my Mercifully Savior. I want to be where You are and do as You say with...More of You God.
(Philippians 2:9-11, Psalm 26:2, 2 Corinthians 13:5, Romans 11:6, James 4:12)

Year One:

_____
_____
_____
_____
_____
_____
_____
_____

Year Two:

_____
_____
_____
_____
_____
_____

January 11

Lord, You are the **Potter,** and I am the **clay.** Lord, Jesus, mold me into what You desire. God, I know, everything You do, You do it good. Today, I'm getting off of my **pity-potty,** saying, "Yes" to You, Lord, "Yes" to Your will, and "Yes" to Your way. Now, I see myself as You see me. I am **fearfully, wonderfully,** and **beautifully** made. From this day forward, regardless of what it looks like, I speak only **positivity** over my life and my situation. You, Lord, have the **final say**. You are working everything in my life to my good, but in Your time. I can feel Your presence; it feels good to be in this place. I have patience, Lord. I'm waiting on You, Lord. Reaching out for...More of You God. (Isaiah 64:8, 1 Timothy 4:4, Psalm 139:14, Psalm 37:7-20)

Year One:

_____
_____
_____
_____
_____
_____
_____
_____
_____

Year Two:

_____
_____
_____
_____
_____
_____
_____

January 12

God, I thank You for always being here for me. I can look to the North, South, East, and West; You are here watching over me. You dispatch Your angels, surrounding me for protection. I'm grateful, I do not have to beg You for all of Your goodness. You say in Your Word, Your **grace is sufficient** and Almighty God, "Yes" it is for sure! Lord, today, I just want to **bask** in Your presence; I feel safe here. Yes, Lord, I have time for You. I promise to make You a **priority** and not an option. You are worthy to be praised….I need You, Jesus….I want You, Lord, pressing into…More of You God.
(Psalm 145:18, 2 Corinthians 12:19, Zephaniah 1:7)

Year One:

_____
_____
_____
_____
_____
_____
_____
_____
_____
_____

Year Two:

_____
_____
_____
_____
_____
_____
_____
_____

January 13

Heavenly Father, the more I praise You, the more You reveal Yourself unto me. Lord, as I bask in Your presence, You are **stripping off** those characteristics that aren't You. Thank You, Lord, for removing depression, anxiety, bitterness, envy, poverty, selfishness, greed, laziness, and hatred. As I see more of You, I have a heart of forgiveness, love, patience, joy, peace, endurance, and perseverance. I know, through You, there is **nothing impossible** for me to accomplish. I want to go **higher** and **higher** with You, Lord, Jesus. In order to grow and change my ways, I must have...More of You God.
(Psalm 19:1-4, Galatians 5:22-23, Mark 9:23, 1 Chronicles 4:10)

Year One:

_____
_____
_____
_____
_____
_____
_____
_____
_____
_____

Year Two:

_____
_____
_____
_____
_____
_____
_____
_____
_____

January 14

Lord, I'm desperate for You. You're all I need to get me through any and every situation. People come and go, but, God, You are always with me. I **cast out** all loneliness; I know, You are always here. Holy Spirit, You are my comforter. As I follow this **unique growth track** You have planned for my life, You keep me **on track**, Lord. I thank You, Lord, for placing a cushion all around me, so when the enemy attacks me, he bounces right down to the pits of hell. Not **one** weapon can stand up against me, when I'm in Your care. I'm condemning every weapon. Jesus, You are my protector. I praise You for who You are, Lord. I just need and live for...More of You God.

(Isaiah 41:10, Isaiah 54:17, Psalm 91, John 17:12)

Year One:

_____
_____
_____
_____
_____
_____
_____
_____
_____

Year Two:

_____
_____
_____
_____
_____
_____
_____
_____
_____

January 15

Another beautiful day in which You have made, Lord; I'm going to be happy and rejoice all day. I thank You, Lord, for the **freedom** You have given me. I **refuse** to let anything or anyone come my way, attempting to hold me captive. With You, God, **I'm free indeed!** There is <u>not</u> one chain holding me down or any strongholds restraining me. I thank You, God, for sending the right people in my life, helping me get to the **destiny,** You have created. I know, I will have to encounter different tests along the way; but they are only working as a **setup** for my **victory**. I will resist the devil and seek Your face, Father. God, I will not get side-tracked with my relationship with You. I'm honored to be in Your presence. I have got to have and love on...More of You God.

(Psalm 118:24, John 8:36, James 4:7, 1 Chronicles 16:27)

Year One:

_____
_____
_____
_____
_____
_____
_____
_____

Year Two:

_____
_____
_____
_____
_____
_____
_____
_____

January 16

"Lord, where are You now, Father?" Right now, so many circumstances and situations are occurring in my life, trying to take me out. "Father, I need to know are You near?" "Are You with me, Lord?" These are questions crossing my mind. However, Lord, today, I know, You are a God, who will **allow** me to be **thrown** into the lion's den, but, the lion **will not** be able to open his mouth; as a matter of fact, You will have the **devouring lion working for my good**. Lord, I trust You with my future, because I know, the Lamb of God, **always wins**. My enemies will be used as footstools, elevating me to my next level. Hallelujah! Lord, I'm praising, rejoicing, and lifting up...More of You God.

(Matthew 28:20, Daniel 6, Luke 20:43, Acts 2:35, Psalm 110:1)

Year One:

_____
_____
_____
_____
_____
_____
_____
_____
_____

Year Two:

_____
_____
_____
_____
_____
_____
_____
_____
_____

January 17

God, the more I get to know You, the closer I get to You; my life just gets **better** and **better**. I'm experiencing a **new season**, I can only get through You. Lord, today, I thank You for the **anointing** on my life. Your **divine favor** is untouchable and impossible without You. Father, I **refuse** to be **stuck**, not moving **forward**; I'm **whole** in You, Lord. I have an **unshakeable faith**. I will stand no matter what the natural says; I'm standing on the supernatural. You have **empowered** me with the Holy Spirit and through Your blood. I know, Lord, Your glory will prevail. **I plead the blood! The Blood!** There is no one like You, Lord. I'm rejoicing and magnifying on...More of You God.
(Jeremiah 23:23-24, 1 John 2:27, Psalm 31:24, Haggai 2:20-23)

Year One:

_____
_____
_____
_____
_____
_____
_____
_____
_____

Year Two:

_____
_____
_____
_____
_____
_____
_____
_____

January 18

Dear Jesus, I need a touch from You, Lord. I have called everyone I know who I think is in my corner, and they cannot help me. The more I talk about the problem, the more I get worked up, frustrated, and disappointed. I'm starting to feel like there isn't any hope for me. I feel like I'm just a loser, and I'm losing this battle. Everything is closing in on me; I feel defeated. But, God, **the Great I Am**, is only a call away, a prayer a way; I'm **shifting** my gear to get in touch with You. Lord, You're all I need; I just start calling on the Name of Jesus, saying, **"Jesus", "Jesus", "Jesus",** and You hear me. Because You are my protector, You never fail me. I have a **shield** around me called **faith** and **salvation**. Further, I have a book called the **Bible**, the **Word** of God; it is **my weapon**. Now, I'm ready for battle; **"Yes" I will win**. Lord, Your presence is heaven on earth. I'm savoring in and thriving with...More of You God.
(Exodus 3:14, John 8:58, John 10:30-33, Psalm 34:17, Psalm 91, Ephesians 6:10-17)

Year One:

_____
_____
_____
_____
_____
_____
_____
_____

Year Two:

_____
_____
_____
_____
_____
_____
_____

January 19

Lord, You say in Your Word, in the Name of Jesus, You have equipped me to **cast out demons** and **lay hands** on the **sick**. I have family and friends, who are suffering with all types of diseases and are in great pain. I have encountered health problems myself, but I have **anointed hands**. Today, Lord, I **tap** into the **power** in which You have put **inside** of me, the **Holy Spirit**. Now, I go forth with the **authority** You have given me. I tap into my **faith** in You, Lord; I **stand** on Your Word. Today, with Your power inside of me, in the Name of Jesus, I lay hands on the sick. In the Mighty Name of Jesus, I even touch myself and speak healing over me. All who come near me with a sickness or in pain, are healed. Father, I know, Your Word **does not lie**; I'm standing on the truth and Your promises. When I get **in Your presence all things change, and I become new**. I'm reborn and restored by...More of You God.
(Mark 3:15, Micah 3:8:10, Acts 2:1-5, Numbers 23:19, Hebrew 6:18, Titus 1:2)

Year One:

_____
_____
_____
_____
_____
_____
_____
_____

Year Two:

_____
_____
_____
_____
_____
_____
_____

January 20

Jesus, my Savior, my soul says, **"Yes"** to You, today. I will continue to **press** toward the mark of the high calling. I will **not turn** back. I have come too far to retreat or give up. My victory is right around the corner; but the enemy wants me to think it is miles away. I will not be deceived; **I will press on**. I know, I'm victorious because You, Father, You're on my side. Lord, all power is in Your hands. You own everything and everybody; You even own Satan. So in the grand scheme of things, he has no power. Moreover, I was made in Your image, so I know, who I am and whose I am. I will operate with the power residing inside of me; **I will not be defeated**. I will stand **tall** and **firm**, walking hand in hand with You, Lord. **Guide** my path, take over these situations, Lord. I'm resting in You. Having great joy and Your peace surpassing all understanding with...More of You God. (Psalm 62:5, Philippians 3:14, Isaiah 62:2, Psalm 95:5, Isaiah 64:8, Job 26:13, 1 chronicles 29:12, Psalm 31:15)

Year One:

_____
_____
_____
_____
_____
_____
_____
_____

Year Two:

_____
_____
_____
_____
_____
_____
_____

January 21

God, thank You, Lord, for loving me unconditionally. Today, I feel Your love wrapped all around me; I know, it never leaves. You love me as much as You loved Your own Son. So I could be **saved,** Yes, Lord, **You gave up Your very own Son's life.** I'm precious to You; I thank You, Lord, for **never giving up** on me. Lord, there are times when I walked away from You, finding myself getting into what the world says is good and acceptable; however, You never stopped loving me. You **keep on forgiving me,** and You **never leave me.** My Precious, Precious, Savior, oh, how I love You, loving on...More of You God.
(Acts 17:11, Isaiah 54:10, Ephesians 3:16-21, John 3:16)

Year One:

_____
_____
_____
_____
_____
_____
_____
_____
_____
_____

Year Two:

_____
_____
_____
_____
_____
_____
_____
_____

January 22

A trick of the enemy comes in the form of confusion. Today, Lord, I **will not move** until I **hear from You** and get **Your approval**. In the meantime, I rebuke Satan, in the Name of Jesus. I'm pleading the blood of Jesus, over and in my life, my mind, every obstacle, and person. I know, I have a God in heaven who loves me. Today, I look **up to the hills** crying out to You, Father. I need Your help; only, You can help me, Lord. I know, You hear me, Lord. Thanks to You, I have a sound mind, and my heart is open for You to **take residence.** I give it all to You, Lord. Less of me, Lord, and....More of You God.
(Luke 21:25-26, Acts 19:32, 1 Corinthians 14:33, Psalm 121:1-8)

Year One:

_____
_____
_____
_____
_____
_____
_____
_____
_____
_____
_____

Year Two:

_____
_____
_____
_____
_____
_____
_____
_____
_____
_____

January 23

Lord, I **refuse** to live in **fear** and **anger** anymore. As of today, I have a **new revelation**. I will not hide my faults. I confess them; now, I have been **set free**. Father, I ask for forgiveness for all wrongs I have done. Through the blood of Jesus, I ask You to wash me white as snow. I know, I'm cleansed by Your Word; so, I will **work Your Word**, Lord, Jesus. There is **not a battle I cannot win** with You, God. I **SHOUT** with triumph and joy unto You, my Lord, my Savior. Joshua fought the battle of Jericho, through listening to what You directed him to do. In his obedience, he won by a shout. I know, I can **knock walls** out of my way, through obedience and shouting unto You, God. Oh, how, powerful You are, my Father. My victory is within reach through You, Father. Grabbing onto…More of You God.
(Isaiah 41:10, James 5:16, 1 John 1:9, Joshua 6:1-27, 1 Corinthians 15:57)

Year One:

_____
_____
_____
_____
_____
_____
_____
_____

Year Two:

_____
_____
_____
_____
_____
_____
_____

23

January 24

Lord, God, today, I'm holding on to You with all my strength, Lord. I'm **not giving up**; everything I have been fighting for will come to pass. I have had enough; **I will not be defeated**. I declare the Word of God, over every area of my life and my circumstances. Right now, I have an unshakable **faith** strong enough to make the **mountains move**. I will continue to open my mouth and speak, calling things into my life **as though it is so, until it is so**. I will walk in **victory**. Your presence, Lord, is so beautiful to me, Father. I have got to have and live with....More of You God.
(Psalm 89:13, Mark 11:23-24, Psalm 2:7, Job 22:28)

Year One:

_____
_____
_____
_____
_____
_____
_____
_____
_____
_____
_____

Year Two:

_____
_____
_____
_____
_____
_____
_____
_____
_____

January 25

Lord, today, I'm going to **re-evaluate** what I'm giving to You. I'm going to stop having a hard time letting go of my finances. **Everything I own is Yours; I want to be a good steward** with what You have given me. Lord, as I give my tithes (first 10%), and my offerings, I know, it is an act of faith, obedience, and a form of **worshiping You**. Lord, I want to have the kind of faith, where I'm an **extraordinary giver**. I want to have my ear and heart, open to You, so when You speak and say, "Give," I give without questioning and any hesitation. Lord, I must **sow a seed** in order to receive a **harvest**. If I do not have anything in the ground, I cannot expect to see anything grow. Lord, I give unto You with a cheerful heart, crying out for...More of You God. (Colossians 3:23, 1 Corinthians 4:2, Matthew 25:20-21, Luke 12:42-46, Proverbs 3:27, Malachi 3:8-18, Matthew 5:17-19, Leviticus 27:30, 1 Samuel 15:22, Revelation 3:18)

Year One:

_____
_____
_____
_____
_____
_____
_____
_____

Year Two:

_____
_____
_____
_____
_____
_____
_____

January 26

Oh Father, God, when I'm in Your presence, I don't want to leave. I could stay here night and day, never leaving You. I **feel strong**. I **feel powerful**. I **have peace**. I **have joy,** and I **feel love**. It's a beautiful place to be in Your presence, just trusting You, God. Today, I just **rest** in You, Lord. I release all torment and burdens. I rejoice in You, Father. I have **no worries** of work, family, health, or my finances; I lay them all down on the altar. I give it all to You, God. All You do, Father, is perfect. **Only, You can do anything and all things perfectly**. As my boat is shaken in the storm, I rest in You. Thank You, God, for giving me the opportunity to truly know You. I trust You, Lord. Leaning on-to...More of You God.
(Exodus 33:14, Psalm 16:11, Joshua 1:9, Psalm 31:20, Romans 8:28, Matthew 6:25-34)

Year One:

_____
_____
_____
_____
_____
_____
_____
_____
_____

Year Two:

_____
_____
_____
_____
_____
_____
_____
_____
_____

January 27

My strength comes from You and only You, Lord. Today, as long as I have You with me, Jesus, I can **withstand** the **fiery furnace**. When I'm released from the furnace all will see, I **will not** even have a **scorch** mark on me; nor will anyone even **smell smoke** on me. Lord, I will go telling the entire world of Your great works and of Your marvelous power. I will let all know of **Your Son, Jesus Christ, who died on the cross for all, giving us eternal life**. It is my choice to believe or not to believe. However, Father, I believe You are who You say You are. Furthermore, I believe You have done what You say You have done. I **am now a new creature in You**. I will not take Your presence for granted; living and breathing with...More of You God.
(Psalm 121:2, Isaiah 40:29, Daniel 3:14-29, Matthew 28:19-20, John 3:16, Acts 4:12, Romans 6:23)

Year One:

_____
_____
_____
_____
_____
_____
_____
_____

Year Two:

_____
_____
_____
_____
_____
_____

January 28

"**G**od, are You in my ear?" *"Can You hear Me?"* Thus, says the, Lord. Lord, today, I hear the sound of an abundance of rain. You're calling me to do Your work. I'm listening closely to get the **intricate details** for **my assignment**. Father, rain down on me with Your Holy Fire. Fill me up, Lord, so I will overflow with the love You have imparted in me. Jesus, You say You will **make room for my gift**. Lord, **open** my eyes, so I can see the gifts in which You have **bestowed** upon me. Lord, let me work on perfecting what You have given me, for the use of Your Kingdom. Father, **I'm working for the Kingdom**. There is nothing more I would rather do, than work for You, telling this **dying world of a living, Savior**. Lord, I will go in **boldness** without fear; I will do what You have called me to do. I love You, Lord. Now, Lord, empower me with...More of You God.

(John 10:27, Romans 10:17, Jeremiah 33:3, John 8:47, Isaiah 30:21, Psalm 32:8-9, James 1:17-19, Proverbs 18:16, Acts 4:31, Ephesians 6:19)

Year One:

_____
_____
_____
_____
_____
_____
_____
_____

Year Two:

_____
_____
_____
_____
_____
_____
_____

January 29

Lord, You created me to praise You. I believe my **praise** will create a **new atmosphere**. Father, today, I had enough of not having enough. I'm ready for my **transformation** into my supernatural, allowing me to flow in my **divine function**. Renew my mind, Father, God; let me understand the mighty power, You have given me. Lord, I want to have what You have promised me. I do not want to miss out on any of what You have for me. I know, my **faith**, my **prayer life,** and my **praise** unto You, is very **powerful**. Now, I'm tapping into Your tools. I'm **activating my faith**, right now. Father, I'm walking with...More of You God.

(Colossians 1:16, 1 Chronicles 16:23-31, John 4:21-24, Psalm 99, Romans 12:1-2, Ephesians 4:23)

Year One:

_____
_____
_____
_____
_____
_____
_____
_____
_____
_____

Year Two:

_____
_____
_____
_____
_____
_____
_____
_____
_____

January 30

I want to see the **manifestations** of the will of God in my life. Lord, today, I do **not** want to **be stuck** in that place called the **natural**. Father, God, I magnify Your Holy Name. Lord, I want to be more like You, Jesus. As my neighbors and friends encounter me, let the Jesus in me, light up my surroundings. Lord, I want You to get all the glory. Father, so I will be equipped to do the assignments You have appointed me to accomplish, let me **tap into the supernatural**. I will not wait for people to tell me what to do, or wait to be accepted by them. Just a **whisper** in my ear from You, God, is all I need. Great are You, Lord; my life changes. I **prosper** and **illuminate** with...More of You God. (Romans 8:19, Colossian 1:25-27, 1 Corinthians 12:7-10)

Year One:

_____
_____
_____
_____
_____
_____
_____
_____
_____
_____

Year Two:

_____
_____
_____
_____
_____
_____
_____
_____

January 31

I love You, Jesus! There is no place I would rather be, than in this place, where You Love me! Today, I'm sitting in Your presence. All I can feel is love, because, Jesus, **You are love**. This place is so cozy, warm, and inviting; I do not want to leave. I feel **freedom** in this place; I feel **joy** and **peace** here. Now, I'm feeling empowered and strong; I do not have any fear. Lord, this place is a place where I make myself **available** to You. Now, You can **create in me a new heart and mind**. Father, I thank You, because You never let me down. Many tempting problems and/or concerns, may come my way to get me off track, but I am on a **one-way highway, straight to be with, my King**. Lord, continue to keep me and guide me. My hope is in...More of You God. (Exodus 33:14, Psalm 16:11, 1 John 4:12, John 15:9, Exodus 16:10, Psalm 139:18, Matthew 28:20, Exodus 25:8, Revelation 4:1-11)

Year One:

_____
_____
_____
_____
_____
_____
_____
_____

Year Two:

_____
_____
_____
_____
_____
_____
_____
_____

February

February 1

Lord, You say, You come near me when I praise You; You **inhabit** my praise. Lord, today, I enter into praise with my hands up in the air. I shout Your name; I sing with a joyful sound, and I clap my hands unto You. God, I want to see Your glory, right here, right now. **I cannot live without You, Lord.** Father, I'm going to keep on praising You, until I enter into **worshipping** You. I want to enter into the **inner courts**; I want to get closer to You. The closer I get, Lord, I start hearing You speak to me. You're telling me how much You love me, what I can do to perfect this life, how I can start living for You, and how You will direct my path. God, **change** my ways, Lord. I want to be more like You. I'm praising, needing, and honoring...More of You God.
(Psalm 22:3, Psalm 100, Psalm 29, 1 Chronicles 16:23-31, Ezekiel 8:16, 1 John 2:6)

Year One:

_____
_____
_____
_____
_____
_____
_____
_____

Year Two:

_____
_____
_____
_____
_____
_____
_____

February 2

God, I dedicate my services to You, the Lord of Lords. Father, first, I'm going to **honor You** and then, I will **honor my family**. Today, I'm going to change the way I think, the way I speak, and the way I act. I'm going to keep seeking You; I know, my mind and ways, will be **transformed**. What I thought was fun and good in the world, I will no longer see it, as so. I will want what You **aspire** for me; then, I will see how my life is so **much more fun** and **rewarding,** to love on You, Lord. Lord, Jesus, I **celebrate** You for who You are, The Great I Am. What a **privilege** it is to know and serve You. I dedicate myself to...More of You God.
(Proverbs 3:9, Deuteronomy 6:5, Matthew 5:37, Exodus 20:12, Numbers 30:2, Philippians 4:6-7, James 4:8, Proverbs 3:5-6)

Year One:

_____
_____
_____
_____
_____
_____
_____
_____
_____
_____

Year Two:

_____
_____
_____
_____
_____
_____
_____
_____
_____

February 3

Jesus, today, I'm **releasing regret**; I forgive myself of **all** wrong doings. I **will not** hold onto what I did in the past, for I know, You have **already forgiven me**, Lord, Jesus. I'm looking at where I am standing right now and **pressing** into the **future**, You have designed, just for me, Father. Lord, You **never** do anything **ordinary**. Therefore, I'm expecting **exceptional**, **conspicuous**, and **striking** changes in my life. I'm walking into my victory, from this day forward. I refuse to be a prisoner to my past. My destiny is going to be phenomenal and extremely good with...More of You God.
(Isaiah 43:18-19, Philippians 3:13-14, 2 Corinthians 5:17, Isaiah 43:25, Galatians 2:20)

Year One:

_____
_____
_____
_____
_____
_____
_____
_____
_____
_____

Year Two:

_____
_____
_____
_____
_____
_____
_____
_____
_____
_____

35

February 4

Lord, I just want to be close to You. Today, I get into my **secret** place with You. I **surrender** all unto You, Father. I now, go into my **prayer closet** with You and only You. I will sit and **meditate** on, the Sweet Name of Jesus. Lord, I know, as I sit in Your presence, You are **breaking the chains** wanting to hold me down. They are falling off one by one. Right now, I can hear the chains hitting the floor. **Boom**! **Bing**! **Bang**! Now, the **sound of freedom** is in my **atmosphere**. This place I'm in is called, peace, love, and joy. This place only comes from You, my Savior, Lord, Jesus. Oh, how I love this place, living with...More of You God.

(James 4:8, Isaiah 55:6-7, Psalm 65:4, Psalm 145:18, Psalm 96:8, Hebrews 10:22, Matthew 6:6)

Year One:

_____
_____
_____
_____
_____
_____
_____
_____
_____
_____

Year Two:

_____
_____
_____
_____
_____
_____
_____
_____
_____

February 5

Father, God, You are all powerful! There is **nothing** You cannot do. Today, Lord, You **changed** my **sadness** into a **joyful dance**. You changed my **sorrow** into a **song** of **happiness**. Now, my **pain** is a very **powerful weapon**. I now, have a **testimony** to shout out, telling the entire world. Others will **overcome** by my testimony. I can do anything and all things with the power of my Mighty King, Jesus Christ, my Savior. **Nothing can stop me**, as long as, I walk with...More of You God. (Psalm 62:11, Job 26:14, 1 Corinthians 6:14, Job 9:4, Zephaniah 3:17, Matthew 19:26, Psalm 30:11, John 16:16-24, Philippians 4:13)

Year One:

_____
_____
_____
_____
_____
_____
_____
_____
_____
_____

Year Two:

_____
_____
_____
_____
_____
_____
_____
_____
_____
_____

February 6

Today, I **rejoice** with a triumph shout for all of my **enemies**. It is through them, Lord, Jesus, You have **built** up my **character**; I am better because of them. I wash my hands of **revenge** and **surrender** to You, Father. I know, Lord, **vengeance** is Yours. I will love my enemies and pray for them. I want to be more Like You, Jesus. I know, I will never measure up to You, Lord; I will strive to be more like You, Father. Right now, Lord, I need Your strength. I pray for...More of You God.

(Proverbs 24:17, Proverbs 25:21, James 4:7, Leviticus 26:3, Deuteronomy 23:14, Romans 12:19, Deuteronomy 32:35, Matthew 5:43-44)

Year One:

_____
_____
_____
_____
_____
_____
_____
_____
_____
_____

Year Two:

_____
_____
_____
_____
_____
_____
_____
_____
_____

February 7

Lord, I'm in awe of You, Jesus. Today, I look up to the hills, crying out to You for help. You hear my cry. You reach out to me, protecting me, **Jehovah Sabaoth**. Lord, thank You. You **devour** the **enemy** as he approaches me. **Yahweh**, is Your name. **The Great I Am**. Thank You, Lord, for shooting arrows at the enemy, stopping him in his tracks. Frightened, he turns and runs away. Lord, I give You all the honor and all the praise, for Your strength. Oh, how powerful You are, Father. I will praise You forever and ever. Rejoicing in...More of You God. (Habakkuk 3:2, Psalm 121:1-8, Psalm 34:17-20, Exodus 15:3-6, Psalm 44:5, Proverbs 26:2, Luke 10:19, Psalm 37:39)

Year One:

_____

_____

_____

_____

_____

_____

_____

_____

_____

Year Two:

_____

_____

_____

_____

_____

_____

_____

_____

_____

February 8

Father, as a child of the Most High, I know, today, **I have the victory**. Lord, defeat does not come to me, as long as I **trust** You. Dear Savior, I am Your student; teach me Your ways and Your will. Lord, I want to **live according** to Your Word, the truth. **Empower** me, Lord, to have a heart and mind, only wanting what You have for me. Lord, I thank You for Your constant love and kindness. Thank You, Lord, for Your gentle hand grabbing and leading me out of darkness, into Your **marvelous light**. Now, I'm **shining** brightly and **glowing** with...More of You God.
(Deuteronomy 20:4, John 16:33, Psalm 3:8, 1 John 5:4, Isaiah 41:13)

Year One:

_____
_____
_____
_____
_____
_____
_____
_____
_____
_____

Year Two:

_____
_____
_____
_____
_____
_____
_____
_____
_____
_____

February 9

Heavenly Father, You are my **hiding place**. Today, I get down on my knees, praying like never before. I need You, Lord; trouble is coming my way. I know, as long as I have You in the equation, it will not reach me. You, Lord, are my **safety net**. Father, You protect the **weak** from those who appear to be strong and powerful. Now, I thank You, Lord, for Your **salvation**. You hide me in Your presence. I trust You, Lord, Jesus. I love You, Lord, for who You are. I love this place, getting and resting in....More of You God.

(Psalm 32:7, Psalm 119:114, Psalm 17:8, Psalm 27:5, Psalm 31:20, Psalm 64:2)

Year One:

_____
_____
_____
_____
_____
_____
_____
_____
_____
_____

Year Two:

_____
_____
_____
_____
_____
_____
_____
_____

41

February 10

Lord, I know, when I fall, You do not let me stay down long. Instead, You **help me back up**; now, everyone sees I'm **victorious**. Today, Lord, I'm thanking You for **never abandoning** me. You say, You will not leave or forsake me. Father, I'm going to concentrate on being a better person, and doing what is good in Your **eyesight**. I will **open** up my heart. I'll start **giving** freely, working at being a **blessing** to others in need. I'm here on this earth for You. It is all about You, Jesus. Lord, I want to be a **faithful servant**, showing the world what I have inside of me…More of You God.

(Psalm 37:24, Psalm 145:14, Deuteronomy 31:8, Deuteronomy 31:6, Hebrews 13:5, Deuteronomy 6:18, Matthew 5:16, Matthew 7:12)

Year One:

_____
_____
_____
_____
_____
_____
_____
_____
_____
_____
_____

Year Two:

_____
_____
_____
_____
_____
_____
_____
_____

February 11

Hallelujah! Lord, Jesus, today, is a **new day** for me; it is my **new season**. I smell the fresh crisp, wintery air. I hear a new tranquil, soothing sound. I have **dreams** still waiting to be fulfilled. Now, I'm **stepping out** on my **faith** of a **mustard seed**. I know, my faith will carry me to the land of **Canaan**; a place where I will be free, where it is **overflowing** with **milk** and **honey**. I will be able to **see the vision** You have for me, God. Through Your divine direction, I will be able to obtain all, You have for me. I'm walking into and receiving, all of the promises You have, awaiting me. Right now, I'm reaching up unto the sky, grabbing a hold of my precious gifts. Lord, I want to be in the right place to receive all, You proclaim is mine. I thrive and mature with...More of You God.

(2 Corinthians 4:16, Ezekiel 43:2, 1 Chronicles 14:15, Job 33:15, Joel 2:28, Matthew 17:20, Luke 17:6, Leviticus 20:24, Genesis 17:8)

Year One:

_____
_____
_____
_____
_____
_____
_____

Year Two:

_____
_____
_____
_____
_____
_____
_____

February 12

Father, this year is a special year for me. Today, I see myself walking into my **unprecedented life-changing season**. What is about to happen in my life will be unparalleled, never before seen, known, or experienced! It is going to be **EPOCH (EPIC)**! It will be divine, and the whole world will see this time, being very distinctive. Notable events are about to happen, for all the glory is Yours, Lord, Jesus. **All the Glory is Yours!** All things are **possible** for me because I love You, Jesus. I believe You, Jesus. My life is going to places **unheard** of and **never seen** with…More of You God.

(Ephesians 1:19, Acts 2:1-4, Acts 19:11-12, 2 Kings 2:11, Joshua 10:13, Joshua 6:20, Acts 8:39, 1 Corinthians 10:31, John 11:40)

Year One:

_____
_____
_____
_____
_____
_____
_____
_____
_____
_____

Year Two:

_____
_____
_____
_____
_____
_____
_____
_____
_____

February 13

Favor! Favor! Favor! Is what I hear in my ear, today. Lord, Your favor is **wrapped** all around me. I'm blessed in every move and step, I take. I am keeping my eyes on the **prize** (my Heavenly Father). I know, what **seems dark** and frightening, is going to turn into a **glorious light**. You, God, are going to **turn all** things into Your **good** for me and all for those near me. Because there is no one like You, I rejoice in You, Lord, Jesus. How wonderful and beautiful You are to me. I **press** forward. **Favor chases** me with...More of You God.
(Genesis 4:4, Genesis 6:8, Genesis 39:21, Proverbs 3:4, Proverbs 8:35, Proverbs 18:22, Luke 1:30, Acts 7:46, Philippians 3:14)

Year One:

_____
_____
_____
_____
_____
_____
_____
_____
_____
_____

Year Two:

_____
_____
_____
_____
_____
_____
_____
_____
_____

February 14

Lord, my God, today, I **press** into Your grace and Your mercy. **Stir** up my heart and mind. **Convict me**, Lord, so I will take every word in the Word (the Bible), **literally**. I will use what You speak over me. I will **stand** on Your promises and Your truth. **I will not relinquish, nor turn around, or quit.** I will persevere until I get to see Your glory. I speak **life** and **not death**. My victory is in Your hands, Father. I just have to be close to You, Lord. Pressing, thriving, and persevering with...More of You God.

(Hebrews 4:16, 2 John 1:3, Romans 8:37-39, Matthew 10:16-22, Galatians 6:9, Proverbs 18:21, Proverbs 10:11)

Year One:

_____
_____
_____
_____
_____
_____
_____
_____
_____
_____

Year Two:

_____
_____
_____
_____
_____
_____
_____
_____
_____

February 15

Father, where You are is bright, beautiful, and flawless. Today, I see Your **star**; it is bright and shining boldly. Lord, I'm glad to be near and dear to You; Your **light is greater than darkness**. Father, now, I'm surrendering, letting Your star **guide** my path, each and every day. **Lead** me, Lord, Jesus, to the precious place You have, just for me. I know, You are with me on this journey called, **life**. How **privileged**, I am to walk with You, Lord. I'm thankful and glad, I have...More of You God. (Isaiah 9:2, Luke 1:79, John 1:5, 2 Corinthians 4:6, 1 Peter 2:9, Ephesians 5:8, John 8:12, Acts 26:18, Matthew 10:27)

Year One:

_____

_____

_____

_____

_____

_____

_____

_____

Year Two:

_____

_____

_____

_____

_____

_____

_____

_____

February 16

Today, Lord, God, my Father, I have a strong desire and passion to **live for You**, Father. God, make my purpose and life plan's You have for me, **very clear.** Lord, as You speak to me, let me have a **receptive** and **obedient spirit. Open my mind** to receive the appointment and assignment, You've placed before me. I know, Lord, if You **call me to it**, You will **see me through it!** Lord, I will plainly **write the vision down and** start **activating my faith**, by my **actions.** I know, my faith is dead, if I do not apply actions to it. Lord, I'm a **willing vessel.** Use me, Lord, so the entire world will see...More of You God.
(Romans 12:1, Ephesians 5:18, 2 Corinthians 12:7-9, 1 Thessalonians 5:24, Matthew 16:24, Habakkuk 2:2, James 2:14-26)

Year One:

_____
_____
_____
_____
_____
_____
_____
_____
_____
_____

Year Two:

_____
_____
_____
_____
_____
_____
_____
_____

February 17

Lord, I want more of You, God. Today, I come before Your throne with a pure heart. I know, **love conquers** all. My heart cries out to You, Father, for this lost world. Lord, I have a **heart** for those **less fortunate**, than me. Those suffering from poor or failing health. Those with not enough food to eat, and those in the prisons. Oh, Lord, **speak to the heart** of the individuals committing crimes, stealing, killing, not loving their neighbors. Lord, I want to be a **part** of the **solution,** instead of part of the problem. I receive the **anointing**, Lord, You have **on my life**. Lord, I go out, now, with Your anointed oil, praying over all in distress. In the Name of the Father, the Son, and the Holy Spirit...Praying for...More of You God.
(Psalm 51:10, Hebrews 4:16, Ephesians 3:20-21, 1 John 2:27, Luke 4:18)

Year One:

_____
_____
_____
_____
_____
_____
_____
_____

Year Two:

_____
_____
_____
_____
_____
_____
_____
_____

February 18

Jesus, move through me, Lord. Today, Lord Jesus, I'm asking You to **enlarge my territory**. Father, touch every area of my life, making me **whole**. Lord, I know, You can, and will, **open doors** for me, no man can **shut**. Yes, Father, when Your hand is in it, what seems to be impossible **is POSSIBLE**. You know, what I need, and You know, what my heart desires; have Your way with me, Lord. As these doors open, I promise to give You all the honor and all the Praise. **The glory is all Yours, Father!** Take me higher and do a new thing in me, as I **endure** with...More of You God.
(1 Chronicles 4:9-10, Psalm 119:32, 2 Samuel 22:37, Luke 1:37, Matthew 19:26, Psalm 37:4)

Year One:

_____
_____
_____
_____
_____
_____
_____
_____
_____
_____

Year Two:

_____
_____
_____
_____
_____
_____
_____
_____
_____

February 19

Today, is a day of **moving forward**, leaving the **past behind**. Father, bombard my enemy, right now, as he tries to wiggle his way in my life, causing horrible situations. Lord, I'm looking to You. I know, You are all powerful and almighty. You are, King of Kings, Lord of Lords, and God of Gods. You are, Alpha and Omega, the Beginning, and the End. My situation **seems** really big to me, Father. However, Lord, You are **GREATER** and **BIGGER** than any problem I may encounter. So, Father, right now, I hand the situation over to You. **I focus on You**, Jesus. I'm seeking Your face, embracing Your power, and thanking You for Your **undeniable** goodness. Lord, Jesus, I need you. I want You. **I WIN** with...More of You God.

(Isaiah 43:18-19, Philippians 3:18, 2 Corinthians 5:17, Deuteronomy 23:14, Luke 10:19, 1 Chronicles 22:19, Isaiah 55:6-7)

Year One:

_____
_____
_____
_____
_____
_____
_____
_____
_____

Year Two:

_____
_____
_____
_____
_____
_____
_____
_____

February 20

Father, I know, You are in **complete control**. Today, no matter what my circumstance looks like, You will position and transition me, to my **perfect destination**. I trust You completely, Lord, Jesus. Lord, let every step I take be a **reflection** of You, **shining** in me. Let me **illuminate** so brightly, the entire world will know, I'm a **child** of the **Most High**. Father, on this journey, guide each and every one, of my steps. As I **crawl**, **step**, and **walk**, Father, You **guide** my path with…More of You God.

(Proverbs 19:21, Joshua 1:9, Jeremiah 29:11, Deuteronomy 7:22, Romans 12:2, Isaiah 41:10, Isaiah 40:28-31)

Year One:

_____
_____
_____
_____
_____
_____
_____
_____
_____

Year Two:

_____
_____
_____
_____
_____
_____
_____
_____
_____

February 21

Lord, Jesus, today, I have made a decision. I will no longer be contained with what the world is trying to offer me. Father, I have **deposited a seed**, in fact, many seeds into Your **Kingdom**. I know, You'll **never** return my **sacrificial efforts, stamped void**. Jesus, in my life, I'm expecting to see a bountiful turnaround season; a season of **not** just enough, but a season of **MORE** than enough. God, You are God Almighty, (El Shaddai). **Everything You do, God, is great**. You have greatness waiting right around the corner for me. I'm walking into my purpose. **Here I come................**I walk greater, confidently, and bolder with...More of You God.
(Romans 12:2, Matthew 7:16-20, Zechariah 8:12, Psalm 126:5-6, Isaiah 55:11, 2 Corinthians 9:8)

Year One:

_____
_____
_____
_____
_____
_____
_____
_____
_____

Year Two:

_____
_____
_____
_____
_____
_____
_____
_____
_____

February 22

Father, I'm feeling a change in my life, today. There is a **shift** taking place. Sometimes I'm feeling overwhelmed; however, I know, You are in the **mix**. What am I really feeling? **Pain!** I call this pain, **growing pains**. Every minute and every day, even when it doesn't appear to be true, I'm being **elevated**. Right now, You are quiet, but I can sense You are here. You are **always near**; I can feel Your calming presence. You'll not let me fall down too far. Lord, You are the **Way Maker**; You will always allow me to **get back up**. Today's **setback** is a **setup** for my <u>victory</u>. While I'm in a holding position, I will seek Your face, trusting You. I'm empowered with...More of You God.
(James 1:17, Psalm 102:13, John 15:3, Habakkuk 3:17-18, 2 Corinthians 2:14, Proverbs 21:31, Psalm 60:11-12)

Year One:

_____
_____
_____
_____
_____
_____
_____
_____
_____

Year Two:

_____
_____
_____
_____
_____
_____
_____
_____

February 23

Lord, today, I'm just sitting here waiting on You. I got to have You! Father, I'm looking for an **outpouring** of Your **divine blessings**. Lord, Jesus, cleanse me; right now, **I repent**. Father, as I bask in Your presence, my life doesn't stay the same; <u>one</u> moment in Your presence changes me. Now, I have a **fullness** only coming from You. Lord, you make me **complete**. Your glory has changed me. I'm so happy to have the most **special treasure residing in me**, the **Holy Spirit**. Holy Spirit, speak to me, now. Speak to my soul and my heart. Thank you for saving me, Lord. In Your presence, I get and breathe...More of You God. (Psalm 27:14, Isaiah 40:31, Psalm 25:4-5, Psalm 37:34, John 3:6-8, Luke 24:45-47)

Year One:

_____
_____
_____
_____
_____
_____
_____
_____
_____
_____

Year Two:

_____
_____
_____
_____
_____
_____
_____
_____

February 24

Jesus, now, I can see what was **invisible** becoming **tangible**. Today, I know, You are with me. I will speak **confidently** to all situations, placing a demand on them. I do not have to forcibly beg for anything. **I'm a child of royalty!** My Father owns the entire world. He is **rich, sits high,** and **looks low.** Therefore, I know, I'm especially, rich and strong. I know, You wrap me in Your wings and hide me; You are my **hiding place.** I will worship You with all my heart. This place I'm in, I'm resting and loving on...More of You God.

(Matthew 21:22, Isaiah 55:11, 2 Corinthians 4:13, 2 Corinthians 4:18, Galatians 4:4-5, Ephesians 1:3-6, Psalm 24:1, Psalm 50:9-12, Psalm 32:7)

Year One:

_____
_____
_____
_____
_____
_____
_____
_____
_____
_____

Year Two:

_____
_____
_____
_____
_____
_____
_____
_____
_____

February 25

Lord, today, I **declare** and **decree**, there is no more sickness in my body. No longer will I battle with mental and/or spiritual issues. Further, I **speak** to my finances saying, I am no longer in debt; I am debt free, in the Name of Jesus. I will take it upon myself to be very careful to **walk** in the steps, You've ordered me, Father. I'm **leaning on** my **faith**; this faith I have is **unstoppable**, **unmovable**, and **transformed**, by the power of the Holy Spirit, living inside of me. My **strength** comes from You, Lord. My **authority** resides in having...More of You God.
(Job 22:28, Isaiah 10:1, Isaiah 40:8, Luke 9:1, Hebrews 11:1, 2 Corinthians 5:6-7, Ephesians 6:16, Exodus 15:2, Philippians 4:13)

Year One:

_____
_____
_____
_____
_____
_____
_____
_____
_____
_____

Year Two:

_____
_____
_____
_____
_____
_____
_____
_____
_____

February 26

Lord, Jesus, today, I'm **taking back** what the enemy has stolen. I am getting my **joy** and **peace** back. Satan, I rebuke you! In the Name of Jesus! You must and will, get out of my life!!! Right now, I'm opening my door, physically escorting you out. There is **no** longer room in my home, or in my life for you. I will **no** longer have destruction in my life. It is a time for **growth** and **prosperity**. Lord, You say, You will give me life **more abundantly**. Father, I'm ready for the life You have for me. Take me, Lord, God, I'm all Yours. I will **win**. My **victory** is with...More of You God.
(Isaiah 61, 2 Timothy 2:26, 1 Peter 3:11, 1 Peter 5:7, Philippians 4:7, Proverbs 16:7, Psalm 29:11, Philippians 4:19, 3 John 1:2, Joshua 1:8)

Year One:

_____
_____
_____
_____
_____
_____
_____
_____
_____
_____

Year Two:

_____
_____
_____
_____
_____
_____
_____
_____
_____
_____

February 27

Jesus, I know, wherever the **Spirit** of the Lord is, there is **liberty**. God, today, my life will never be the same. Lord, I want You with me all day, every day. I have found **freedom**; now, **I am free forever**. I'm **totally consumed** with You, Lord. I cannot be in a better place this very moment. In my life, Father, I need Your **guidance** and **direction**. I know, as I rest in You, I will hear Your voice, directing me. My **reward** in life comes through You, Jesus. Lord, I'm **opening** myself to receive, all **knowledge** and **wisdom** from You. Father, I'm living and growing with...More of You God.

(2 Corinthians 3:17, Deuteronomy 3:12,   Psalm 37:7, Psalm 62:5, 2 Chronicles 14:11)

Year One:

_____
_____
_____
_____
_____
_____
_____
_____
_____
_____

Year Two:

_____
_____
_____
_____
_____
_____
_____
_____
_____

February 28

Father, today, I want to thank You for **keeping** me. What I thought was going to **take me out**, You **used it** to **lift** and take me, to **another level**. Lord, this victory is all about edifying Your Holy Name. Yes, Father, You used it to **bring me** into what You have for me, **my best life**. Lord, I'm so sorry for being so hard headed; I had to get my head banged around many times, over and over, before submitting to You. However, Lord, Jesus, **I hear You, and I'm intensively listening**. Take me to where You want me to go. Just a little higher, Father. Reaching up for...More of You God.

(Psalm 102:13, Psalm 147:5, Job 38:35-36, Proverbs 3:5-6, Isaiah 43:1-3, Psalm 193:1-6, Psalm 25:4-5, Hebrews 10:35-36)

Year One:

_____
_____
_____
_____
_____
_____
_____
_____
_____
_____

Year Two:

_____
_____
_____
_____
_____
_____
_____
_____

February 29

Lord, I hear a **sound of victory** in my life, today. I know, Your **living Word** will get me to the **next season** of my life. I **block out** what the world is saying to me; now, I'm only hearing from the kingdom. I'm hearing the kingdom say, "**Victory! I win! I have power! I have authority!**" My tongue is powerful; I can speak things into existence. I'm standing on Your Word. I will submerge myself into Your Word. **Now, I am building my faith.** I know, my faith is increasing through **reading** and **hearing** Your **Word**. <u>I will not be shaken</u>. I will **stand** tall, firm, and strong. This is why I'm grabbing onto Your right hand and depending on...More of You God.

(Nehemiah 4:20, Psalm 47:5, Psalm 89:15, Proverbs 18:21, 1 Peter 3:10, Ephesians 4:29, Psalm 62:6, Psalm 16:8, Romans 10:17)

Year One:

_____

_____

_____

_____

_____

_____

_____

_____

Year Two:

_____

_____

_____

_____

_____

_____

_____

_____

March

March 1

Father, living in this beautiful world, I'm approaching a changing Season. A new day and fresh beginning, I'm going to **press** into more of You, God. I do not care what, or who, is in the way; all things must get out of my space. I'm going to be like the **woman** with the **issue of blood,** pressing into **touch** the **hem** of Your **garment. She received her healing through Your grace.** Yes, Lord, I'm going to build my life on Your Word. I know, You give me grace. But what, I really need to understand, Your **grace empowers** me to **do better** than before I received it. Now, I will be able to **operate** in what You're asking and requesting of me, Father. Lord, **transform** my mind, so it is more like You, Jesus. I long to do Your will and live Your way. **Striving** to tap into...More of You God.

(Luke 8:43-48, Romans 13:8-10, John 13:34, 2 Corinthians 12:8-9, Hebrews 4:16, 1 Peter 5:10, Romans 12:2, Ephesians 4:23)

Year One:

_____
_____
_____
_____
_____
_____
_____
_____

Year Two:

_____
_____
_____
_____
_____
_____
_____
_____

March 2

Lord, I'm feeling a little uncomfortable, today. I can feel You **stretching** and **changing** me. It feels really weird; it gives me a feeling of being **totally** out of control. However, I know, You are taking and **launching** me to a place, I can only go with Your help and guidance. Father, You have given me a **vision**; now, I have a **dream**. Lord, until recently, for so long, I could not even dream. Now, I have **written** the **vision** on **paper**; it is **plain** and **clear**. I will **adhere** to what You want me to do. You, Lord, have an **appointed time** for me. Father, I'm making myself **available** to You, Lord. I'm working with and thankful for…More of You God.
(Exodus 9:16, Jeremiah 29:11, Proverbs 20:5, Micah 6:8, Habakkuk 2:2)

Year One:

_____
_____
_____
_____
_____
_____
_____
_____
_____
_____

Year Two:

_____
_____
_____
_____
_____
_____
_____
_____

March 3

Jesus, I have a spirit of **gratitude**. Today, I see You so vividly in my life. Lord, You are **alive**, **well**, and I see You cleaning out my house. Father, **remove** what does not need to stay, Lord. You know which friends and family, mean me well. Also, You know, which ones are trying to destroy me. **Clean me up, Lord**, so I can walk and talk like You. I want to be **more** like You, Lord, Jesus. **Create** in me a **pure heart**. You, Lord, only You, can **transform** me and **rewire** me. My change will come, only in operating with...More of You God.
(Psalm 28:7, Psalm 107:29-32, Colossians 2:6-7, Psalm 51:10)

Year One:

_____
_____
_____
_____
_____
_____
_____
_____
_____
_____

Year Two:

_____
_____
_____
_____
_____
_____
_____
_____
_____
_____

March 4

Lord, this is a season and period of time in my life, I will **give up** something unto You. I'm giving more of my **time**. Today, I'm going to commit to creating a very **robust** and **healthy prayer life** with You, **daily**. I ask you to forgive me of my sins. I come humbly laying before Your feet worshipping You. You are worthy, Lord! I **meditate** on who You are-Your power, Your unconditional love, Your holiness, Your perfection, and Your sacrifice, to save my life. Father, I want to spend the rest of my life **focusing** on giving unto You and giving to others. Lord, I am so thankful for all You have given me. **I want to care for others, as You care for me**. Lord, **work** through me. I'm feeling **transformed** with...More of You God.
(Romans 12:1-21, Ephesians 6:18, 1 Thessalonians 5:17, Matthew 6:9-13, 1 Corinthians 14:15, James 5:16, 2 Chronicles 7:14)

Year One:

_____
_____
_____
_____
_____
_____
_____
_____
_____
_____

Year Two:

_____
_____
_____
_____
_____
_____
_____
_____

March 5

God, I'm entering into **more** of You and **less** of me. Today, in honor of You, I will **give up** a **food,** or an **activity** for the rest of this **month.** Lord, Jesus, I love You so much; I just want to be saturated with Your presence. I want to be closer to You, Father. I know, the more I praise You, You come near. Lord, I want to **decrease,** so You will **increase** in my life. There **isn't any room** for my selfishness, nor my controlling attitude in Your presence. Right now, in the Name of Jesus, I **release** all **not** of You. **Rain** on me, Lord, Jesus. **Reveal** unto me, Father...More of You God.

(Joel 2:12, Matthew 6:16-18, Mark 9:29, Isaiah 58:6, Jeremiah 29:13, Psalm 16:11, Psalm 73:28, 2 Chronicles 5:13-14, Psalm 27-4)

Year One:

_____
_____
_____
_____
_____
_____
_____
_____
_____

Year Two:

_____
_____
_____
_____
_____
_____
_____
_____

67

March 6

Lord, I thank You for **paying** the **full price** for **life everlasting**, just for me. You didn't have to do it, but You did it anyway. Today, I sing praises unto my King, Jesus. There is **nobody** like You, Lord. In my life, You **turn the night into day**. Wow! Just too really grasp this concept is simply amazing. Only You, Lord, Jesus, can **turn water into wine or part the Red Sea**. Lord, I see You **splitting** the **sea** and **opening up a path for me** to walk right into, a **land of prosperity**. I'm not just referring to money; I'm speaking of health, a sound mind, family, unity, overcoming depression, and of course, finances. Whatever I need, Lord, You have already done it for me, in the Name of Jesus. I praise You, God. I **can't stop** and **won't stop,** praising You. My life depends on...More of You God.

(1 Corinthians 6:20, 1 Peter 2:24, Romans 6:23, 1 Corinthians 7:23, John 2:1-11, Exodus 14:21-31, Isaiah 43:12-21)

Year One:

_____
_____
_____
_____
_____
_____
_____
_____
_____

Year Two:

_____
_____
_____
_____
_____
_____
_____
_____

March 7

Jesus! Jesus! Jesus! Today, Lord, I thank you for **choosing me** when no one else wanted me. I **almost lost** my mind, but You were there and **saved** me. I'm now, putting on my **garment of praise** unto You. Holy! Holy! Holy! Is the Lamb of God. I sing with the angels, **lifting up holy hands** unto, my King. Lord, Jesus, I put You first in my life. I will seek You day and night. I **bow down** before Your throne. My heart is filled with **admiration** for You, my Savior. Lord, Jesus, I **can't stop** praising on and **digging deeply** into...More of You God.
(Ephesians 1:4, John 15:16, 1 Peter 2:9, 2 Timothy 1:7, Colossians 3:2, Revelation 4:8-11)

Year One:

_____
_____
_____
_____
_____
_____
_____
_____
_____
_____

Year Two:

_____
_____
_____
_____
_____
_____
_____
_____
_____

March 8

Father, I know, You are **preparing** me for a **greater** life. Lord, with and through You, I know, I can **fly**. There isn't a storm or mountain holding me down. I see all difficulties as **opportunities** to strengthen me. They will help to better **enhance** my capabilities to take me to **another level** in You, Lord. My lips are filled with praises unto You, Lord, Jesus. I will serve You forever and ever. Father, the assignment You have for me, only You can take me there. I will hold onto Your hand, letting You guide my steps, one by one. I'm **completely depended** upon You, most gracious, God. I'm seeking and searching. Wanting to fly with...More of You God.

(Ephesians 2:10, 2 Corinthians 12:8, Hebrews 11:24-27, Deuteronomy 31:6, Psalm 107:29, 2 Timothy 2:1-2, 2 Chronicles 14:11-12, Psalm 5:3, Psalm 37:5, Psalm 73:23-25)

Year One:

_____
_____
_____
_____
_____
_____
_____
_____
_____

Year Two:

_____
_____
_____
_____
_____
_____
_____
_____
_____

March 9

God, today and throughout my life, I'm going to **put a praise** on **every situation** good or bad. I will **not** live by fear, it is only a demon. I **will** live by **faith**. Lord, I know, the **giants** I'm facing, today, are **little ants** to You, Father. I will **stay focused** on who, as well as, what matters. Praising You, Lord, all the days of my life definitely is most important to me. Lord, I will stay in **constant communication** with You, through **prayer**. **Prayer** is one of the most **powerful tools** You have given me. Thank You, Lord, for loving me so much. I'm praying to have...More of You God.
(1 Chronicles 16:23-31, Psalm 29, 1 Samuel 17:1-58, 1 Thessalonians 5:17)

Year One:

_____
_____
_____
_____
_____
_____
_____
_____
_____

Year Two:

_____
_____
_____
_____
_____
_____
_____
_____

71

March 10

Lord, Jesus, today, I have the **victory**! I will only keep my eyes to where You are taking me. I'm not focusing on where I am, right now. Father, I'm **positioning myself** by staying **fixated** on You. Jesus, I thank You. You **paid the price** allowing for me to **transform** and **transition**. I am never a failure in Your sight. Lord, I thank You for making me **righteous through Your blood**. Oh, how grateful I am to You! **You are a Wonder! You are a Wonder!** In Your victory, I'm pressing into and going higher with...More of You God.
(Deuteronomy 20:4, Romans 8:31-32, Psalm 3:8, Proverbs 21:31 1 Corinthians 15:57, 2 Corinthians 5:1, Ephesians 4:22-24)

Year One:

_____
_____
_____
_____
_____
_____
_____
_____
_____

Year Two:

_____
_____
_____
_____
_____
_____
_____
_____
_____

March 11

Heavenly Father, I'm **changing** my **atmosphere**. I'm going to **set** myself **up for miracles** to start happening. Today, I am **activating my faith** and through having faith in You, Lord, Jesus, I know, my life will never be the same. Faith will change my atmosphere, allowing what **seems** to be impossible to the human eye, **possible** for me. I have faith, and I **trust in You**. My Father, my Lord, and my Savior, I **welcome** You into my life. I must have faith if I want to **please** You. You **reign** and have full **control** over me. **I'm getting ready for a miracle in my life**, with the greatest of all...More of You God.
(Mark 4:37-40, Genesis 1:26, Matthew 21:21, John 14:12, Matthew 15:28, Luke 17:5, Acts 6:5-8, Romans 4:20, Matthew 9:29)

Year One:

_____
_____
_____
_____
_____
_____
_____
_____
_____

Year Two:

_____
_____
_____
_____
_____
_____
_____
_____
_____

March 12

My Savior, as I enter into this day, I am **declaring a supernatural blessing** over my life. Father, You have given me the **power** to **speak** things into **existence**, as if it is so. **I am a child of royalty.** A child of, the King of Kings, the Lord of Lords, and the God of Gods. I know, all of my blessings come from You, Lord. Now, I'm asking You to have **favor** on me, in the Name of Jesus. I'm **pleading the blood** of Jesus, over every **obstacle** or **situation** trying to **destroy** and **hold** me from receiving all the blessings You have for me, Lord, Jesus. My heart is full of joy in You, Lord. I just need You. Singing praises to...More of You God.

(Isaiah 43:11, Exodus 6:6-7, Hosea 13:4, Luke 3:4-6, Psalm 18:46, Psalm 28:8, Revelation 3:10)

Year One:

_____
_____
_____
_____
_____
_____
_____
_____
_____
_____

Year Two:

_____
_____
_____
_____
_____
_____
_____
_____
_____

March 13

Jesus, Jesus, Jesus, **You are so beautiful to me!** Today, I come humbly kneeled at Your throne, saying, "Thank You, Lord, Jesus." You are a-mazing to me. **Oh, how I love You, Jesus!** You gave Your life, just for me. I know, through Your blood, I am **made complete**. Thank You, Lord, for making me **afresh** and **anew**. Lord, I am no longer blue; I have joy unspeakable joy. I have peace surpassing all understanding, through You, my Savior. Right now, I'm rejoicing in You. I have You by my side. Loving this experience having...More of You God.
(1 Chronicles 16:29, Isaiah 4:2, Isaiah 28:5, Isaiah 33:17, James 4:10, Nehemiah 9:6, Psalm 138:2)

Year One:

_____
_____
_____
_____
_____
_____
_____
_____
_____
_____

Year Two:

_____
_____
_____
_____
_____
_____
_____
_____

March 14

Lord, today, I'm seeking after all You have in store for me. I'm **stepping out** on my **faith**. I'm saying, "Have Your way with me, Lord." In order for me to obtain all You have for me on this earth, I **must** take a **risk**. Therefore, today, I'm changing my way of thinking, my way of acting, and my way of performing. I will open my ears unto You, Father. I need You to **impart** the **wisdom** needed to take the risk lying ahead. I know, **I can do all things through** Christ, who strengthens me. Now, I walk with **more knowledge**, **power**, and **authority**. More reasons inspiring me to tap into the source of...More of You God. (2 Corinthians 5:7, Proverbs 3:5-6, Romans 10:17, Hebrews 11:1-40, Romans 1:17, Ephesians 4:23, Proverbs 4:6-7, Philippians 4:13)

Year One:

_____
_____
_____
_____
_____
_____
_____
_____
_____
_____

Year Two:

_____
_____
_____
_____
_____
_____
_____

March 15

Father, today, I will **pay** very **close attention** to my **tongue** and the **words** coming out of my mouth. I will speak **prosperity, healing,** and **victory.** Right now, I am looking at my **future, giving it notice;** I have the victory. Lord, You are just waiting on me to change my ways and actions. There is **power** in the tongue. There is **life** and there is **death** in this sharp weapon. Exactly, the reasons why I am speaking of blessings, goodness, love, peace, and joy. From now on, I will keep a positive attitude. It shall be reflected through my words and actions. **I shall live and not die! I am the head and not the tail! I am above and not beneath! Yes! Yes! Yes! I have the victory!** Crying and shouting in triumph. My victory is with...More of You God.
(Proverbs 18:21, 1 Peter 3:10, Ephesians 4:29, Proverbs 12:18, James 3:6, Psalm 19:14, Psalm 118:17, Deuteronomy 28:13)

Year One:

_____
_____
_____
_____
_____
_____
_____
_____
_____
_____

Year Two:

_____
_____
_____
_____
_____
_____
_____

March 16

Lord, God, today, I will focus on Your promises. In Your Word, You state, my **latter will be greater**. Therefore, I am rejoicing and singing, Glory! Hallelujah! Hallelujah! Hallelujah! I am now joint heirs with, You, Jesus; therefore, I know, I am great. Father, when I take the **first step**, You take the **next one**. Lord, **lead** and **guide** me to my **destiny**, my **purpose**. Without a doubt, I can count on You. You are my **Anchor! My Foundation and my Rock!** Thank You, Lord, for Your direction. My **victory** is **right around** the **corner**. My joy will come in the morning. I'm holding on, crying out, and looking up into the hills for...More of You God.

(Haggai 2:9, Job 8:7, Galatians 3:29, Galatians 3:16, Jeremiah 29:11, Hebrews 6:13-20, 2 Timothy 2:19, Deuteronomy 32:4)

Year One:

_____
_____
_____
_____
_____
_____
_____
_____
_____

Year Two:

_____
_____
_____
_____
_____
_____
_____
_____

March 17

Abba, today, I surrender unto You. I submit, because I belong to You. "Lord, what do You want me to do?" "Lord, how do You want me to do it?" "Lord, when do You want me to do it?" All I need is You, Father. Take me, I am all of Yours. I know, all I have to do is seek Your face; You will add all things unto me. I love You, Lord! I thank You, Lord, You **do not keep count of my sins. You forgive me of all my sins. All I have to do is ask and believe, in the Father, the Son, and the Holy Spirit.** Abba, Father, I belong to You. You're all I'm seeking after...More of You God.

(Romans 8:12-17, Galatians 4:6, 1 Chronicles 16:11, Hebrews 11:6, Isaiah 55:6-7, Zephaniah 2:3, Proverbs 8:17, Job 14:16, Psalm 32:2)

Year One:

_____
_____
_____
_____
_____
_____
_____
_____
_____
_____

Year Two:

_____
_____
_____
_____
_____
_____
_____
_____

March 18

Lord, today, I have a **now-faith**. Father, I know, You are a **now-God** and Your Word is the **now-living Word**. Your Word never changes. It is the same as yesterday, today, and forever more. This is why I trust You, Lord. I can go to Your Word and read it, building my faith, daily. **Faith only comes by hearing and reading of Your Word.** I am ready to take off and fly. Therefore, I need to **take my faith to a completely different frequency.** Lord, Your Word says, You will take me from **glory to glory**. Father, I want to get on Your boat to take a trip with You. Lord, stop by, and let me on; don't leave me on this troubled shore, Lord. Dear, Lord, Jesus, I have got to go with and will only sail with...More of You God.
(Hebrews 11:1, Isaiah 1:18, Hebrews 4:7, Romans 10:17, Hebrews 4:12, 2 Corinthians 3:16-18, Matthew 14:32-33)

Year One:

_____
_____
_____
_____
_____
_____
_____
_____
_____
_____

Year Two:

_____
_____
_____
_____
_____
_____
_____
_____

March 19

Holy Spirit, today, I **welcome** You in my heart **wholeheartedly**. I need You to transform me, making me all new. You wrap me in Your arms and comfort me. Holy Spirit, **I am nothing without You**. I need You. At all times, You give me direction. You direct me to what I need. You direct me away from all harm and danger. Holy Spirit, I want to get to know You better. I **must** have a relationship with You. I have a **strong desire** to hear Your voice. Speak to me, now. I promise to **take special quiet time daily** to hear from You. Holy Spirit, You live inside of me; I'm **depending** on You. You are the reason, I have got to have and commune with...More of You God.

(Romans 8:9, Ephesians 5:18, Revelation 21:5, Psalm 51:10, Psalm 37:23, Psalm 32:8, John 10:27-30, 1 Corinthians 3:16, 2 Corinthians 6:16, Ezekiel 36:27, 2 Timothy 1:14)

Year One:

_____
_____
_____
_____
_____
_____
_____
_____

Year Two:

_____
_____
_____
_____
_____
_____
_____
_____

March 20

Jesus, today, I am cleaning out my house. God, **holiness is what I am after**; I want to be more like You, Jesus. I know, You have a special purpose for me on this earth. Lord, **I am available to You**, so **use me**, Father. Do what You want to do, **through me** and **to me**. I want to fulfill the **divine purpose** You have for me to achieve and accomplish. **All for Your glory**. Lord, all the glory is Yours. I am just a **humble vessel**, waiting for direction from You. Lord, I want the world to know of Your **power**, **goodness**, **grace,** and **mercy**. Father, **clean me up** and use me. I want my house full of...More of You God.
(1 Peter 2, Luke 11:25, Matthew 12:44, 2 Timothy 1:9, Romans 8:28, 2 Corinthians 3:18, Ephesians 2:10, Ephesians 1:11)

Year One:

_____
_____
_____
_____
_____
_____
_____
_____
_____
_____

Year Two:

_____
_____
_____
_____
_____
_____
_____
_____
_____

March 21

Oh, Lord, Jesus, **how excellent is Your Name!** Today, I am grateful for You **paying my debt in Full**. All of my sins are washed away; the past, present, and future sins have been cleansed by the blood of Jesus. Thank You, Lord, "**It is finished**." Lord, You sacrificed Your Son Jesus, on the cross, just for me; **He paid the price in full**. What a mighty God, I serve! I choose to worship You and only You. You are my Lord, my Savior, and my King. Lord, Jesus, You are my everything! I rejoice in You and shout, Hallelujah to Your Holy Name! Hallelujah to the King! I bow down to You, worshipping You in spirit and in truth. Lord, Jesus, now, I sacrifice my life to worship You, Father. You are worthy, and my life depends on...More of You God.
(1 Corinthians 6:20, John 19:30, John 1:1-14, 1 Peter 2:24, Romans 6:23, John 4:24, Hebrews 12:28-29, Psalm 86:9-10)

Year One:

_____
_____
_____
_____
_____
_____
_____
_____
_____

Year Two:

_____
_____
_____
_____
_____
_____

March 22

Lord, today, I cry out to You. Jesus, my heart is heavy, but my spirit is well. When I try to comprehend what You have done for me, I cannot explain the **admiration** and **appreciation**, I have for You. My heart cries out, thinking of all the **pain You endured**, just for me. There isn't anyone in this world who loves me the way You do. I thank You, Lord, Jesus. Jesus, **You are my Hero**. You are my example of how I'm supposed to live my life. I give everything I have unto You. Use me, now, for Your glory, Lord. I make myself **available** to the **purpose** and **plan,** You have for me. Now, take me, Father, with Your right hand, directing my path. Jesus, the only way I'm going to make it, is by having...More of You God.

(Psalm 57:2, Psalm 18:6, Psalm 22:2, Jeremiah 29:11, Micah 6:8, 2 Timothy 1:9, Romans 8:28)

Year One:

_____
_____
_____
_____
_____
_____
_____
_____

Year Two:

_____
_____
_____
_____
_____
_____
_____
_____

March 23

God, I'm going to put on the **garment of praise** today. Lord, I praise You in the morning. I praise You in the noon time. Oh! My Father, I praise in the evening; You are worthy to be praised. All the praises belong to You, Lord. You are, Alpha and Omega; the First and the Last; the Beginning and the End. I know, when I lift the praises up to You, You pour my blessings down. Father, first and foremost, I praise You because of who You are, the Great I Am. You are my **protector**, my **healer**, my **deliverer**, my **provider**, my **redeemer**, and my **Savior**. There is **no me without You**, Father. Quicken me, Father. Accelerate and ignite me in You, Father. Lord I'm on fire for...More of You God. (Isaiah 61:3, Isaiah 52:1-5, Revelation 19:16, Revelation 22:13, Revelation 1:8, Psalm 143:11, Psalm 119:107, Psalm 142:7)

Year One:

_____
_____
_____
_____
_____
_____
_____
_____
_____
_____

Year Two:

_____
_____
_____
_____
_____
_____
_____
_____

March 24

Lord, another day of praise unto You. I praise You no matter what is going on in my life. As I seek You, You **knock out my giant,** and **I win.** There is **victory in my praise.** I cannot be shaken or moved. I am unstoppable as I praise You, Lord. I'm **positioning** myself in You; You are my friend. You're my best friend who I can always count on no matter what is happening in my life. **I speak!** I have **dominion** over <u>all</u> situations trying to come up against me, right now, in the Name of Jesus. My praise will prevail as long as I have the breath of life. I will praise You when all else seems to fail, and I do not know what else to do; praise will run off of my lips. I will enter into Your gates with thanksgiving and into Your courts with praise. Praise is what I do, because I love being with...More of You God.

(1 Chronicles 16:23-31, Psalm 99, Revelation 4:8-11, Deuteronomy 20:4, Ephesians 6:13, James 1, Psalm 100:4-5)

Year One:

_____
_____
_____
_____
_____
_____
_____
_____
_____

Year Two:

_____
_____
_____
_____
_____
_____
_____

March 25

Father, today, **every** stronghold trying to bind me is **broken**, in the Name of Jesus. Today, I cleanse my mind, because the only stronghold holding me back **is myself**. I refuse to let the enemy in my mind, having control. I rebuke Satan on every hand; I'm pleading the blood of Jesus. Lord, I surrender to You. You are my **strong tower**. You are my **peace**. You are my **joy**. You are my **shepherd,** and there is nobody like You, Father. Right now, I'm standing still, Father, watching You **work on** my behalf. I am standing on Your truth and Your promises. Lord, I know, **nothing is impossible for You and You are going to do, what I cannot do in my own power**. Thank You, Lord, for knocking my giant down and slaying him. All the glory belongs to You. I'm going to keep praising...More of You God.
(2 Corinthians 10:3-5, Romans 12:2, Ephesians 6:12, 1 John 4:1, Psalm 103:2-4)

Year One:

_____
_____
_____
_____
_____
_____
_____
_____

Year Two:

_____
_____
_____
_____
_____
_____
_____

March 26

Jesus, Jesus, today, I'm praising You for **where You are taking me**. I refuse to look at my, now-situation. I'm going to glorify You for where I am going. I have a **spirit of expectancy**, expecting to have a new-life in You. Expecting to **see new, be new,** and **live a new life**. Lord, I pray, right now, You will **remove all** stuff from me that does not bear fruit. Lord, Jesus, prune me. Take a knife and cut off what needs to be removed, so, I can have more plentiful fruit. Lord, You say in Your Word, You will give me life more abundantly. Lord, I know, as long as I stay with You, You will make me more prosperous in all areas of my life. Lord, thank You for the abundancy; it continues to come with...More of You God.

(Psalm 51:10, Psalm 31:15, Acts 17:26, John 15:2, John 10:10, Matthew 6:33, Luke 6:38, Isaiah 48:17)

Year One:

_____
_____
_____
_____
_____
_____
_____
_____

Year Two:

_____
_____
_____
_____
_____
_____
_____
_____

March 27

God, today, I thank You for being a good God. Lord, everything You do is good. You are the God, who **takes my mistakes**, my **mess**, and You **turn them around** for Your glory. I thank You, Lord, You **restore, refresh** and **renew** me daily. Also, I thank You for the **new benefits** You provide to me daily. Lord, without You, I have no purpose here on this earth. You took me and put my life back together. It was **only** by Your mercy and Your grace, I have a strong mind. Lord, as long as I do what You require of me (believe), You will **restore the years I've lost**. I thank You, Jesus! Only a great God, can do such works. I praise You! I praise You! I praise You! You are a good God! I cannot live without...More of You God.

(Deuteronomy 4:31, Numbers 23:19, Deuteronomy 3:24, Joshua 23:3, 2 Samuel 22:32-34, Psalm 48:14, Psalm 54:4)

Year One:

_____

_____

_____

_____

_____

_____

_____

_____

_____

Year Two:

_____

_____

_____

_____

_____

_____

_____

_____

March 28

God, today, I thank You for being a God, who **watches over Your Word, to perform it**. I thank You, God, You are not like man. You are a God, who **does not lie**. Father, all of my trust is in You. Lord, I know, anytime You speak over me, a **supernatural life change** is about to occur in my life. Lord, breathe over me, my life, and all situations. I promise to **not** curse my crisis. I will let you mend the broken pieces. Therefore, I will blossom to a level that no man has seen. The world will not be able to comprehend my life's growth. But, Father, I will be a witness for You. I will let the entire world know, if it wasn't for my Lord and Savior, there would not be this great harvest I'm enjoying. Lord, it's a pleasure and a blessing to have...More of You God. (Jeremiah 1:12, Isaiah 55:10-13, Numbers 23:19, Titus 1:2, 1 Samuel 15:29, Hebrews 6:18, Psalm 89:35, Job 33:4, John 20:22, 1 Peter 5:10, Psalm 34:18, Isaiah 41:10)

Year One:

_____
_____
_____
_____
_____
_____
_____
_____

Year Two:

_____
_____
_____
_____
_____
_____
_____
_____

March 29

Lord, today and forevermore, I will s-t-r-e-t-c-h myself. I know, the **spectacular plans** You have for me. Father, You say in Your Word, You will prosper me and give me good health. So, today, I'm going to **another level** in You, Father. I know, as I stretch myself, it's going to hurt. As a child is growing, they will have growing pains. Therefore, I will experience some growing pains too. Father, if I do not experience any pain, I am not growing. But, Lord, God, this pain is only for **my gain**. All I do for You is **never** in vain. I refuse to stay the same! Lord, I know, You are a **great rewarder**; I can never out give You. So, Lord, I give myself to You. I love experiencing and growing with...More of You God.
(Jeremiah 29:11-13, 2 Peter 3:18, 1 Peter 2:2, 1 Timothy 4:15, 1 Corinthians 13:11, Colossians 2:6-7, James 1:2-4)

Year One:

_____

_____

_____

_____

_____

_____

_____

_____

_____

Year Two:

_____

_____

_____

_____

_____

_____

_____

March 30

Savior, today, I hear a **sound of a rushing wind**; it's taking me to a **greater dimension** in You, God. **I'm going higher**. I refuse to have fear. Right now, I rebuke it, in the Name of Jesus. No man has heard or seen, what You are about to do in my life. Lord, this sound I hear is **motivating** me to look at my life, seeing myself at a completely different place/position/and level. I know, right before my victory, the enemy will come like a lion, trying to destroy me. However, I refuse to hear him. **My faith is in You** and only You. My victory is **within** reach; I will not stop until I have it. Right now, I speak to this situation and say, **"Peace be still."** I am about to step into the **promised land**. I hear the sound of victory; victory is mine today. I continue to move forward, having victory, as long as I get to...More of You God. (Acts 2:2, John 3:8, Isaiah 43:1, Psalm 34:4, Psalm 27:1, 1 Peter 5:6-7, Deuteronomy 31:6, Isaiah 54:4, Mark 4:39-41, Psalm 118:15, Exodus 23:20-23, Deuteronomy 20:1-4)

Year One:

Year Two:

March 31

Jesus, thank You for **paving the way**, today. I might be in a storm, but I know, You are using this storm to **mold** and **form** me into what You want me to become. Lord, You are doing a **new thing** in my life. Again, I thank You for shedding Your blood on the cross, so I am **now delivered**. I realize before I receive my deliverance in any situation, a distraction is going to try to stop me from receiving my blessing. However, today, I'm going to **press in harder** and **deeper,** into You. I refuse to be destroyed and lost. Lord, strengthen me, encourage me, define me, hold me, and speak to me, for I need Your help. I'm on the battle field; it is not easy, but I know, as long as I hold onto You, **I win**. My victory exist, as long as, I hold onto…More of You God.

(John 14:6, Psalm 8:3-8, Genesis 1:26-28, Genesis 45:7, Deuteronomy 31:8, Isaiah 45:2, Isaiah 52:12, Jeremiah 18:3-4, Isaiah 45:9, Exodus 15:2, Psalm 18:32-34)

Year One:

_____
_____
_____
_____
_____
_____
_____

Year Two:

_____
_____
_____
_____
_____
_____
_____

April

April 1

Father, You reign! You reign! You reign over the entire Universe; **everything** belongs to You. Today, Father, I am like a flower, just waiting for You to rain on me. My leaves will sprout; I will blossom during this season. Lord, I'm getting stronger in You each and every day. Continue to outpour on me, letting my spirit continue to grow with You, daily. **It is now, time for my seasonal transition**; I will spring into a new-season. A season of **growth, maturity, prosperity, abundancy,** and **breakthroughs**. Lord, it is my time to spring forth; I will see the beauty of the works You have imparted. Now, **my victory is manifesting, coming into fruition**. Thank You, Lord, for my transition and an incredible season, only because I have...More of You God.

(Psalm 47:8, Revelation 15:3, Isaiah 45:8, Ezekiel 34:26, Joshua 1:9, Philippians 4:6-7, Ephesians 3:20, 1 Corinthians 12:7)

Year One:

_____
_____
_____
_____
_____
_____
_____
_____
_____

Year Two:

_____
_____
_____
_____
_____
_____
_____
_____
_____

April 2

Jehovah, today, I am **turning** my life <u>completely</u> over to You, Lord. I'm putting You in the **driver's seat of my all**. God, I know, I can do all things through You. Yes! You will strengthen me. I thank You for always being by my side, never leaving or forsaking me. What a wonderful Savior, You are to me. Whatever direction You are positioning me, be it North, South, East, or West, I will go. Yes, **I'm in the midst of a new season**, Hallelujah! Lord, **I am Your willing vessel**, use me to Your glory, Father. Jehovah, You are my everything. I'm **desperate** for...More of You God.

(Exodus 6:3, Exodus 17:6, 2 Corinthians 10:1-4, Esther 3:13-15, Philippians 4:13, Deuteronomy 31:6, Isaiah 52:11, 2 Timothy 2:21, Isaiah 43:5-6)

Year One:

_____

_____

_____

_____

_____

_____

_____

_____

Year Two:

_____

_____

_____

_____

_____

_____

_____

_____

April 3

Today, is a day of **letting go of the past** and **stepping into my future.** Father, I thank You for **forgiving me** for what I did, yesterday. I thank You for not having to stand on my yesterday, to get to what You have for me now and tomorrow. You are so gracious to me. Oh, how I love You for being so loving and kind to me. Lord, show me a **healthier approach** to achieve all You have for me. You tell me to **forget my past, pressing onto my future.** Now, Lord, Jesus, I am all in, ready for a new-thing. Because I have **faith** in You, Father, I will **take the risk.** I'm committed to being victorious in my life, as long as I have...More of You God.

(2 Corinthians 5:17, Galatians 2:20, Philippians 3:13-15, Numbers 6:24-26, Isaiah 43:19, Matthew 21:22, Hebrews 11:1, Proverbs 3:5-6)

Year One:

_____
_____
_____
_____
_____
_____
_____
_____
_____

Year Two:

_____
_____
_____
_____
_____
_____
_____
_____

April 4

Lord, Jesus, I just want to tell You I love You; I will never stop loving You. Today and forevermore, I **cannot live without You**. Jesus, You are so precious to me. Every moment I spend with You, is like heaven to me. Father, from now on, I choose to **cherish** every one of these **special moments** with You. I promise to make sure I have **on-going time with You**, each and every day. Moreover, I will continue to work at **building** a **special relationship** with You. Father, I want to be able to hear You. I never want to allow myself to have so many distractions around me, hindering me from my time for You, Lord. Lord, God, I want to **hear Your sweet voice** directing me. Lord, Jesus, I want to rest in...More of You God.
(Mark 12:28-30, Matthew 6:24-25, John 14:21-24, John 15:9-17, 1 John 1:9, Revelation 3:20, Jeremiah 29:11)

Year One:

_____
_____
_____
_____
_____
_____
_____
_____
_____
_____

Year Two:

_____
_____
_____
_____
_____
_____
_____
_____

April 5

Jesus, Jesus, Jesus, today, I'm **cleaning up** my house. I'm talking about a serious spring cleaning. I am going to look inside of my heart, cleaning it, making sure it is a **reflection of You**, Father. I'm talking about my mouth, that **what I speak** is only of You, Father. Oh, Lord, I'm talking about **what I watch** and allow in my sight; I am going to start protecting my eyes. Lord, I know, what I let in my auditory and visual gates, have a big influence on my being. **What I allow in me, is what comes out.** Father, I want to be more like You, Jesus. God, let me **practice what Your Word** tells me to accomplish. I must live in this world, however, not be of this world. Lord, I can only get enhanced and wiser with getting...More of You God.

(Psalm 51:10, Luke 6:45, Psalm 51:7, Psalm 119:105, Romans 12:1-2, Ephesians 2:10, Ephesians 4:22-24, Ephesians 5:1-2, Proverbs 3:5-6)

Year One:

_____
_____
_____
_____
_____
_____
_____
_____
_____

Year Two:

_____
_____
_____
_____
_____
_____
_____
_____
_____

April 6

Lord, today, I'm here to **worship You in spirit and in truth.** I come humbly, as I know how, worshipping Your Holy Name. Oh, Father, You are so worthy to be praised! Father, as I come, I ask You to strengthen me mentally, enabling me to walk hand and hand with You, Father. I want to have the kind of communication I have, only with my BFF (Best Friend Forever). Yes, Lord **You are my BFF** and no one can come before You, Father. I want to have a closer walk with You, Lord. "Satan, get behind me. I have an amazing Father, who is Holy." He **can** and **will win** the **battle** for me, each and every time, as long as, I walk with...More of You God.

(John 4:23-24, Psalm 29, Hebrews 12:28-29, Nehemiah 9:5-6, Psalm 100, Deuteronomy 5:33, 2 Corinthians 5:7, Ephesians 2:10, Matthew 16:23, Matthew 4:10)

Year One:

_____
_____
_____
_____
_____
_____
_____
_____

Year Two:

_____
_____
_____
_____
_____
_____
_____

April 7

Father, I want to **be more like Jesus**. Lord, please help me, today, to have a **lifestyle reflecting the Jesus inside of me**. Lord, purify my heart and cleanse me. Lord, wash me clean as glistening white snow. I want to have a light so bright, the reflection from me glows only of You, Lord. I want **my little light to shine splendidly bright**, so the world can see, I work hard at **pleasing You, Father**. From this day forward, I **avoid doing the things You hate**, such as: lying, arrogance, dirty hands, wickedness, evilness, false witness of Your Word, and sowing the wrong seeds in the ground of discord. Jesus, I want to **be a reflection of You**. Therefore, it is imperative, my light gleams fiercely with...More of You God.
(Psalm 51:7, Isaiah 1:18, 1 John 1:1-10, Hebrews 9:14, Ephesians 5:26, 2 Chronicles 7:14-16, Psalm 19:14, Psalm 119:18)

Year One:

_____
_____
_____
_____
_____
_____
_____
_____
_____

Year Two:

_____
_____
_____
_____
_____
_____
_____

April 8

Heavenly Father, today, I **speak** a word over my life. **I declare and decree blessings are coming** to me from the East, West, North, and South, as I come and as I go. Right now, in the Name of Jesus, I re-move all **curses off** of my life. I'm getting ready for breakthroughs in every area of my life. A **breaking** of **strongholds** and a **life filled** with **abundant blessings.** I thank You, Lord, You take pleasure in my pros-perity. My Father, my Lord, as the blessings come down and my barns are filled up with Your goodness, I will **give You the first fruits of all I produce**, because **my first belongs to You and only You.** My precious Savior, oh, how I crave for...More of You God.
(Genesis 28:14, Isaiah 43:5-6, Job 22:28, Psalm 2:7, Proverbs 18:21, Proverbs 3:9-10, Deuteronomy 28:8, Matthew 6:25-26, Luke 12:23-24)

Year One:

_____
_____
_____
_____
_____
_____
_____
_____
_____

Year Two:

_____
_____
_____
_____
_____
_____
_____
_____

April 9

My Savior, I just want to **meditate on You**, all day and night. I want to have a **mindset of Christ**, my Savior. Lord, I want to be where You are. Yes, very near to You. Father, I love You so much; You are so very near and dear to my heart. Right now, Father, Your Word is music to my ears and beauty to my eyes. You bring me peace and joy; I can only get from my precious, King. **Holy Spirit, enter me, now, filling me with Your anointing**. Lord, anoint me from the crown of my head, to the sole of my feet. Father, I want to be in that **secret place with You**, my hiding place. Lord, You are my Rock! My Salvation! Holy, Holy, Holy is the Lamb of God! I cry out for...More of You God. (Psalm 19:14, Psalm 104:3-4, 2 Timothy 2:7, Psalm 119: 15-16, Joshua 1:8, Psalm 77:12, Psalm 145:5, Psalm 119:148, Job 22:22)

Year One:

_____
_____
_____
_____
_____
_____
_____

Year Two:

_____
_____
_____
_____
_____
_____

April 10

Savior, today, I ask You to forgive me of all my worries and slow my mind from racing. Lord, I will **not be anxious for anything,** anymore; I will keep my mind on You, my God. **I rebuke the spirit of nervousness, uneasiness, apprehensiveness, and/or of having so much interest in something, I lose myself in it.** There is **nothing** in this whole wide-world worth more than my relationship with You, Lord. Jesus, I want to go to a place where I grow, learning to lean, and depend solely on You, my Lord, my Savior. Father, take me to a place where, only I can get there through You, Lord. Take me there! Please take me there! I'm hungry and excited to have...More of You God. (Matthew 6:25-27, Mathew 6:34, Matthew 11:28-30, Luke 12:25, John 14:27, Colossians 3:15, 2 Thessalonians 3:16, Psalm 55:22)

Year One:

_____
_____
_____
_____
_____
_____
_____
_____
_____

Year Two:

_____
_____
_____
_____
_____
_____
_____
_____

April 11

Lord, Jesus, today, I'm working on having **stronger faith**. If I am to please You, Lord, I know, I must have faith of a mustard seed. God, Dear Savior, I must walk by faith and not by sight. Faith is me, **believing before receiving** and knowing, I will get it. **It shall be done! It will be done, all in the Name of Jesus!** Faith is getting out on the water, knowing man says, "I cannot walk on water", but with God, I can do all things, because You strengthen me. Therefore, I can walk on water with Your strength and guidance. **Faith is closing my ears to what the world is telling me and listening to what You are saying.** Lord, I have an ear for You. My faith only will come with...More of You God.

(Hebrews 11:1, Hebrews 11:6, Matthew 21:22, Luke 1:37, Ephesians 2:8-9, Proverbs 3:5-6, 2 Corinthians 5:7, Matthew 14:22-33, Mark 6:45-52, John 6:16-21)

Year One:

_____

_____

_____

_____

_____

_____

_____

_____

Year Two:

_____

_____

_____

_____

_____

_____

April 12

Father, I **trust** You, Lord, with all of my life. Lord, Jesus, I have read of Your **many great works**. Lord, today, I have a **spirit of expectancy**. Jesus, perform a new-thing in me and in my life.   Now, I surrender all I have and all I am to You, Lord, Jesus. Father, You give me power and strength; You are my Savior, my King, my everything. As I come to You, today, I say, "**Rain down on me, Lord, I want to see Your Glory**." Oh my Lord, my Savior, I want **more** of You, Father, and **less** of me! Fill me up, Lord! Fill me up with...More of You God...my heart longs for...More of You God.
(2 Corinthians 3:4-6, Psalm 18:2, Psalm 91:2, Nahum 1:7, 2 Samuel 22:31, Psalm 7:1, Psalm 25:1-2, Proverbs 30:5)

Year One:

_____
_____
_____
_____
_____
_____
_____
_____
_____
_____

Year Two:

_____
_____
_____
_____
_____
_____
_____
_____
_____
_____

April 13

Your Majesty, today, I sit at Your feet. I worship You, Lord, because of who You are, my Heavenly Father. I bow down, reverencing You as, my King. Lord, I would not live to see another promising day without You, Jesus. Without You there is no me. It's another reason, to just say, "Thank You, Lord." The moon doesn't shine, nor is the sun bright without You, Lord. My heart does not beat, nor does blood run through my veins, without You, Lord. The wind does not blow, nor does the rain come down, without You, Lord. I shall not prosper or soar, without You, Lord, Jesus. So today, I just want to say, "Thank You, Lord. I love You, Lord." I just want to be close to You. I can only truly live with...More of You God.

(Hebrews 8:1, Psalm 24:10, Hebrews 1:3-4, 1 Chronicles 29:11, Psalm 145:12, Job 37:22, Psalm 93:1, Exodus 15:6-11, Psalm 111:3)

Year One:

_____
_____
_____
_____
_____
_____
_____
_____
_____

Year Two:

_____
_____
_____
_____
_____
_____

April 14

Lord, today, I ask You to release Your miraculous power, revealing Your glory to me. I know, Father, **You reveal Your resurrecting power in everything You undertake.** Lord, I'm asking You to make me new. Create in me a clean heart and change my evil ways. I will walk this earth as an empty vessel for You and only You, Lord, Jesus. Father, my life is in Your hands. I know, it cannot be in better hands than in my Creator. Lord, **I want to walk new, look new, and act new.** Father, I surrender unto You, for **this life I walk, is not about me, it is all about You, Lord, Jesus.** I was created by You. **To praise You! To worship You! To be a disciple for You!** I will go, telling the entire world who You are to me and to the rest of the world. Lord, use me, filling me up supernaturally with...More of You God.

(Psalm 62:11, Job 26:14, 1 Corinthians 6:14, 2 Corinthians 13:4, Psalm 8:1, 1 Chronicles 16:24, Philippians 1:11, Psalm 108, James 4:7-10, 1 Peter 5:6-10)

Year One:

_____
_____
_____
_____
_____
_____
_____
_____
_____

Year Two:

_____
_____
_____
_____
_____
_____
_____

April 15

Father, You are **my Rock**! Today, I walk in <u>complete</u> authority. Lord, I'm asking You to put a **boldness** in me, one I can only get from You. I want the kind of boldness where, I have **no fear** to accomplish what You have called me to execute on this earth. Lord, give me a boldness where I will be able to feel comfortable being a **witness for You**, Father. Lord, **send me, and I shall go**! Lord, **use me, and I will be willing**! Lord, **fill me up, and I will share**! Lord, **pour out to me, and I will give unto others**! My foundation is in my Lord, my Savior; fear will no longer be a part of my life. Now, I will walk with my head up high. Not exemplifying arrogance, but it's because I know, who I am and whose I am. I go now, sharing with the world...More of You God. (Psalm 31:3, Psalm 18:2, Psalm 78:35, Psalm 42:9, Habakkuk, 1:12, 2 Samuel 22:32, Acts 4:29, Ephesians 3:12, Ephesians 6:19, Hebrews 4:16, Psalm 127:3, 2 Corinthians 10:2)

Year One:

_____
_____
_____
_____
_____
_____
_____
_____

Year Two:

_____
_____
_____
_____
_____
_____

April 16

Lord, where You reside is **where the light shines**. Today, I see the light over my life, Lord. There can be **no darkness** wherever You exist. This is even more of a reason why I call Your Name out loud, "Jesus, Jesus, Jesus." **Demons flee at Your powerful Name.** There is power in Your Name. You shine brightly over all that You execute and all You plan to undertake. I know, **when Your Son died on the cross for me, everything I could ever ask for was already made possible.** Now, Father, in order for me to receive all the blessings You have for me, it is time for me to accomplish what You have called me to conquer. Lord, I'm living with a changed heart and mind, because I have stepped into...More of You God.

(John 8:12, 1 John 1:5-17, Matthew 5:16, Psalm 27:1, 1 Peter 2:9, Matthew 8:16, Mathew 8:28-34, Mark 9:29, Matthew 17:18)

Year One:

_____
_____
_____
_____
_____
_____
_____
_____

Year Two:

_____
_____
_____
_____
_____
_____
_____

110

April 17

Creator, my Savior, You created me to **love, love,** and **love**. Today, I'm going out into the world to show Your divine and unconditional love. I refuse to let the enemy have his way. Therefore, I **will pray for my enemies showing love**. To everyone who crosses my path, I will greet them with a warm smile, saying, "Hello and how are you today?" It is an amazing feeling to say, "I love you," to people who have never heard it from a stranger and/or someone who is just not expecting to hear such kindness come from my mouth. **Yes, it is so refreshing and much easier to show love, rather than to show or have a hateful spirit.** God, touch me, filling me with Your loving kindness; so I will be a **reflection** of who You are in **all** my ways. Lord, let love radiate off of me, as I walk this day with...More of You God. (1 John 4:10, Luke 2:11, Matthew 5:44, Luke 6:25-31, Mark 12:31, 1 Corinthians 13, 1 Peter 4:8)

Year One:

_____
_____
_____
_____
_____
_____
_____
_____

Year Two:

_____
_____
_____
_____
_____
_____

April 18

Lord, today, I thank You for how You made me, so unique and beautiful. Father, I thank You for the special gift You have created inside of me. Lord, You say, You **will make room for my gift**. I guarantee, I'm available for Your use. Today, Father, I completely open myself up to You. Lord, make a way for me this day, guide and direct my path. I know, my gift is **not** what You are after, because **You are the one who gave it to me**. You have given me a free will, and it is up to me to accept You as my Lord and Savior. Also, to work for Your kingdom. Today, I offer up to You, all You have given me, Father. Lord, God, You are worthy! I praise Your Holy Name and give all the honor to You, my Father. Lord, **my gift shall glorify Your Name**, as I grow with...More of You God.

(Jeremiah 1:5, Genesis 1:27, Ephesians 2:10, Matthew 10:30, Proverbs 18:16, Proverbs 16:9, Joshua 24:15, Revelation 3:20, Mark 8:34)

Year One:

_____
_____
_____
_____
_____
_____
_____
_____

Year Two:

_____
_____
_____
_____
_____
_____
_____
_____

April 19

Father, today, I thank You for **Your Word**. You talk about how a **bountiful garden** may have some weeds and what it represents. Lord, I know, You are talking about me, Father. I am imperfect, even if I do Your good works all day, I once was a sinner, but through Your blood, I'm now a saint. Holy Spirit continue to work in me day and night, so I will become a better person, living a healthier life. I also know, **if my garden has some tares and I pull the weeds, I will lose the wheat (good) planted.** I will wait on You for **Your pruning**. Lord, today, I continue to press toward a higher and deeper, place in You. I will wait on **You to mold me**, the way You want me, Father. I'm planning to stay on the Potter's wheel **until** You move me, Lord. I do not want to get off too soon and not be **completely** formed. Lord, I am nothing without...More of You God.
(Matthew 13:24-30, Psalm 27:13-14, Philippians 3:14, Jeremiah 18:1-6, Isaiah 64:8, John 15:4-5, John 5:19, John 1:3)

Year One:

_____

_____

_____

_____

_____

_____

_____

_____

Year Two:

_____

_____

_____

_____

_____

_____

April 20

As long as I have You, Father, today, I praise You because I have no wants or needs. I thank You that **You are fully stocked.** As long as I have You, there is **no** emptiness or void in my life. **Because I have You and all of my answers are in You,** I will **no longer look to man for any answers.** Lord, God, thank You for making a way for me and answering my prayers. Your Word says, Your promise in my prayer, the answer is, **"Yes and Amen."** Lord, I can do all things through You who strengthens and lives inside of me. I know, I will **always win** as long as I have You. Lord, I grab on to You for Your Word says, **as long as I seek, I shall find.** Lord, God, I shall continually seek after...More of You God.

(Psalm 95:1-11, 2 Samuel 22:50, Philippians 4:19, Matthew 6:8, Psalm 34:10, Psalm 24:1, 2 Corinthians 1:20, Matthew 7:7)

Year One:

_____
_____
_____
_____
_____
_____
_____
_____

Year Two:

_____
_____
_____
_____
_____
_____
_____
_____

April 21

Hallelujah! Lord, Jesus, today, my **praise is my weapon**. I have a spirit of praise built all up inside of me; I can feel it in my bones. I have got to release it, all to my Father. My heart is **on fire** for You, Lord, Jesus, and my **eyes are fixed** on You, Jesus. As I praise You, today, Father, I can see Your image and feel Your presence; You're revealing Yourself to me. **My praise is setting my mind free**; I have freedom in my praise. Right now, this praise I have, today, is a **lifetime ministry**. It is **my new lifestyle,** and it sure looks good on me. Oh Father, my God, **my praise is my response to revelation**. Lord, I know, my praise **will break chains** off of any situation. I thank You, Father, for the response You reciprocate, when I give, what is due to You. Lord, Jesus, all the praise belongs to You! My praise I offer You, Lord, You are all I need. I'm worshipping...More of You God.

(2 Chronicles 20:21-22, Hebrews 13:15-6, Exodus 15:1-2, Deuteronomy 32:3-4, 1 Samuel 2:1-2, 1 Chronicles 29:11-13, Jeremiah 20:9, Psalm 39:3)

Year One:

_____
_____
_____
_____
_____
_____
_____
_____

Year Two:

_____
_____
_____
_____
_____
_____

April 22

Lord, I'm amazed by You. Holy, holy, holy You are and there is no one else who has Your holiness. Today, I rejoice and I'm basking in Your presence. In Your presence, sickness is being healed and deliverance is taking place. As I'm sitting here with You, Lord, I have all the protection I need. Now, in Your presence, all bondage is falling off of me. I thank You for being my **Redeemer**; I can always count on You, Father. Lord, when everyone around seems to fail me, You are still here. Jesus, You are so compassionate; I feel Your Love. I thank You for living inside of me, Holy Spirit; oh, how You comfort me. I will sit before Your throne, praising Your Name forever. Yes, because You are Holy! Yes, You are worthy! This is why I am falling more in love with...More of You God.

(Revelation 4:8, Leviticus 14:13, 1 John 4:12, Acts 3:19-20, Acts 2:1-47, Romans 8:28, John 3:16, Psalm 23:4)

Year One:

_____
_____
_____
_____
_____
_____
_____
_____
_____

Year Two:

_____
_____
_____
_____
_____
_____
_____
_____

April 23

New blessings are coming to me. Today, so I can get to You, God, I'm **tapping into Your invisible world, where Your supernatural powers reside**. You are where the <u>impossible is possible</u>. As Your Word says, all things are possible for them who love the Lord. Thank You, Lord, for not giving up on me. Thank You, Lord, Jesus, for making a way out of no way. You did not have to do it, but You did it anyhow- just for me, Lord. Oh, how I love You, Lord, Jesus! What a mighty God, I serve! I thank You, Lord. Father, You are **about to elevate me to another level**. I'm so grateful this current cycle is about to end. Father, here I am, holding onto, praising, and trusting...More of You God.

(2 Corinthians 9:8, Philippians 4:19, James 1:17, John 1:16, Mark 9:23, Luke 1:37, Matthew 17:20, Deuteronomy 10:17)

Year One:

_____

_____

_____

_____

_____

_____

_____

_____

_____

Year Two:

_____

_____

_____

_____

_____

_____

_____

April 24

My breakthrough is already here. Today, I'm going to walk and tap into all the blessings You have for me, Father. Your Word says, You **will break forth and build me a paved road right through the ocean,** Hallelujah! Lord, Jesus. **I now, <u>forget the old</u>, letting go of what has happened and I <u>grab ahold to the new</u>, what is about to happen.** I will stop talking about what did happen, unless it is to glorify Your Name, Father. I refuse to sit around here asking for a pity-party, it's not what I need. My hope and my faith is in You, Almighty God. You said You're about to do a new-thing. Therefore, I will **keep a praise in my mouth at all times**. All the glory belongs to You, Lord! My heart is full of praise. My breakthrough comes with…More of You God. (Ephesians 6:12, Revelation 1:3, Isaiah 53:1-12, Romans 5:1, Isaiah 14:21, Psalm 39:7, Psalm 34, Ephesians 3:20-21, Philippians 4:20)

Year One:

_____
_____
_____
_____
_____
_____
_____
_____
_____

Year Two:

_____
_____
_____
_____
_____
_____

April 25

Father, for so many days I have asked, "Why me Lord?" "Why do I have to be the one to go through this and that situation?" Today, I just give You all the honor, all the glory for choosing me, to endure this journey. Now, I realize **what I have been going through is not a-bout me**. I step out of myself, because **this pain and suffering was for someone else.** **Right now, my testimony is** helping the next person, to hold onto Your unchanging hand. Your Word says, You are no respect of person; therefore, if You did it for me, You will do it for them. Glory! Glory! Glory! To the Most High! All of my worship is for You, Lord. Praising and singing, Lord, thanking You for...More of You God.

(Deuteronomy 2:7, Numbers 9:13, 1 Kings 19:4, Genesis 24:42, 2 Timothy 3:12, Philippians 1:29, Revelation 2:10, Matthew 5:10-12, 1 Peter 4:12-16, Revelation 12:11)

Year One:

_____
_____
_____
_____
_____
_____
_____
_____
_____

Year Two:

_____
_____
_____
_____
_____
_____
_____
_____

119

April 26

The battle **is not** mine. Today, Lord, Jesus, I know, **You are** fighting my battle. You are fighting cancer, high blood pressure, depression, diabetes, heart problems, neurological problems, and weight problems. All diseases are not of You, Lord, Jesus. Thank You, Lord, for **rebuking all of these illnesses.** Lord, help me to **fight** these battles **in my mind.** It is so hard to let them go. They are trying to consume me, and I feel like I am drowning in problems, problems, and more problems. But, I have a God, who is a **BIG** God. Lord, I thank You! **You are bigger than any situation or problem I will ever face in this lifetime.** I **speak** to the situation, problem, and/or illness, right now, and say, "Be thou removed, in the Name of Jesus." Lord, I thank You for Your power. Hallelujah Lord! You are the reason why I have to have and flow in...More of You God.

(2 Chronicles 20:1-29, Ephesians 6:12-17, 1 Samuel 17:47, Job 26:14, Isaiah 40:28, Psalm 147:5, Jeremiah 1:5, Mark 11:22-24, Proverbs 18:21)

Year One:

_____
_____
_____
_____
_____
_____
_____

Year Two:

_____
_____
_____
_____
_____
_____
_____

April 27

This day is a day of **courage**. Because with You, God, You are my strength; I will be strong and courageous. Lord, Jesus, **with You I can move mountains**. I **can** **fight any giant and <u>win</u>**. "Why am I courageous?" You **have** given me the **power** and **authority**, to **cast** out **demons and to heal the sick**. When You, Jesus, ascended back into heaven to sit by the Father, to intercede on my behalf, You left me with **more power** than what Your Son had on this earth, per Your Word. Today, I'm walking in authority, because I know, who I am and whose I am. I'm made in Your image, and You reside inside of me. My Father is the King and yes, He owns it all. I will press on, as I seek, and operate with...More of You God.

(1 Chronicles 28:20, 1 Corinthians 15:58, Psalm 27:1, Psalm 56:3-4, 2 Timothy 1:7, Joshua 1:9-11, Proverbs 3:5-6, Mark 5:36, John 14:12-14)

Year One:

_____
_____
_____
_____
_____
_____
_____
_____

Year Two:

_____
_____
_____
_____
_____
_____
_____
_____

April 28

Today, I'm **changing** my ways; I want to be more like You, Lord, Jesus. Your Word says, it **is better to give than to receive.** I do not want to miss my whole entire life's purpose. I want to **be a giver and not a taker.** From this day forward, I will give from my heart. I will **give to those who are less fortunate than me.** I will give through, **my service to others, my finances, clothing, and time.** Lord, work with me and through me, Father. Lord, You gave Your only begotten Son's life, just for me, "So what more can I do?" You came to show and paved the way. I just want to say, thank You, Lord! You're so good! You're so good to me! This is the reason why my heart yearns for...More of You God.

(Romans 12:2, 1 Corinthians 15:35-58, Isaiah 40:31, 2 Corinthians 5:17, 1 Corinthians 10:13, Acts 20:35, John 3:16)

Year One:

_____

_____

_____

_____

_____

_____

_____

_____

_____

Year Two:

_____

_____

_____

_____

_____

_____

_____

April 29

Jesus, You came down here on this earth, serving us, **instead of us serving You**. Father, You are the **greatest servant of all**. Lord, You **led by example,** and You **never** complained or turned anyone away. Jesus, today, place in my heart and soul, **how to be a better servant** for Your kingdom and Your people. Lord, I need Your help; sometimes I just get tired. My mind, my feet, and my hands, just want to quit. But, Father, I look up to You. As Your Word tells me, to **look up to the hills for my help**, Lord, Jesus, I need You, now. I cannot do it without You! My spirit cries out and up unto the hills, for...More of You God. (Luke 22:24-30, Mark 10:45, Philippians 2:5-8, 1 Corinthians 10:24, 1 Corinthians 4:1, John 13:12-15, Proverbs 3:5-6, Psalm 121:1-8)

Year One:

_____

_____

_____

_____

_____

_____

_____

_____

Year Two:

_____

_____

_____

_____

_____

_____

April 30

Holy Spirit, You are welcome here. Today, Lord, come and **rain on me. I declare and decree, in the Name of Jesus, it is my time to bloom.** I'm ready to blossom into the beautiful flower, You have design me to be. Lord, let the entire world see what You are doing in me. I have a **changed attitude,** that only reveals the Jesus in me. **I'm taking leaps, bounds, growing, and evolving into the stunning image, You've created me to become.** Father, everywhere I go I will shine for You, Lord-for Your glory, Lord, Jesus. My light is shining more each day, as I wrap my heart and mind into...More of You God. (John 4:6-8, Micah 3:8-10, Acts 2:1-5, 1 John 2:19-27, Matthew 5:13-16, Romans 13:11-14, Ephesians 5:7-14, John 12:35, Isaiah 60:1)

Year One:

_____
_____
_____
_____
_____
_____
_____
_____
_____

Year Two:

_____
_____
_____
_____
_____
_____
_____
_____

May

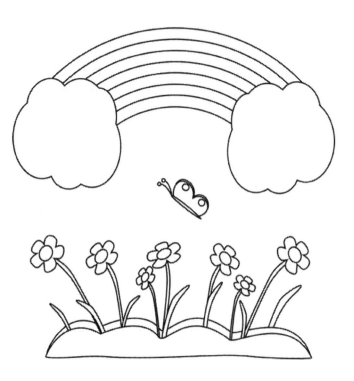

May 1

Dear, Lord, Jesus, thank You for the **Holy Spirit, who speaks on my behalf**. Lord, it is so wonderful to have **Your Spirit inside of me**, speaking on my behalf; especially, when I do not even know what to say. Today, Father, I just want You to know how I appreciate my gift of speaking in tongues (for those who do not have the gift you can pray and ask God for it). It is so powerful to be able to speak to You in tongues; **even the devil doesn't know what I am saying to You**. Holy Spirit, You know, what I need **better than I know myself**. Please **intervene** on my behalf. I need You! I want You! I have got to have You! I'm blessed to have this precious relationship with You, and I'm **more powerful** with the Holy Ghost. I have more depth, strength, and power with…More of You God.

(Matthew 10:20, John 14:26, Acts 2-4, Galatians 5:16, Romans 8:26, John 20:22, Luke 11:13, 1 Corinthians 14:2)

Year One:

_____
_____
_____
_____
_____
_____
_____
_____
_____

Year Two:

_____
_____
_____
_____
_____
_____
_____
_____

May 2

Lord, today, I want to **praise You** for thinking so much of me. Father, You thought enough to save little-old-me. You **sent Your only Son Jesus, to die on the cross, just for me, a sinner.** You thought I was worth it; oh, how grateful I am. I'm so glad You are in my life, You have **cleansed** me of my many sins; now, I am **free**; I am **whole.** Oh Hallelujah, Lord, Jesus! Now, I must go telling the entire world, of Your goodness, Your greatness, and Your power. What a powerful and Mighty God, I serve! I give You all the honor, all the glory, and all the praise. You are worthy, Lord, Jesus! You are worthy! **My heart is grateful; You felt I was worthy.** It's an honor to have...More of You God.
(John 3:16, Romans 5:8, 1 John 4:9-11, Ephesians 2:4-5, Mark 16:15, Luke 8:38-39, Psalm 145)

Year One:

_____
_____
_____
_____
_____
_____
_____
_____
_____

Year Two:

_____
_____
_____
_____
_____
_____
_____

May 3

Glory hallelujah to my King! Today, I am singing praises and shouting unto You, God, my Savior; **You saved me**. There is none like You, my Savior, my Lord, and my King. You came to give me a **greater life, filled with abundance** and prosperity. Oh, how I thank You, Lord! **Your sacrifice allowed my life to be complete and full of purpose**. I thank You for loving me first and for the uniquely-created plan You have for me. I know, I have fallen short from Your glory, but You still continually call me **Your friend**. <u>God, Your Son, Jesus, is the only way to get to You</u>. Your Word states, Jesus is the way, the truth, and the life. No one can come to You without going through Your Son, Jesus Christ. I continue to pray through Your Son, Jesus Christ, seeking for...More of You God.

(Psalm 96:1-2, Ezra 3:1, Psalm 81:1-2, Isaiah 44:23, John 10:10, 3 John 1:2, 1 John 4:19, Romans 3:23, John 15:15, John 14:6)

Year One:

_____
_____
_____
_____
_____
_____
_____
_____

Year Two:

_____
_____
_____
_____
_____
_____
_____

128

May 4

Where the **grace of God abounds, there is freedom**. Lord, today, I'm grateful Your **love is plentiful**. I just want to be full of You, night and day, Lord, Jesus. Lord, I know, where Your spirit is, there is liberty. This means, I am free because Your spirit lives inside of me. Holy Spirit, have Your way in me, right now; it is Your will I am seeking after, forever. Father, according to the New Testament of Your Word, now, I am **under Your law of Love**. Lord, all of Your Words **will** be fulfilled. The heaven and the earth, will pass away, but Your Words will never pass away. My Father, **You are the same God, in the New Testament as in the Old Testament; you have not changed Your mind about right and wrong**. Therefore, Holy Spirit, You have Your way in me; please tell me what it is You want me to achieve. Use me Lord! Use me Lord! Crying out for...More of You God.
(Romans 5:17-20, Romans 6:14, 2 Corinthians 3:17, James 2:8, Matthew 24:35, Hebrews 13:8)

Year One:

_____
_____
_____
_____
_____
_____
_____
_____
_____

Year Two:

_____
_____
_____
_____
_____
_____

May 5

This **dream** in my heart, Lord, Jesus, I know, is who You have **created** me **to become**. Father, today, I have a **fire burning** in my heart, giving me **goals** and a **clear vision**. Now, my soul is saturated with an unspeakable joy, wrapped around my future. Lord, **take my dreams, and draw me to a place You have prearranged, just for me**. Father, Your Word tells me, I must have a vision because if I don't, I will perish. Today, Lord, to get my dream's instructions, I draw my attention to You; only You can make sense of them. Father, I want to follow Your instructions; **I will be <u>unstoppable</u>**. My dream was created from You, Lord, Jesus. Lord, convey Your power inside of me. I know, the creativity and energy I need to fulfill my dreams, will only come from You. Lord, Jesus, my dreams **will come to pass,** as long as I am escorted with...More of You God.
(Job 33:15, Judges 7, Psalm 39:3, Isaiah 9:3, Ecclesiastes 9:7, Habakkuk 2:2, Isaiah 26:4, Ephesians 6:10, Matthew 19:26)

Year One:

_____
_____
_____
_____
_____
_____
_____
_____

Year Two:

_____
_____
_____
_____
_____
_____
_____

May 6

Father, God, **I will bless You, Lord, at all times**. Today, I recognize who I am blessing, the highest King; I give my all to You, Jesus. Father, You **always** reward me, as I strive to do what is Your will and Your way. You are a blessing to me; therefore, **I will be a blessing for someone else**. Father, as I bless others, You **always** take care of all of my needs and heart's desires. I thank You, Lord, Jesus, for Your loving kindness. Lord, **You are the greatest giver of all**. Every good and perfect thing comes from You, Lord. Father, my trust is in You. I will always have consideration for the poor. My ear is **tuned** into You for Your guidance; I will follow Your ways and continue working through enduring temptations. I appreciate that **all of Your blessings come from spiritual places**. Glory! Glory! Glory! To my King, my blessings come from...More of You God.

(Psalm 34, Hebrews 11:6, Galatians 6:9, Matthew 6:33, Jeremiah 17:10, Ephesians 6:8, Revelation 22:12, Isaiah 41:10, 2 Corinthians 3:4-6, Proverbs 3:5, Isaiah 61:1)

Year One:

_____
_____
_____
_____
_____
_____
_____
_____

Year Two:

_____
_____
_____
_____
_____
_____
_____

May 7

Today, I have a **faith surpassing all human understanding**. Lord, my faith **doesn't have any boundaries, nor any limits**. Father, my soul, my body, and my mind, is chasing after You, Lord, Jesus. Lord, the more I read Your Word, my faith continues to grow. Father, as I look back over my life, I **remind myself of what You have already done for me**; my faith increases substantially. Right now, I can tell any mountain to move and it will move! I have the kind of faith where I can accomplish whatever is put in front of me. Father, I can do any, and everything, as long as You strengthen me. **I believe, therefore, I know, I will achieve all You have for me, Lord**. Thank You, Lord, for acknowledging and rewarding my faith, **taking me somewhere limitless**! Through and with You, I will achieve and succeed, as long as I put my faith in...More of You God.

(Ephesians 3:19, 2 Corinthians 5:7, Romans 10:17, Proverbs 3:5-6, Hebrews 11:1, Luke 1:37, Matthew 17:20, Philippians 4:13)

Year One:

_____
_____
_____
_____
_____
_____
_____
_____

Year Two:

_____
_____
_____
_____
_____
_____
_____

May 8

Jesus, You made a way for me. Today, I **look back when I was lost; but now, I am found**. I look at **when I was in darkness**; but You, Lord, Jesus, **brought the light, directly to me**. Father, I remember **when I was bound; You set me free**. Oh Yes, Father, You made a way for me! Thank You, Lord. You loved me enough to save and care for me. Jesus, **You are the way maker**; You made a way for peace, joy, and my victory. Lord, You saw my spiritual brokenness and had mercy on me. Thank You, Lord, for **wrecking** Satan's plans for me. I am still on the battle field, however, I will win this battle, as long as I have and fight with...More of You God.

(1 Corinthians 10:3, Isaiah 43:19, John 8:12, Ephesians 5:8, Romans 7:6, John 3:16, Psalm 18:30, Psalm 34:18, Ephesians 6:11)

Year One:

_____
_____
_____
_____
_____
_____
_____
_____
_____

Year Two:

_____
_____
_____
_____
_____
_____
_____
_____

May 9

Lord, I exalt You for who You are, Father! You reign! You reign! Today, Lord, Jesus, I **will wait on You**; all the power is in Your divine hands. Father, You know how the human mind works. You created me; therefore, You know, how extremely hard it is for me to wait. I have such an inpatient habit of wanting to take matters into my own hands. You see, Lord, I have a desire to have instant gratification, always wanting things at my fingertips. However, Lord, You have spoken, and I know, **patience is the virtue**. Patience is one of the fruits of the spirit; I must have patience to wait on You. Father, **You are going to do all things, on Your time. It is always the right time.** I <u>will</u> <u>not</u> grow weary in doing well; for in due season, **I will have the victory. I will reap a bountiful harvest.** Father, I'm waiting on You, Lord, for...More of You God.

(Psalm 99:5, Isaiah 25:1, Lamentations 5:19, Psalm 110:1, Psalm 27:14, Job 33:3, Habakkuk 2:3, Galatians 5:22-23, Galatians 6:9, 1 John 5:4)

Year One:

_____
_____
_____
_____
_____
_____
_____
_____

Year Two:

_____
_____
_____
_____
_____
_____
_____

May 10

Father, Your Word is the **guiding light** in my life. Today, I concur, I have **never** been able to do anything in my life, worthy, **without** You, Lord. Savior, **Your Word is the light, directing me straight to heaven.** Through my acceptance of Your Word, I am born again, my soul is purified, and I am saved. Hallelujah! Hallelujah! Hallelujah! Father, use me as Your vessel to be a light to the world, showing others the right walk of life and path, to get them to Your Kingdom. Glory! Glory! Hallelujah! Lord, I just want to tell You how much Your Word is truly a blessing to me. **I cannot live without it.** Until the day I die, I will **continue** to **read it, act on it, live it, and share it.** Hallelujah, Lord, Jesus, Hallelujah! My light will luminously sparkle, as long as I walk with and spread...More of You God.

(Psalm 16:11, John 15:5, John 3:3, 2 Timothy 2:21, 2 Corinthians 4:7)

Year One:

_____
_____
_____
_____
_____
_____
_____
_____
_____

Year Two:

_____
_____
_____
_____
_____
_____

May 11

Today, Lord, I'm **depending** on You. I know, there isn't any mountain too high, You cannot tear down and move. **There is deliverance in my worship**. It is an honor for me to come before Your throne, praising Your Holy Name. Hallelujah! Hallelujah! This is the highest praise, all the Hallelujahs belong to You, Father. I glorify You and only You. Lord, I **thank You for honoring my worship; You put tremendous value on it**. Lord, You sit high and look low. Your presence comes near me, as I glorify Your precious Holy Name. I invite You to be with me day and night. Oh, **how sweet it is to be in Your presence; You start breaking confining chains off of me and completely cleaning me up**. Your Presence! Your Presence is what I'm after! Desiring to be closer to You, Lord, Jesus. I have got to get closer to...More of You God. (Psalm 34:17, John 8:32, Psalm 34:4, Joel 2:25-27, Psalm 113, Genesis 28:15, Psalm 16:11, 2 Chronicles 5:13-14, Psalm 27:4)

Year One:

_____
_____
_____
_____
_____
_____
_____
_____
_____

Year Two:

_____
_____
_____
_____
_____
_____
_____

May 12

I'm ready to **take off** like an eagle. Today, I am ready to **soarrrrrr**. Father, in Your Word, You **compare** us to an eagle. The mother eagle **stirs up the nest** for her babies, and this is what You do for me, Lord. You allow situations to become so uncomfortable for me. Therefore, I have a **get up spirit** to change myself to help others change, and I have an impact on changing the world around me. As this affliction is on me, God, You **flutter over** me just like the eagle does with her babies. Lord, You do this to **draw my attention** to You, and once, I look to You, a change comes over my life. Then, You **spread Your wings to reveal Your glory and to release Your power**. Your grace is sufficient. Father, You always show up in my life mightily. Yes, Lord, I will mount up like an eagle, spread my wings, and fly with...More of You God.

(Isaiah 40:31, Job 9:26, Job 39:27-29, Proverbs 23:5, Deuteronomy 32:11, Jeremiah 48:40, Psalm 103:5, 2 Corinthians 12:9)

Year One:

_____
_____
_____
_____
_____
_____
_____
_____

Year Two:

_____
_____
_____
_____
_____
_____
_____
_____

May 13

Father, God, thank You for **hiding me in Your wings**, keeping me safe and sound. Today, I'm thankful for waking up with another breath of life. Lord, I'm grateful. This is just the beginning of what You have in store for my life. Your Word says, my latter will be greater; so I'm excited and I'm looking forward to **walking into my blueprint, You've designed**. Lord, Jesus, I must tap into Your tools and stand firmly on Your Word, the promises You laid out for me. I must **stand securely on the truth, Your Word,** and not on the precarious facts of this world. **If You said it, it shall be done, and I believe it**. So, **no matter what test** I have gone through: the loss, the sadness, the oppression and/or failure, **it was all done for Your glory, Lord, Jesus, and my life's promotion**. Father, I'm so happy for Your **divine favor, bless-ings,** and **increase,** in my life. I will continue to flourish, as long as I experience...More of You God.

(Psalm 91:4, Psalm 17:8, Psalm 57:1, Psalm 63:7, Acts 17:25, Haggai 2:9, Psalm 90:17, Psalm 5:12, Luke 2:52, John 1:16)

Year One:

_____
_____
_____
_____
_____
_____
_____
_____

Year Two:

_____
_____
_____
_____
_____
_____
_____

May 14

My heart is genuinely in love with You, today and forevermore, Lord, Jesus. Father, preserve my spirit, soul, and body, for You, my Savior. My **spirit** is the component receiving **You**, God; it makes **intimate contact** with You. It is my **innermost quality of my being**. Lord, my **soul makes up my mind to worship and praise You**. It is my **free will and psychological source, which directs me**. Last, but not least, is **my body, Your temple!** My physical character encompasses all of my senses and this is how I express my most inward uniqueness to You. So, Father, God, today, **with my entire** being, I want to tell You how much I love You, wholeheartedly and absolutely, Lord. Jesus, **You command me to love You** and yes, You loved me first. Lord, my heart cries out to You and surely, most definitely, I'm in love with...More of You God.

(Romans 12:9, 1 Thessalonians 5:23, Matthew 10:28, James 2:26, Hebrews 4:12, Galatians 5:16-17, 1 Corinthians 6:19-20, Luke 1:46-47)

Year One:

_____
_____
_____
_____
_____
_____
_____
_____

Year Two:

_____
_____
_____
_____
_____

May 15

Savior, today, I am in <u>total</u> agreement with You. I **will not relinquish Your truth;** I **will stand firm on what Your Word speaks** to me. Right now, I will speak blessings over my life, in the Name of Jesus. For the glory of the Lord is here; I will live; I shall not die. As I look at my life, all **weapons** trying to form against me, <u>have no power</u>. I'm putting on the **full armor of the Lord** and <u>I shall win</u>. **No** devil in hell has any power over me. I cry out Your Holy Name. Jesus! Jesus! Jesus! **For there is power in Your Great Name.** I thank You, Lord, for **giving** me the **authority** to **use** Your Name to cover me, anoint me, and keep me, as I endure trials, throughout my life. What an awesome, God, You are to me! **I can walk through fire,** as long as I walk with...More of You God.

(Matthew 18:19, Acts 2:1-47, Psalm 118:17, Isaiah 54:17, Acts 4:12, John 14:13, Matthew 1:21, Matthew 21:22, Isaiah 55:11, 2 Corinthians 4:18, Romans 4:17, Daniel 3:1-30)

Year One:

_____
_____
_____
_____
_____
_____
_____
_____

Year Two:

_____
_____
_____
_____
_____
_____
_____

May 16

What a mighty God, I serve! Today, I will make a promise to go out, telling the whole wide-world of Your goodness, mercy, and grace. Father, **I will spread Your Word** to all who come near me. I will **step out** of my **comfort zone, letting go** of my **fearful** and **weird feelings.** It's time to **tell** my neighbors about **a God,** who is my **Savior.** I will **tell** them about a **God,** who is **compassionate** and **unconditionally loves us** all. Moreover, I will tell them about a **God,** who **sent His only Son to die on the cross for the entire world** and **three days later, He rose** up from the **dead.** Yes, I will tell them about a **God,** who has **paved the way** for <u>all</u> of **my needs.** Hallelujah Lord, Jesus! How mighty You are! Everything You do is great! How marvelous and Holy are You! My Precious, Precious, Savior, oh, how I cherish You. It's an honor to know...More of You God.

(Mark 16:15, Matthew 24:14, 1 John 4:16, 1 John 4:7-10, Romans 8:39, Jeremiah 29:11, 1 Timothy 4:4, Romans 8:28, Psalm 86:10)

Year One:

_____
_____
_____
_____
_____
_____
_____
_____

Year Two:

_____
_____
_____
_____
_____
_____
_____
_____

May 17

Laughter is the **best medicine** for my **soul** and my **heart**. God, today, I am able to **laugh** at what happened **yesterday**; You came, **turning my life from upside-down** to <u>joy</u>. Now, I can see Your light twinkling brightly in my life and in every situation I encounter. This laughter, in my soul, is a **cheap medicine**. I <u>do not have</u> to go see a doctor to get a prescription for it; I just come to You, Father, the <u>**Great Physician**</u>. I have a joy just locked up inside my bones; I have to let it out. I dance unto You! I shout unto to You! Jesus! Jesus! Jesus! The Great Messiah, You are to the entire world! There is none like You! You hold the entire earth in the palm of Your hand. How big You are! I have a great spark inside of me and I'm using it for Your glory, to reach others in need. Father, use this laughter and joy inside of me, to build Your kingdom. This joy I have is because of...More of You God.
(Proverbs 17:22, Ecclesiastes 2:26, Philippians 1:3-5, 1 John 1:5, John 5:1-9, Psalm 95:4)

Year One:

_____
_____
_____
_____
_____
_____
_____
_____

Year Two:

_____
_____
_____
_____
_____
_____
_____

May 18

You are the God of **turning burdens into blessings**. Today, I see Your goodness in my life. For Your glory, Father, You take **my bad** and **turn it into Your good**. Oh, how grateful and thankful I am, for **deliverance, mercy, and grace**. Your grace has found me just as I am. Now, I am changed by Your great love for me. Thank You, God, for **sending Your Son into this world to bring hope, light, and reconciliation**. Sometimes, my life is difficult and filled with unexpected hardships, causing me pain. But, **I have a God, who is a nothing-impossible God!** Now, I have faith in the plans You have for me, Lord. Father, I commit myself to You, there is nothing and no one, I shall fear. Lord, Jesus, You are my **safety net**. Jesus, I will seek Your face and build my relationship with You. As my faith grows, I press into…More of You God. (James 1:12, Revelation 2:10, 2 Corinthians 12:10, James 4:6, Hebrews 4:16, Luke 1:37, Matthew 19:26, Philippians 4:13, Jeremiah 29:11, Psalm 27:1, Psalm 32:7)

Year One:

_____
_____
_____
_____
_____
_____
_____
_____

Year Two:

_____
_____
_____
_____
_____
_____
_____

May 19

Lord, I am **staying** on the course. I'm staying on Your wheel until You have me **perfectly molded**. Today, I have a **changed mindset** and **attitude**. I know, while I am on Your Potter's wheel it gets hot and scary, but, You have me by Your right hand. You tell me in Your Word, I will go through some obstacles, but, **You will be with me during the process**. These oppositions I'm facing, are just an indicator, the devil is not happy with how You plan to use my life. God, continue to form me, so, I can be more Christ-like. Build my character, Father. Lord, Jesus, I realize **my timetable is not Your timetable**. Thank You, Lord, for **transforming my burdens into blessings**. I will wait for...More of You God.

(Psalm 119:1-8, Jeremiah 18:2-4, Genesis 2:7-8, Psalm 94:9, Isaiah 29:16, Romans 12:2, Isaiah 40:31, Isaiah 41:10, John 16:33)

Year One:

_____
_____
_____
_____
_____
_____
_____
_____
_____
_____

Year Two:

_____
_____
_____
_____
_____
_____
_____
_____

May 20

Your, Majesty, I'm here to worship You. Lord, Jesus, today, my **purpose is to worship You** and only You. I just want to love on You. I can't help but to praise You. You are the Great I Am; You are **greatly to be praised**. **My worship is for You; it is not about me.** I humble myself before Your throne, crying out, Holy! Holy! Holy is the Lamb of God! I adore You, Lord, Jesus! Within my life, **I decrease so You will increase.** You **specifically** **created me for this sole purpose,** to worship You. Here I am, Lord, to bow down to, my King. I clap my hands to, the God of Gods and I lift up my hands to, the Lord of Lords. I'm after a new experience in You, Lord, God, and I'm getting there with...More of You God.

(Psalm 93:1, Hebrews 8:1, 1 Chronicles 29:11, Psalm 145:12, Job 37:22, Isaiah 2:10, Revelation 5:12, John 1:29, Revelation 13:8, Revelation 17:14)

Year One:

_____
_____
_____
_____
_____
_____
_____
_____

Year Two:

_____
_____
_____
_____
_____
_____
_____

May 21

Jesus, today, I'm asking You to fill me up. I want to be **full of You**, so, wherever I go, I will be able to **set the atmosphere**. I want my heart to be pure; I want to glorify You, Lord. Therefore, I will commit to **studying Your Word daily**. I will listen to praise and worship songs, around my home. I will have an **appointed set time to spend with only You**, Lord, Jesus. Yes, I will exhibit humility and not pride, allowing for Your Gospel to flourish. With sincere praise and heartfelt worship, I'm here to express my love and adoration for You, Lord. Father, the **primary reason I attend Your church body** is to **worship You together as Your Church**, **one body**, **one mindset,** and **on one accord**. Lord, I am the church. When I worship You, I get near to...More of You God. (Proverbs 31, Psalm 16:11, Psalm 81:10, Psalm 51:10, 2 Timothy 3:15-17, Proverbs 30:5-6, Revelation 22:18-19, Romans 15:6, Philippians 2:2, 1 Corinthians 12:27, Romans 12:4-5)

Year One:

_____
_____
_____
_____
_____
_____
_____
_____

Year Two:

_____
_____
_____
_____
_____
_____
_____
_____

May 22

Oh, what a happy day. I have **my mind made up**; I'm going to rejoice in this beautiful day You have made, Lord. My praise to You does not depend on the place or the condition I am in; it is where my mind is right now; I am happy. I refuse to rely on my happiness from things, circumstances, and people, I encounter today. Lord, my Father, **I rejoice in You and in Your will**. I am glad in You, Lord; I have joy. I know, the **reward** You have for me is great and mighty. I will **stay focused on spiritual things,** having the right understanding of reality. I **will not have** an **envious spirit** of my neighbors; I **will have** Godly contentment. Lord, I came into this world without anything; I will leave without anything. Father, You are all I need, chasing after...More of You God.

(Ecclesiastes 3:12, Proverbs 15:13, Psalm 103:1-2, Psalm 118:24, Philippians 4:4, Colossians 3:23-24, Romans 2:6, 1 Corinthians 15:58, 1 Timothy 6:7)

Year One:

_____
_____
_____
_____
_____
_____
_____

Year Two:

_____
_____
_____
_____
_____
_____

May 23

Today, is a day to **break off chains**. I <u>refuse</u> to let the devil steal my joy. I'm going to **evaluate** <u>all</u> of my past and current relationships, making sure I do not have any **resentment**. Once I **release all resentment** bounded up inside of me, **I <u>will</u> get my joy back**. Today, I forgive every person who has caused pain and hurt in my life. I will not hold onto or ignore these intense, deeply-rooted feelings, any longer. Now, it's time for me to **relinquish this unresolved, consuming fire, causing me deep anger**. I <u>will</u> look at the <u>truth</u>, asking God to **cleanse my heart** of these terrible feelings and **release this pain** harnessed inside of me. <u>Resentment is a silent destroyer</u>. Right now, Father, I confess of my sins and repent. Forgive me, Lord, Jesus, and forgive my neighbors, as well. Lord, now, I pray for my enemies, asking You to bless them. Father, as I release this resentment, I am blessed and filled with...More of You God.

(Psalm 2:3, Acts 16:26, John 16:16-24, Ephesians 4:32, Colossians 3:13, Genesis 50:15-21, Psalm 51:7-10, 1 John 1:9, Acts 3:19, Matthew 5:44)

Year One:

_____
_____
_____
_____
_____
_____
_____

Year Two:

_____
_____
_____
_____
_____

148

May 24

Father, today, I **will get into Your Sanctuary**; I want to be near You, Lord. I know, Father, where You are is, only, Holy. I come now, with pure worship on my heart and a humble spirit. Lord, You are **great, awesome, amazing, magnificent, majestic, and beautiful to me.** Jesus, I know, as I'm here in Your Sanctuary, I am **setting myself up** for miracles, signs, and wonders to occur, in my life and others. I'm ready Lord! I'm ready! Here I am! This is an **opportunity** for **chains to be broken, breakthroughs to occur,** and **strongholds to be released.** Hallelujah to the Most High! Healing is taking place in my body, right now, in the Name of Jesus. Glory Hallelujah! I am free indeed, as I enter into Your gates, I receive...More of You God.

(Exodus 15:17, Exodus 25:8, Leviticus 19:30, Psalm 73:17, Romans 15:19, 2 Corinthians 12:12, Isaiah 8:18, Psalm 100:4)

Year One:

_____
_____
_____
_____
_____
_____
_____
_____
_____

Year Two:

_____
_____
_____
_____
_____
_____
_____

May 25

God, You are **not the Author of confusion**; You are the **Lord of Peace**. Today, no matter what I encounter, I will have a peaceful day. **If You are not in it**, Lord, Jesus, **I do not want to be a part of it**. God, **impart wisdom** in me this day as I move forward in my life, my destiny, and my purpose, You have for me. **Guide** my feet as I take **each step** moving closer and closer to the prize. Father, God, I want to have peace that surpasses all understanding; it comes only from You. I **do not care** what the **doctor's report is**, I'm **standing on Your Word**. Moreover, I do not care what other people say about me. I know, I'm wonderfully and beautifully made, by my Creator, my Savior. I thank You, Lord, for who You are and I, **now**, know who I am and whose I am. Lord, just a closer walk with...More of You God.

(1 Corinthians 14:33, Romans 15:13, Philippians 4:4-7, James 1:15, Proverbs 2:6, Psalm 119:105, Psalm 139:14, Micah 6:8, Deuteronomy 5:33)

Year One:

_____
_____
_____
_____
_____
_____
_____
_____
_____

Year Two:

_____
_____
_____
_____
_____
_____
_____

May 26

God, I thank You today, You are a **God of possibilities.** I have been **wishing, wanting, and dreaming.** As long as I hold onto Your unchanging hand, I know, **my desires are within reach.** Right now, Father, let Your will be done in me. Lord, Jesus, **my hope is in You,** Father. No one **has seen, heard, or can imagine what You are about to do in my life,** Hallelujah! Father, please, Savior, do a new thing in me. I use to want what the world had for me, but now, I am found. **I want to live for Y**ou and only You, Lord, Jesus. Father, You are a wonder! You are a wonder! My life keeps changing and growing with...More of You God.

(Genesis 18:14, Jeremiah 32:17, Matthew 19:26, Luke 1:37, Mark 14:36, Job 42:2, Matthew 26:39, Psalm 62:5, Isaiah 43:19, 2 Corinthians 12:12, Isaiah 8:18, Revelation 12:1, Deuteronomy 4:19)

Year One:

_____
_____
_____
_____
_____
_____
_____
_____

Year Two:

_____
_____
_____
_____
_____
_____
_____
_____

151

May 27

Elevation is the word for today; it is **time for my upgrade**. Lord, Jesus, I'm **keeping** my eyes on You. Father, You sit up high and as long as I continue to **keep seeking Your face, I can only go one way**, Up! Up! Up! Lord, God, I know, as long as You are in me and I am in You, **I will** accomplish great things. I am going higher and **higher** in You, Lord, Jesus. I **cannot do anything** without You, Lord. I once felt hopeless; **now,** I can see. My eyes are wide open; I have an **unstoppable vision**. Yes, **I will reach** the mountain top! I may be in the valley right now, but, I'm **on my way to victory**. Yes, Lord, victory is mine! Victory is mine! My victory and elevation comes with seeking after...More of You God.

(2 Corinthians 4:18, Deuteronomy 31:6, Hebrews 12:2, Hebrews 3:1, Isaiah 26:3, Proverbs 3:5-6, Philippians 4:6-7, James 5:16, John 9:25)

Year One:

_____
_____
_____
_____
_____
_____
_____
_____
_____
_____

Year Two:

_____
_____
_____
_____
_____
_____
_____
_____

May 28

Today, Father, I have the kind of **faith cultivating** my life for **success.** This faith I have **will achieve mastery.** I **will not** let fear creep into my plans, my mind, or my life. This faith I have **will allow** me to **walk a-cross the sea.** It **will allow** me to **touch the hem of Your garment.** It **will allow** me to **enter into the burning furnace** and **not** burn, **nor** have any scourge marks on me. It **will allow** me to be **thrown in the lions' den** and **not** be bitten, **nor** eaten. This faith I have, Lord, Jesus, **will cast out demons** and **heal the sick,** all in the Name of Jesus. Father, thank you for strengthening me, equipping me, and inspiring me. I cannot do anything without You. I am walking and running with...More of You God.

(Hebrews 11:1, 1 Corinthians 2:5, Proverbs 3:5-6, Matthew 14:29, Matthew 14:36, Matthew 9:20, Daniel 3:1-30, Daniel 6, Matthew 10:8, John 15:5, Philippians 4:13)

Year One:

_____
_____
_____
_____
_____
_____
_____
_____
_____

Year Two:

_____
_____
_____
_____
_____
_____
_____
_____

May 29

My Savior, today, I have an **attitude of gratitude**. I just want to say, thank You, Lord. I thank You, Father, for the trials, the problems, the hurts, and the pains. I know, Lord, Jesus, <u>without</u> **encountering troubles, I have no growth**. Father, You allow these things to come up against me, **to prepare me for the special place, You have for me**. Lord, Jesus, I know, everything happening to me gets me a step closer to achieving something bigger and better, than my current situation. Lord, today, I'm **investing in You**, Lord. I get a **greater return from You**, Father. Lord, I will not have room enough to store all of the blessings You have for me. I give my offerings of time and money, investing into...More of You God.

(Colossians 2:7, Psalm 118:24, 1 Chronicles 16:34, 1 Corinthians 15:57, Psalm 23:4, Psalm 37:7, Proverbs 19:17, Matthew 6:19-21)

Year One:

_____

_____

_____

_____

_____

_____

_____

_____

_____

Year Two:

_____

_____

_____

_____

_____

_____

_____

May 30

Hallelujah! Hallelujah! Hallelujah! Today, Lord, Jesus, I **usher into Your** underlined **presence.** Lord, God, **meet me here**; I want to be with You, Lord. It is in Your presence, **I am revived**; I **have peace**; I **have joy**; I **am strong** and **I have a Holy Ghost boldness.** Father, as You meet me here, I **can feel Your** unwavering **love.** It feels so good to get into this place with You, Lord. I don't want to leave. Lord, please stay here with me, Father. You comfort me in my time of need. This place I'm in, right now, **feels like heaven.** Wow! My Savior, You are so beautiful to me! **Your presence is warm; it is inviting; it is magnificent.** The King has enter into my room. I reverence You with a bow and shout out...More of You God.

(Psalm 42:1-2, Psalm 84:1-2, James 4:8, John 15:5, Psalm 27:8, Hebrews 10:19-22, Isaiah 50:4, Jeremiah 33:3, Psalm 46:10)

Year One:

_____

_____

_____

_____

_____

_____

_____

_____

_____

Year Two:

_____

_____

_____

_____

_____

_____

_____

May 31

Sovereign, Savior, today, I want to thank You for taking this heavy load and burden off of me. Lord, God, I **thank You for removing every yoke**, right now. Father, I'm **standing on Your promises** and I surrender. I cannot save the day. I refuse to live another day succumbing to fear. I am a child of the highest God and I know, You love me dearly. I remember, **love conquers all**, and **perfect love casts out all fear**. My Sovereign Savior, I am going to **practice** putting **my peace to work. Not only will I preach Your Word, I will live Your Word.** I have a changed mentality and a new attitude. My victory is in the will of the Lord. I will continue to prosper with...More of You God. (Psalm 115:3, Proverbs 16:9, Romans 8:28, Isaiah 40:23, 2 Chronicles 20:6, Psalm 71, Matthew 11:29-30, Acts 15:10, Matthew 23:4, 1 Corinthians 13, 1 Peter 4:8)

Year One:

_____
_____
_____
_____
_____
_____
_____
_____

Year Two:

_____
_____
_____
_____
_____
_____
_____

June

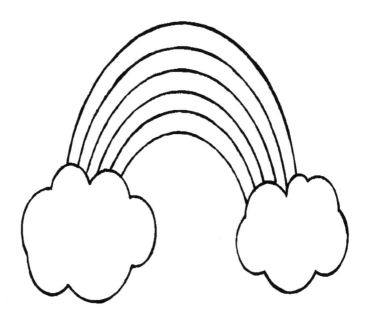

June 1

Father, my Lord, today, I'm **moving forward** and **believing** there is **nothing I cannot accomplish**. Yes, Lord, I believe, You, God! Father, You are faithful and You are willing. Therefore, I believe You, God! I believe, **I will** be **very successful** in my life. I believe, I will be **blessed abundantly, exceedingly, and more than what I can ever ask for**, Lord. Father, **I believe as I continue to sow seeds, financially, physically, and mentally, they will come back, pressed down, shaken together, and overflowing**. Yes, Lord, I believe, You, God! I believe, I **am the lender** and **not the borrower**. I believe, You, God! Hallelujah! **I am the head** and **not the tail**. **I will experience and see enormous measures of greatness in my lifetime**. Yes, God, I believe, the more I get in Your presence, the more my life will prosper with...More of You God.
(Matthew 21:22, John 3:16, John 6:35, Ephesians 3:20-21, Luke 6:38, Deuteronomy 28:13, Exodus 33:14)

Year One:

_____
_____
_____
_____
_____
_____
_____

Year Two:

_____
_____
_____
_____
_____
_____
_____

158

June 2

Lord, today, I want to thank You for **opening my eyes**, allowing me to see such an **awesome view**. What **appears** to be impossible, I know, it **is possible with You**, my Savior. Father, thank You for letting me **see clearly**, this **dream**; it can only be achieved through the power of my God. Lord, I see You **breaking restrictive chains off of me**. I see the opening of doors which are leading me to what I once thought **was impossible, becoming conceivable**. Father, I now see, what I though was going to take me out of here, You are **using it as a setup for my success**. Only a Great God, can do the impossible. Now, Lord, I see the **pain and suffering I went through, was for my victory and for Your glory**. My victory is near! My victory is within reach! My victory is in Your hands! I can only progress forward and receive it, as long as I keep seeking after...More of You God.
(Matthew 19:26, Luke 1:37, Philippians 4:13, Mark 10:27, Revelation 3:7-13, Deuteronomy 20:4, Ephesians 6:10)

Year One:

_____
_____
_____
_____
_____
_____
_____
_____

Year Two:

_____
_____
_____
_____
_____
_____
_____
_____

June 3

Creator, You **crafted me** to do great things for Your kingdom. Today, I have a spirit of thankfulness, growth, and prosperity. I will **not despise the small beginnings**, for it is in these moments, You are molding, building, and preparing me, to take on my mountain. Father, I know, I am in a **stage of preparation**, right now. As long as I'm here on this earth, You are working on my inner being and taking me from **stage to stage, to stage, or better yet, glory to glory**. Lord, I know, my one day is like 1000 years for You; You already know my tomorrow. You say, it is going to be greater; therefore, I trust You, Lord. I can do all things through You, Lord, Jesus. I **will continue to climb this mountain; my success is up there waiting on me**. I'm climbing to get closer to You; I must have...More of You God.

(Exodus 9:16, Jeremiah 29:11, Micah 6:8, Zechariah 4:10, 2 Corinthians 3:16-18, Psalm 90:4, Philippians 4:13)

Year One:

_____
_____
_____
_____
_____
_____
_____
_____
_____

Year Two:

_____
_____
_____
_____
_____
_____
_____
_____

June 4

Jesus, thank You for **saving me**. You didn't have to do it, but Yes, You did it. Today, I'm thankful for You **removing all baggage**, in my way trying to hold me down. Father, sometimes, I get so caught up in this world and in my life; I forget what is my purpose and plan. Thank You, Father, for **getting me back on course** and for removing all garbage trying to invade my space. You have taken me and striped me, as well as, pruned me. Sometimes, I feel like, "Why me Lord?", but, then You tell me, *"Hold on, I have great work for You to do."* Lord, now, **You've removed, people, situations, jobs, and circumstances, out of my life. All of these things were just distractions, keeping me from You.** Now, I'm moving in the **right direction for my victory**. I will keep pressing my way through, reaching towards...More of You God. (Romans 10:9-10, 1 Peter 3:18, John 15:2-6, Isaiah 18:5, Hebrews 13:21, Psalm 90:17, Colossians 3:24, Genesis 2:3, Philippians 3:14)

Year One:

_____

_____

_____

_____

_____

_____

_____

_____

Year Two:

_____

_____

_____

_____

_____

_____

June 5

A shift is taking place. Lord, today, I can see and feel You **shifting my atmosphere**. Father, I am so excited about this **new season**, the new place You are taking me to, for Your glory. It is a place where **milk and honey will plentifully flow**. I will not have to worry about my bills, finances, health, relationships, etc. Everywhere I look, blessings are coming, from the North, South, East, and West. I just cannot keep up, they are coming so fast. Father, God, I will just rest in You, right now, Lord. I have a peace, I know, only comes from You. **All I can see is simply incredible**; it is a gift from my Savior. **My life is changing from anxiety, fear, not having enough, to overflowing-joy, with more than enough**. I will walk in this new season, while equipping myself with...More of You God.

(Luke 2:13, Amos 9:13-15, Psalm 37:7, Matthew 11:28-30, Psalm 55:6, Psalm 4:8, Philippians 4:7, 2 Timothy 1:7, Exodus 15:2)

Year One:

_____
_____
_____
_____
_____
_____
_____
_____
_____

Year Two:

_____
_____
_____
_____
_____
_____
_____
_____

June 6

Beloved, Savior, today, I refer to myself as the **disciple God, loves;
just as Your disciple John referred to himself.** I am the child You
love, Lord, Jesus. Yes, I am special and yes, You especially, love me.
Your Words says, You first loved me, and Jesus is love. Therefore, I
can go out and tell the entire world, You love me and I am a child of
the Most High God. **As royalty, I am a queen/king, and I will be re-
spected.** I refuse to be treated less than who I am and whose I am. I
will **walk with authority**, the authority that You have given me, Lord,
Jesus. I'm filled up with boundless bliss, joy, and peace. Father, Your
love lives inside of me; there is comfort in knowing I have Your love.
Lord, let me continue to show Your love to everyone I encounter. My
love will flourish, as long as, I feed off of...More of You God.
(John 13:23, John 19:26, John 20:2, John 21:7, John 21:20, Romans
5:8, John 3:16, Romans 8:35-39, 1 John 4:16, Luke 10:19, Matthew
7:29, Matthew 10:1, Mark 1:22, Mark 3:14-15)

Year One:

_____
_____
_____
_____
_____
_____
_____
_____

Year Two:

_____
_____
_____
_____
_____
_____
_____

June 7

Lord, God, **how excellent is Your name!** Father, You are good and very good. Today, I am grateful for **every name given to You** in Your Word. Each name reveals something about Your character, and I have been blessed by each one of them. Yes, **Jesus**, You are my **Salvation**; You **saved me**. You are the Precious **Lamb of God**. **Yahweh, Jehovah,** You are **my Lord**, and **my Master**. **El Shaddai, Lord, God, Almighty,** You are **my Provider**, supplier, and my sustainer. **Jehovah Jireh**, Yes, Lord, You **provide for me**; You always have a ram in the bush waiting, just for me. **Jehovah Rapha**, You are **my Healer**, my Great Physician. **Jehovah Shalom**, the Lord, of **my Peace**, I turn to You for comfort and strength. **Jehovah Mekoddishkem**, my Lord, **who sanctifies me**. You set me apart as Your child, sanctifying and You make me holy. **Jehovah Raah**, my Lord, **my Shepherd**, You are my friend, indeed. **Jehovah Tsidkenu**, You are my Lord, **my Righteousness**. You provide me with victory and prosperity. **Jehovah Shammah**, You are, my Lord, who is **always there**; You never leave me or forsake me. Regardless of what I am going through, or heading into, Lord, Jesus, my Father, I must go with...More of You God.
(Psalm 8, John 14:6, Genesis 2:4, Genesis 17:1, Genesis 22:14, Exodus 15:26, Judges 6:24, Exodus 31:13, Psalm 23:1, Jeremiah 23:6, Ezekiel 48:35)

Year One:

_____
_____
_____
_____
_____

Year Two:

_____
_____
_____
_____

June 8

Jesus! Jesus! Jesus! I'm going to **have good manners** and **let You know I'm thankful.** Today, I'm going to **be like the one Leper out of the ten, who came back to tell You, thank You, Lord.** Father, I realize **my obedience** unto You is **my duty to serve You.** God, You are deserving of gratitude because of Your mercy and grace. Lord, each and every day, **You give freely to me, and I do not deserve it.** Lord, God, You **sent Your only Son to die on the cross for my sins.** Now, I have life everlasting and words cannot express how thankful, I am unto You, Jesus. I do not have enough tongues to tell You, thank You, Lord. Hallelujah! Hallelujah! Hallelujah! I give You the highest praise. Lord, Jesus, You are worthy to be praised! My life depends on...More of You God.
(1 Thessalonians 5:18, Psalm 107:1, Ephesians 5:20, Luke 17:11-19, John 3:16, 1 John 4:9, 1 Corinthians 14:19, Psalm 103:2, Psalm 95:1-11)

Year One:

_____
_____
_____
_____
_____
_____
_____
_____

Year Two:

_____
_____
_____
_____
_____
_____
_____
_____

June 9

Most gracious, God, today, I come to **lift up my Savior.** My heart cries out, Hallelujah! Hallelujah! Hallelujah! Hosanna! Hosanna! Hosanna, to the King! Lord, **You are the ruler of the entire world.** Save me I pray, my Lord, my King, and my Savior. Father, hear my cry out to You. This **world is in chaos,** and everywhere I turn, I see evilness. Lord, God, **I want more of You.** This **world needs more of You. My family needs more of You. My friends need more of You.** You tell us in Your Word, all we have to do is **humble ourselves, pray, and turn away, from our evil ways.** Then, we will **hear from You.** This land will not be healed unless we all change our ways and tap into...More of You God

(1 Timothy 6:15, 1 Timothy 2:1-2, Proverbs 29:2, Psalm 39:12, Psalm 116:1, Psalm 61:1-4, 2 Chronicles 7:14)

Year One:

_____
_____
_____
_____
_____
_____
_____
_____
_____
_____

Year Two:

_____
_____
_____
_____
_____
_____
_____
_____

June 10

Heavenly Father, today, with all of my might, **I'm going to praise You like King David praised You**. I will **not limit my praise**; I will **not be ashamed of my praise**. Oh, bless the Lord, oh my soul, I cannot contain the adoration I have for You, nor can I control it. Like David, I'm going to praise You so hard I will dance out of my clothes. Lord, I am in awe of all of Your marvelous attributes. Compelled by Your power and majesty, all I can do is praise You. Father, **You are from everlasting to everlasting; You are timeless**. Lord, God, everything I know about You, causes me to praise You. You are **great!** You're **omnipotent!** You're **omnipresent!** You're the **first and the last!** You're the **beginning and the end!** Hallelujah, my Savior, all power, glory, and salvation belongs to You, Lord, God. You are worthy to be praised! Glory! Glory! Hallelujah! Hallelujah! Hallelujah! My God is awesome and I cannot help, but to keep praising...More of You God. (Psalm 149:1-9, Psalm 150:1-6, Psalm 146:2, Psalm 135:3, Psalm 105:1-45, 2 Samuel 6:14-23)

Year One:

_____
_____
_____
_____
_____
_____
_____

Year Two:

_____
_____
_____
_____
_____
_____

June 11

Hallelujah, Lord, I'm so thankful, today, knowing **every good and perfect blessings comes from You**, God. Lord, You are the "Father of Lights"; You **created all things**. Father, I am here to give credit to where credit is due. You created the moon, the sun, the stars, and the sky. No man can do what You have done and what You continue to do. Lord, Your Word says, You give me **benefits daily**. I can, surely, testify to this being true; every gift You give me it benefits me daily. My dear, Father, thank You for **the gifts You give me, to perfect Your church, enhance Your ministry, and edify Your body**. Lord, God, I know, Your gift is perfect, and it is **complete**. I will ask for Your gifts and wait on You. As I receive them I will use them to Your glory. Thank You, Lord, for pouring into me, my spirit says yes to...More of You God.

(James 1:17, Job 42:2, Matthew 19:26, Mark 10:27, Psalm 68:19, Ephesians 4:12, Acts 2:17, Titus 3:6)

Year One:

_____
_____
_____
_____
_____
_____
_____
_____
_____

Year Two:

_____
_____
_____
_____
_____
_____
_____

June 12

Mighty Creator, today, I'm **crying out** for **our country** and this **entire world**. We need You, Lord, Jesus. Nowhere is safe, we are **fighting against principalities in high places**. I know, I can only fight with Your armor, Lord. It's time for an awakening of our people. I'm **crying out** for all of Your **people to come together, humble ourselves, and pray**. Right now, we are amongst evil times. Satan is running rampant, but he has **no** power over You, Lord, God, **because You created him**. Let me **step into my calling, my purpose and pray…pray…pray**. I submit to You, Father, and I will **now prioritize** what is really important. I surrender! I surrender! I surrender unto You, my King! I can only move forward with…More of You God.

(Psalm 57:2, Judges 3:9, 1 Chronicles 5:20, 2 Chronicles 13:14, Psalm 34:6, Lamentations 2:18, Matthew 27:46, Ephesians 6:12)

Year One:

_____
_____
_____
_____
_____
_____
_____
_____
_____

Year Two:

_____
_____
_____
_____
_____
_____

June 13

In all sincerity, Lord, Jesus, today, I **believe every word You have spoken to me**. I'm praying and believing for a miracle. Jesus! Jesus! Jesus! I need Your **divine intervention**; something supernatural is about to happen in my life. This miracle is going to **substantially benefit my life**. Yes, this **miracle will be a non-natural phenomenon occuring, all for my good**. It will take me to another level in You, Lord. The world will speak to me and say it is impossible, but, God, I know, nothing is impossible with You, Lord, Jesus. The **possibility and probability of miracles are all through Your blood and existence, in my Life**. All I have to do is believe and wait on You. While I'm waiting, I'm grabbing a hold to...More of You God.
(Acts 4:30, John 4:48, Acts 3:16, Acts 19:11, 2 Thessalonians 2:9, John 14:12, Mark 16:17, Mark 11:24, Jeremiah 32:17, Proverbs 3:6)

Year One:

_____
_____
_____
_____
_____
_____
_____
_____
_____
_____

Year Two:

_____
_____
_____
_____
_____
_____
_____

170

June 14

God, I thank You for **shielding me** from all of **my falls.** <u>I am victorious</u>; that's why people look at me calling me victory. Today, I <u>refuse</u> to let any of **my past failures defeat me or dictate my future.** I will hold onto my passion, taking each day forward to work towards the life You established for me. Lord, I thank You. Your eyes erase all that is ugly. **You sent Your, Son, Jesus, to seal the deal on giving me eternal life.** Wow, Lord, Jesus, I'm so grateful unto You, my Savior. **You lift me in all of my times of need.** Lord, God, You have <u>**never**</u> **failed me**, as a matter of fact, You **carry me when I fall.** Hallelujah! Lord, Jesus! I thank You for loving me so much. I love You, Lord, God, I'm falling more and more in love with...More of You God.

(Psalm 28:7, Psalm 18:2, Genesis 15:1, Deuteronomy 33:29, Psalm 33:20, Psalm 84:11, Proverbs 30:5, Psalm 115:9, Psalm 3:3)

Year One:

_____

_____

_____

_____

_____

_____

_____

_____

_____

Year Two:

_____

_____

_____

_____

_____

_____

_____

June 15

Father, today, I thank You for **strategically placing me** in You, Lord. You have looked down on me and have **given me a touch from heaven.** I can feel it in the air; Your presence is all around me. I'm **mesmerized by Your love, grace, and mercy.** Lord, You have ministered to my soul, renewed me, revived me, and rebirthed me. My Savior, thank You for **breathing** into me, **rebirthing** what was dead, and **bringing it back to life.** Now, I am **glowing. I'm like a beautiful flower, blooming and blossoming.** The light of You, Lord, Jesus, is shining through me. I now, have a **purpose to move forward** with what is inside of me; Your just **waiting for me to activate it.** Lord, God, I'm on my way to my destiny with...More of You God.

(Esther 2:16-17, Jeremiah 31:2-3, Acts 15:39-40, 2 Corinthians 12:8-9, Hebrews 4:16, John 1:14, Acts 4:33, Acts 6:8, Acts 11:22-24)

Year One:

_____
_____
_____
_____
_____
_____
_____
_____

Year Two:

_____
_____
_____
_____
_____
_____
_____
_____

June 16

Oh, what a happy day-today! When the enemy tried to come in like a rushing flood, to destroy me, Father, God, you used it to cure me, Hallelujah! Lord, **You continue to motivate me.** You <u>keep</u> me fight-**ing and dreaming fearlessly.** I once thought that I could create my experience, but since, I have found out I must live it. **I'm unstoppable with You,** Lord, Jesus. Now, I can better help my neighbor, since I am rooted in You and know who I am.   This life I'm moving into is **spec-tacular, outstanding, unbelievable, and magnificent; it is only be-cause of You,** Father. My dreams and future is evolving because of...More of You God.

(Micah 7:8, Deuteronomy 20:4, John 16:33, Ephesians 6:10-13, James 1, 2 Peter 3:9, 1 John 5:4, Romans 8:31-32, Joshua 10:8, Philippians 4:1)

Year One:

_____
_____
_____
_____
_____
_____
_____
_____

Year Two:

_____
_____
_____
_____
_____
_____
_____
_____

June 17

You are so great, God, I **will never figure You out**. Today, I rebuke the **spirit of trying to put You into a box**, limiting Your power. Lord, I can't even wrap my mind around the magnitude of **how big of a God, You are to me**. The world cannot even use all the logic, nor are we studious enough, or even intellectually capable of knowing, imaging, guessing and/or describing Your greatness, Lord, Jesus. Therefore, God, I **will not treat You commonly**. I will **not subject to praising You in a common way**. You are the King and when You enter into the room, I will always bow down to You and submit to, my Lord. Your love for me has shown me **You are a God without limits; nothing is impossible for You**. Hallelujah, Lord, Jesus! What a mighty God, I serve! I just want to sit at the feet of my Savior, submitting un-to...More of You God.

(Psalm 147:5, Psalm 77:13, Psalm 62:11, Job 26:14, Psalm 79:11, 1 Corinthians 6:14, Luke 11:20, 2 Corinthians 13:4, Job 9:4, Isaiah 26:4, Zephaniah 3:17, Ephesians 6:10)

Year One:

_____
_____
_____
_____
_____
_____
_____
_____

Year Two:

_____
_____
_____
_____
_____
_____
_____

June 18

I Praise You! Praise You! Praise You! Lord, Jesus. I'm going to **praise You in all circumstances.** It does not matter what my today looks like; it can be my best or worse day; but it's not going to dictate my praise to You, Lord. Hallelujah! From this day forward, I'm **walking into kingdom living.** I'm having **an attitude of joy, thanksgiving,** and **praying, at all times.** Lord, because I have You, I know, whatever comes my way, I will be able to overcome it with Your strength, therefore, I shall rejoice. No matter what the devil tries conjuring up, I will love and rejoice in You, Lord, Jesus. Father, I **will not question You, nor become infuriated with You,** for You are my Rock and my foundation is in You, Lord. My victory is in...More of You God.
(Psalm 22:3, 2 Samuel 22:50, Psalm 103:2, Deuteronomy 28:1-68, Psalm 24:8-10, Psalm 127:1-5, Psalm 95:1-11)

Year One:

_____
_____
_____
_____
_____
_____
_____
_____
_____

Year Two:

_____
_____
_____
_____
_____
_____
_____

175

June 19

"The prayers of the righteous availeth much," says the, Lord. Today, I can shout out, "**It is over, and I made it.**" Lord, thank You for **seeing me through every trial and tribulation.** Sometimes, I start losing hope, but You extend Your right hand out to me, keeping me stable. Now, I'm leaping over many of my situations and circumstances. Through You, I'm **not bound to my faults**, Lord, Jesus. It's reassuring, knowing You hear my prayer, Father. I get down on my knees day in and day out, fervently praying to You. You hear me, and You answer me. Father, I know, my prayer is merely a request to Your sovereign will. I will wait on You, Lord, for **a good, Father, doesn't always do what I ask; He does what is good for and to me.** Thank You, Lord, for loving me enough to protect me from all harm and danger. I can't help but love on...More of You God.

(James 5:16, Psalm 65:2, Psalm 34:15, Proverbs 15:29, 2 Chronicles 7:14-15, Psalm 66:19-20, John 14:6, John 16:23-24, Matthew 7:7-8, 1 John 5:14-15)

Year One:

_____
_____
_____
_____
_____
_____
_____
_____

Year Two:

_____
_____
_____
_____
_____
_____
_____

June 20

Father, today, **this fire inside of me is blazing red hot**. Lord, what You have put inside of me is ready to flame brightly, rapidly and bursting outside of me. What a tremendous impact I'll have on this world! Father, my ears are still open to You. I need a whisper from You, now. Lord, Jesus, **give me a rhema word-a spoken word, to edify Your people and to draw unbelievers to You**. Now, Father, do a supernatural thing in me, Lord. To receive all You have for me, **open my spiritual eyes, ears, and heart**. I promise to **remain grounded in Your Word**, the Holy Bible. I want a heart like Yours, Lord, Jesus. My heart will transform and shape with ...More of You God.

(Jeremiah 20:9, Leviticus 9:24, Genesis 3:24, Exodus 9:23, Revelation 4:5, 2 Timothy 4:2-5, 1 Thessalonians 1:5, 2 Timothy 3:16-17, Psalm 119:50, Luke 8:11-15, Psalm 119:9-11)

Year One:

_____
_____
_____
_____
_____
_____
_____
_____
_____

Year Two:

_____
_____
_____
_____
_____
_____
_____

June 21

God, Your Word stands forever and ever. Today, I look at the grass, the flowers, and the buzzing bees. I realize **all things will pass away, but Your Word will always remain.** Lord, Jesus, Your Word will not change, and Your benefits will not change. Father, every Word that You send forth will accomplish what You say it will. Lord, God, Your Word is eternal; it is sure and steadfast. My Savior, **Your Word is my sword**, and I take it with me, everywhere I go. I use Your Word to fight my battles and, Yes, I win every time. **Your Word never comes back void.** Until I stand before Your almighty throne, I'm equipped to fight the good fight of faith. Lord, **Your Word is my sustaining food.** I will continue to feed off of...More of You God.

(Isaiah 40:6-8, 1 Peter 1:25, Matthew 24:35, Malachi 3:6, Hebrews 13:8, Lamentations 3:21-23, Hebrews 4:12, Ephesians 6:17, Isaiah 55:11)

Year One:

_____
_____
_____
_____
_____
_____
_____
_____
_____
_____

Year Two:

_____
_____
_____
_____
_____
_____
_____

June 22

My life is a lesson in humility; I **can only grow with You, Lord**. Today, Father, I know, **I'm nothing without You**, Lord, Jesus. Every gift I have comes from you and only You, Lord. I **do not deserve** any of these blessings You have bestowed upon me. You are so gracious, and You honor me with so much. I am very thankful unto You, my King. **God, You gave Your Son's life for me; therefore, I will give up some of my prize possessions to my neighbors, so it will benefit them and glorify You**. Lord, I know, as I humble myself, You give what You have promised. It doesn't get any better than this, to receive Your blessing as I am always trying to be obedient to You, my Savior, my King. I want to be more like You, Jesus. I can only have this humble spirit with...More of You God.
(John 5:19, John 15:4-5, John 1:3, Jeremiah 10:23, Philippians 4:13, Deuteronomy 31:8, Genesis 1:27, Matthew 7:21, Joshua 1:8, 1 Samuel 15:22)

Year One:

_____
_____
_____
_____
_____
_____
_____
_____
_____

Year Two:

_____
_____
_____
_____
_____
_____
_____

June 23

Today, **like a lion, I feel fiercely strong**. I'm feeling courageous because I have the **power of God inside of me**. Holy Spirit, **take control of my every move**. As I take each step today, guide me. **Impart Your wisdom** to speak and perform, only, what is of You, Lord, Jesus. No matter what the earthly cost may charge me, Lord, **don't let me fail You**. Father, lift my head, and keep me on the right path, the path of righteousness. Lord, God, I need courage to be indestructible, so I will spread and preserve Your Word. By standing on Your Word and Your truth, I know, I may endure some pain and afflicttion. But, **in the end I will come out victorious**. Lord, God, I can only live courageously and be strong with keeping my eye on the prize. Yes, Lord, having...More of You God.
(Philippians 1:6, Philippians 4:13, Hebrews 4:16, Deuteronomy 31:6, Proverbs 3:26, Proverbs 3:5-6, John 1:12, Romans 8:28)

Year One:

_____
_____
_____
_____
_____
_____
_____
_____
_____

Year Two:

_____
_____
_____
_____
_____
_____
_____
_____

June 24

Your sovereign monarchy, is all about You, Father. Today, Lord, Jesus, **I do not look to man's government, I look to You, Lord**. You are the **Godhead and there is no one above You**. Oh, yes, You are the **King of the universe, for You hold the whole wide-world in Your hand**. All things were made through You, God. Without You nothing would exist. God, **You are the light of the world**. Father, You are life. Lord, You are eternal. You are infinite. You are omnipotent. You are omniscient; You are, my Savior. Lord, God, You are, the author and the finisher. My King, You are the Father, the Son, and the Holy Spirit (all three in one). Lord, Jesus, You are my all. I must live this life without compromising You. I'm thirsty for...More of You God.
(1 Chronicles 29:11-12, Isaiah 46:9-10, Psalm 103:19, Proverbs 16:4, John 5:21-30, Matthew 5:14, Hebrews 12:2, Matthew 28:9, 1 John 5:7, Romans 8:5-11)

Year One:

_____
_____
_____
_____
_____
_____
_____
_____
_____

Year Two:

_____
_____
_____
_____
_____
_____

June 25

Father, there are so many **trappings I cannot change**. I can't change people, my past, and the inevitable. However, today, I will start with a **changed attitude towards my future**. Whatever I set out to do in this life, **the bible speaks on, and I should work hard, be diligent, and perform, doing my best**. Now, Lord, I commit to having an attitude allowing me to seek all things of You. In pursuit of Your righteous will, for the rest of my life, I am **setting my heart on heavenly things**. This day forward, I will have a positive attitude; I know, it will directly contribute to my life's success. Even when I have to endure challenges, this new positive attitude will assist me in dealing with all situations; **I will have a successful outcome**. Lord, Jesus, my success is in tapping into...More of You God.

(Colossians 3:23-24, Psalm 90:17, Proverbs 12:11, Proverbs 13:4, Philippians 4:13, Matthew 6:33, Deuteronomy 4:29, 2 Chronicles 30:18-20, Psalm 14:2, Psalm 63:1)

Year One:

_____
_____
_____
_____
_____
_____
_____
_____

Year Two:

_____
_____
_____
_____
_____
_____

June 26

Heavenly Father, You are the **head of my life**. Today, I am overjoyed to find true joy, fulfillment, and faithfulness in You, Lord, Jesus. Lord, each day You have so much for me. I am **challenged with adventure, purpose, and new lessons**. Father, I **trust You completely with every area of my life**. I know, You love me more than anyone I know. **Your love is perfect**. Lord, there have been many times in my life I have gone astray, but **You always find and bring me back home**. Lord, I will seek Your will, so I will be able to receive Your best. I **will stop allowing myself to take a chance on influencing my decisions**; moreover, I will **rely, solely, on You**. God, I now know, You are **my settled peace**; I'm going to do all You have directed of me. Lord, Jesus, You are the **center of my joy,** and I will always look to You to direct my path. I cannot move ahead without...More of You God.
(Joshua 24:15, Psalm 103:17-18, Psalm 137:2-4, Psalm 27:5-7, James 1:2-3, Psalm 4:6-8, Philippians 4:4-5, Psalm 16:11, Psalm 21:5-7)

Year One:

_____

_____

_____

_____

_____

_____

_____

Year Two:

_____

_____

_____

_____

_____

June 27

Lord, God, today, I thank You for being the **God of chances**. Father, throughout this life's journey, I continue to stumble and fall. Circumstances come my way trying to overcome me and I get tired, I want to quit. However, I have You, Lord, Jesus, who **renews my strength daily**. I can **stand on Your Word which never fails**. Your Word is the **glue holding me together**. My **life is a mysterious puzzle**; but You, Father, <u>know what is and what is to come</u>. Before I was even conceived, You already knew me. How can I not serve a God like You! As I appear to fail Lord, **You step in and intervene on my behalf**. You save me, lead me, and direct me, to my victory. I'm so thankful for You, **giving me chance after chance**. I have a victorious life, living with...More of You God.

(1 John 1:9, Matthew 18:21-22, 2 Peter 3:9, Jonah 2:1-10, John 3:16, 2 Corinthians 4:16, Isaiah 40:31, Psalm 51:10, Ephesians 4:23)

Year One:

_____
_____
_____
_____
_____
_____
_____
_____

Year Two:

_____
_____
_____
_____
_____
_____
_____
_____

June 28

Jesus, there isn't any other place I would rather **be**, than **in Your presence**. Today, I just want to reverence You, Father. I just want to be in Your arms. Here in Your arms, I have peace, joy, contentment, relief, and love. Lord, I can rest comfortably, without a lot of chaos, going on inside my head. This place, is a place **I'm not relying on what the world is dictating to me; it is where the truth is spoken**. I rely on **Your Word**, Father, to **mandate my future**. If **You said it, it shall come to pass**. All I have to do is rest in You and trust You, Lord. Lord, I thank You because I can trust You, Father, **You are unchanging**. My faith gets stronger, and I **go to unheard places** with...More of You God. (Psalm 37:7-9, John 14:26, Hebrews 13:5, John 4:24, Psalm 25:5-9, Psalm 16:11, 1 Peter 1:25, Joshua 21:45, Isaiah 55:11, Numbers 23:19, Deuteronomy 28)

Year One:

_____
_____
_____
_____
_____
_____
_____
_____
_____

Year Two:

_____
_____
_____
_____
_____
_____

June 29

I'm **led by the Spirit of God**, therefore, I **am a child** of the **Most High**. Today, I will **be sensitive to You**, Father, as You alert me to the direction I must be obedient to follow. Holy Spirit, You are my prompter, You give me the understanding and acceptance to follow Your will. Thank You, Holy Spirit, for alerting and keeping me away from all harm and danger. You speak to my heart, **empowering me to resist things I should not do or say**. Whatever situation I'm currently addressing, Holy Spirit, as I read my Bible daily, You **impart to me a Word** from Your scripture speaking directly to me. My **intimate relationship with You**, Lord, Jesus, is all about me getting closer to...More of You God.

(Romans 8:14-17, Matthew 1:18, John 14:16-26, John 16:7-15, Isaiah 61:1-3, Joel 2:28, Acts 1:8, Matthew 28:19, Genesis 1:1-2)

Year One:

_____
_____
_____
_____
_____
_____
_____
_____

Year Two:

_____
_____
_____
_____
_____
_____
_____
_____

June 30

You are **my shield**, Lord, Jesus. Today, I realize this life I'm actually living consist of **dealing with a daily war**. The enemy is at his usual trickery of destruction. But, oh no Satan, **You cannot steal my joy. You can't have anything belonging to me**. Not my family, finances, peace, not even, my increase. I have the power and authority, to rebuke You, right now, in the Name of Jesus. This **battle is not mine**, it is Yours, Lord, Jesus. Satan is **no match** for You, my Lord, my Savior. I submit to You, God, and **I resist the enemy**. In order for me to conquer Satan, Father, I'm relying on Your strength. Lord, God, as evil crosses my path, I will come to You, Lord, in prayer, asking You for Your help. I can overcome evil and sin, as long as, I submit to...More of You God.

(2 Chronicles 20:15, Ephesians 6:12, 1 Samuel 17:47, Zechariah 4:6, Romans 8:28, James 4:7, Hebrews 13:6, Psalm 86)

Year One:

_____
_____
_____
_____
_____
_____
_____
_____
_____

Year Two:

_____
_____
_____
_____
_____
_____
_____

187

July

July 1

Abba, Father, today, I **look up to You**. I **honor You** because You are my Father. I **call You Daddy** for I am Your child. God, You sent me here. Father, I thank You for loving me enough to hold me when I'm sad, crying, and in distress. You are always here to catch me as I make mistakes, **giving me substantial (limitless) chances to get it right**. You even scold and chastise me when I do wrong, not adhering to You, Holy Spirit. When I succeed, through You, Holy Spirit, **You reward me greater than what I could ever imagine**. I'm so grateful to You, because You let me make choices. You give me enough rope to find my own way. Father, thank You for always being here; **You never fail me**. Abba, it is awesome having You as my Daddy. My life depends on...More of You God.
(Romans 8:15, Mark 14:36, Galatians 4:1-7, Jeremiah 31:3, Psalm 136, Hebrews 13:5-8)

Year One:

_____
_____
_____
_____
_____
_____
_____
_____

Year Two:

_____
_____
_____
_____
_____
_____
_____

189

July 2

My Lord, Adonai, today, I'm looking at Your **superiority**. You are **supreme over everyone and everything**. Adonai, You are the Lord of my life. You are my everything; I cannot live without You. Lord, Jesus, You are the **Divine owner of all existence** and the **Master of Creation**. Jesus, You gave up Your deity, just for me; You took upon Yourself humanity. How could I not serve a God like You! I submit unto You, Lord. I bow down at Your feet. You are definitely my Boss, Lord, Jesus. **My allegiance is unto You, God**. Lord, my life depends on You. You take care of my family, my health, my finances, and every situation coming my way. It is my honor and duty to serve a God like You. Oh Sovereign Lord, it is imperative for me to have...More of You God. (Psalm 110:1, Deuteronomy 9:26, Psalm 2:1-4, Psalm 8:1-8, Psalm 37:12-13, Psalm 97:5, Psalm 114:7, Malachi 1:1-14)

Year One:

_____
_____
_____
_____
_____
_____
_____
_____

Year Two:

_____
_____
_____
_____
_____
_____
_____
_____

July 3

You are the First and the Last, the Beginning and the End. Yes, Lord, You are Alpha and Omega. Today, I look at my Lord, who is the Author and the Finisher of all things. **In the beginning was God and when everything is all said and done, You will still be here, Lord**. You are **all knowing**, for You knew me when I was in my mother's womb. Father, You know the numbers of hair on my head. Lord, You knew my yesterday, today, and my tomorrow. Father, today, I want to get closer to You in order to have the kind of **intimate relationship where I can hear Your wisdom and guidance**. Lord, Jesus, it is hard staying on Your narrow path. My road is crooked, but I want to be more like You, Jesus. My path can only be straightened with...More of You God. (Revelation 1:8, Revelation 22:13, Revelation 21:6-7, Revelation 1:17-18, Isaiah 44:6, Isaiah 48:12)

Year One:

_____
_____
_____
_____
_____
_____
_____
_____

Year Two:

_____
_____
_____
_____
_____
_____
_____

July 4

Christ, Jesus, You are **the Chosen One.** Let Your anointing fall on me this day. I am a **willing vessel ready for You to use me**, Lord. I'm excited; it gives me pure satisfaction and fulfillment to do Your work, Father. **Use me now, Lord, as Your instrument to change someone's life, so they may be saved, having eternal life with You, Lord, Jesus.** It is an honor being chosen by You, Lord, to do Your will and Your way. Father, I know, I was **born for a distinctive purpose**, for You to get the glory from my life. I was lost; but now I am found. I'm ready for a transformation to take place in my life, and I will impart this transformation to all people along my journey. **Miracles**, **signs**, and **wonders** all come with...More of You God.

(2 Corinthians 5:17-18, Luke 23:35, Luke 9:20, Acts 19:4, Romans 3:24, Romans 8:1, 1 Corinthians 1:2, Hebrews 3:1, 1 Peter 5:10-14)

Year One:

_____
_____
_____
_____
_____
_____
_____
_____
_____

Year Two:

_____
_____
_____
_____
_____
_____
_____
_____

July 5

I'm praising, God Almighty, El Shaddai, for **You reign, Lord**. As I look around, today, I can see Your power, Your Majesty. Many, many, years ago El Shaddai was the name You first used to identify Yourself to Abraham. You are **still the same God, today, who possess overwhelming strength**. No one can stop You, move You, or change You. El Shaddai, You are the **God, of all mountains**. You declared Your promises to Abraham. I live by every promise in Your Word as I have been adopted into the royal family. As I walk each day and stand on Your Word, or better yet, when **I work Your Word (submit to it)**, Your Word actually **manifests in my life**. When I **believe for healing, I receive it**. When I **believe for prosperity, I get it**. When I **believe for favor, I get it**. I'm **walking in my victory daily** with my Almighty God. I lift up holy hands unto You. I'm living with and enjoying...More of You God.

(Genesis 17:1, Exodus 6:2-3, Genesis 1:16, John 1:1-5, John 17:3-6, Philippians 2:12-15, John 8:33, 2 Thessalonians 1:10-12, 2 Corinthians 3:18, Colossians 1:27-28)

Year One:

_____
_____
_____
_____
_____
_____
_____

Year Two:

_____
_____
_____
_____
_____
_____
_____

July 6

Glorious Lord, I know, through Your daily sustenance, **my battle is not mine**; it is Yours. This day forth, Lord, I have a desire to get closer and closer to You, Father. Father, I'm asking You to reveal Your glory; the closer I get to You, I see Your glory. **Where Your presence is, it is holy.** Release Your power all over my life. As Your light brightly shines down on me, I'm taking off my shoes, because I'm standing on holy ground. **I enter into Your gates with thanksgiving and into Your courts with praise.** Glorious Savior, I bow down before, my King. You are worthy to be praised. All the glory is Yours, Lord. **I have faith in all You do**, Lord, Jesus. **Your brightness illuminates this room. Your robe's train fills this temple.** Now, all I want to do is cry out to You with honor and praise. Yes, Lord, You are worthy to be praised! I give You all the glory, the honor, and the praise, as I enter into...More of You God.

(Psalm 66:2, Isaiah 28:5, Romans 11:25, Psalm 8:1, 1 Chronicles 16:24, Philippians 1:11, Psalm 145:11-12, 2 Peter 1:3)

Year One:

_____
_____
_____
_____
_____
_____
_____

Year Two:

_____
_____
_____
_____
_____
_____
_____

July 7

Jehovah Jireh, how awesome You are to me! I'm so thankful, today, for all You provide in my life, daily. Jehovah, You know my needs better than I do myself. **Jehovah Jireh, You are my Provider.** When problems come my way, I look up to the hills; I cry out for Your help. You hear me and answer my cry, with Your divine help. **You tell me not to worry about tomorrow, for it has its own worries.** Your Word tells me, if You take care of the birds and the flowers, why should I worry? I thank You, Lord, **You bring people into my life to help.** I understand, **they come for specific reasons, seasons, and some are for a lifetime.** Father, give me discernment to know what their purpose is in my life. Help me accept what the provision they are to bring forth, as Your gift. Jehovah Jireh, thank you for putting a gladness and a spirit of hope, inside of me. I appreciate You, Lord, Jesus, for my heart is filled with...More of You God.
(Genesis 22:14, Philippians 4:19, Ephesians 3:20, Isaiah 12:2, Philippians 4:7, Psalm 65:9-13, Luke 12:22-24, Matthew 6:25-34)

Year One:

_____

_____

_____

_____

_____

_____

_____

_____

Year Two:

_____

_____

_____

_____

_____

_____

_____

July 8

The Lord is my banner; Jehovah Nissi, **You are my Victory**. Today, I have hope in You, Lord. I will stay focused, and keep my eyes on the prize of the high calling. I know, I do not have to worry about uncomfortable situations attacking and taking me out, because **You are the one who wins all of my battles**. Now, I surrender unto You. **I release defeat. I release failure. I release I'm not good enough to obtain success. I release I'm not smart enough to accomplish all goals.** Right now, in the Mighty Name of Jesus, I rebuke all things coming against me, trying to make me crumble and fall. Jehovah Nissi, **You are my flag and my banner**, wrapping me up with Your divine protecttion. Shielding me daily, **my flag is the color red, representing the blood of Jesus**. My victory is with You, Lord; my victory is in You, Father. Right now, I'm pleading the blood of Jesus. I'm walking victoriously with...More of You God.
(Exodus 17:8-16, Deuteronomy 20:4, John 16:33, Ephesians 6:10, 1 John 5:4, Romans 8:31-32, Joshua 10:8, Zechariah 9:15)

Year One:

_____
_____
_____
_____
_____
_____
_____

Year Two:

_____
_____
_____
_____
_____
_____
_____

July 9

Jehovah Mekoddishkem, You are the Lord, **who sanctifies me.** Today, Father, I'm looking at how **You have set me apart**, for such a time as this. I'm Your child; I believe in all You do and all You are. Therefore, You make me holy; I'm not capable of it on my own. I cannot conjure up sanctification. **It was only through Your blood, Lord, Jesus, I am clean**. Throughout this life, I'm dealing with heaviness, intense discomfort, and uneasiness, but all of these obstacles allow me to call on, Jehovah Mekoddishkem. **Lord, You enter into my situation; You enter into me, and You make me whole.** There is nothing in this world taking Your place, there is no substitution for You, my Savior. My thirst to be purified, can only be accomplish through You, Lord. Therefore, I get on my knees, seeking after...More of You God.

(Exodus 31:13-15, Leviticus 20:7-11, Genesis 2:3, Exodus 13:1-2, Numbers 29:12, Exodus 12:16, Exodus 35:2, 1 Kings 8:8)

Year One:

_____
_____
_____
_____
_____
_____
_____
_____

Year Two:

_____
_____
_____
_____
_____
_____

July 10

"Peace be still," says the, Lord. Jehovah Shalom, **You are the God of peace**. Today, I rebuke all confusion from my mind and out of my life. I say, "Satan, go back to the pits of hell. There is no room for you here." Jehovah, I know, **You are not the Author of confusion**. All of my joy and peace comes from, my Savior, the Mighty Comforter, who gives me my enduring strength. **Because I have You, Jehovah Shalom, I thank You, Lord, for when I am weak, I will say I am strong.** You bring unto me the peace surpassing all understanding. Sometimes, I really do not understand how and why I'm not losing my mind. But, I now know, it is truly because of Your presence in my life. I will overcome all things with and through You, Lord, Jesus. When it seems like the whole world is against me, I grab a hold to...More of You God. (Judges 6:24, Philippians 4:6-7, 2 Thessalonians 3:16, 1 Corinthians 14:33, John 14:27, John 16:33, Matthew 11:28-30, Isaiah 54:10, Isaiah 26:3-12, Isaiah 9:6)

Year One:

_____
_____
_____
_____
_____
_____
_____
_____

Year Two:

_____
_____
_____
_____
_____
_____
_____

July 11

Jehovah Raah, You are my Shepherd, **I shall not want.** Today, Lord, Jesus, I am so happy **You call me friend.** **Yes , Lord, You are my friend.** You are always right on time. You always show up and show out on my behalf. Oh, how grateful I am unto You, Jehovah Raah. Father, **You provide me with extravagant nourishment.** You watch over me with Your divine protection, as well as, You give me rest for this weary body and soul. Thank You, Lord, **for providing me with food to eat, spiritually, as well as, tangibly.** Lord, I thank You, **I am one of Your sheep. I will listen closely for Your quiet whisper; the sound of Your sweet voice, guiding me through the pastures of this unpredictable life.** But, I have a Savior, who knows my everything, today, and tomorrow. Therefore, I am holding onto Your unchanging hand, for I know, where my help cometh from, tapping into...More of You God. (Psalm 23:1, 1 Samuel 25:25, Genesis 48:15, Genesis 49:24, Psalm 80:1, Psalm 95:7, Psalm 79:13, Psalm 100:3, Ezekiel 34:31, 1 Peter 5:2)

Year One:

_____
_____
_____
_____
_____
_____
_____
_____

Year Two:

_____
_____
_____
_____
_____
_____
_____

July 12

Jehovah Tsidkenyu, through You my righteous Savior, **I am made whole**. Today, I know, You are giving unto me life more abundantly, my cup is overflowing. **Because of Your gift of elevation, Lord, I get all of these benefits**. Now, folks look at me and wonder...What? How? And Why? It is all by Your grace and mercy, dear, Lord. I thank You, Lord, **You loved me so much You sent Your only, Son, Jesus, to save me from eternal hell, allowing me an eternal life with You**, Lord, Jesus. Jehovah Tisidkenyu, I will praise You for all the days of my life. I only have a life worth living because of You, Lord. Father, You are a sovereign, all-sufficient, eternally righteous, Savior. All of my righteousness comes from You, and through You, it sustains me. Jehovah Tsidkenyu, through You, I get justice, righteousness, deliverance, victory, and prosperity. Lord I continue to prosper with...More of You God.

(Jeremiah 23:6, Jeremiah 33:16, Psalm 119:137, Deuteronomy 32:4, Psalm 48:10, Psalm 97:2, Psalm 119:142, Psalm 145:17, Isaiah 45:21)

Year One:

_____
_____
_____
_____
_____
_____
_____

Year Two:

_____
_____
_____
_____
_____
_____
_____

July 13

Today, I tap into the Lord who heals. Jehovah Rapha, Lord, Jesus, **You are my Healer**. Father, You are the Great Physician, and You heal Your people. **You heal me physically, mentally, and emotionally**. Lord, You say, all I have to do is ask and it will be given unto me; seek, I will find; knock and the door will be opened for me. You also, say, I have not because I ask not. But, today, I'm tapping into all You have made available to me. I know, by the **blood of Jesus (Your stripes), I am cleansed, restored, and renewed**. I'm ready to walk in my purpose and plan You have for my life, Lord, Jesus. Jehovah Rapha, I will wait on You. Your timing is not my timing, nor are Your thoughts my thoughts. Father, I thank You for caring enough to heal me from all of my resentfulness, bitterness, shame, and pride. I trust You, Lord. I will walk hand in hand with You. Holy Spirit, with You, I will work at being obedient to Your commands, Father. My faith is in You, Lord, Jesus. My healing comes with...More of You God.

(Exodus 15:26, Matthew 8:2-3, Matthew 8:17, Isaiah 53:4-10, Isaiah 58:8, 1 Peter 2:24, Matthew 14:4, Matthew 9:12, Matthew 9:27-30)

Year One:

_____
_____
_____
_____
_____
_____

Year Two:

_____
_____
_____
_____
_____

July 14

Father, I know, **You are here with me**. Today, I stand on the Lord, who is there, Jehovah Shammah. No matter what is transpiring in my life, right now, it will **not overtake me**. Lord, You will never leave me or forsake me; You are always here. Sometimes, Father, You are very quiet during my storm; but, I trust <u>in Your timing; You will avail</u>. **You will come right in the nick of time**, as always. For You are the Lord of Hosts, the God of Jacob, and my Fortress. I know, Lord, **I am never a-lone**, even though at times, I feel I am. Father, I thank You, Jehovah Shammah, You are present in my plans, and You guide me through with Your love. You are present in my heart, delivering Your eternal hope to this dying world. I plan to walk this journey with...More of You God.

(Ezekiel 48:35, 2 Corinthians 3:17, Psalm 118:6, Psalm 42:5-6, Psalm 124:8, Psalm 107:29, Psalm 46:7-11, Hebrews 13:5)

Year One:

_____
_____
_____
_____
_____
_____
_____
_____
_____

Year Two:

_____
_____
_____
_____
_____
_____
_____
_____

July 15

Yahweh, (Lord Jehovah), **You are my Lord and my Master.** Yahweh, Lord, Jesus, today, I want to tell You Your name is the sweetest name I know. How **excellent** is Your name, Father! It's the most **sacred** name which will ever be: yesterday, today, and forevermore. You are **the Great, I Am!** Lord, God, You absolutely are or is. Yahweh, You are the beginning and the end. As You please, You created all and do all. God, You are the truth, the way, and the life. Lord, You are the standard for what is right and perfect; I cannot look anywhere else, for **You are my answer.** I solely depend on You, God. **You made the entire universe, and it depends on You too.** Lord, I am so glad I know You, for You are God all by Yourself. What an honor and privilege to get to know...More of You God.

(Revelation 1:8, Exodus 3:14, John 4:24, Isaiah 41:4, Matthew 4:14, Isaiah 42:8, Psalm 91:14-16, Isaiah 52:5-6, Jeremiah 16:21, Jeremiah 23:26-27)

Year One:

_____
_____
_____
_____
_____
_____
_____

Year Two:

_____
_____
_____
_____
_____
_____

July 16

You are the Most High, God, El Elyon, <u>nothing</u> takes You by surprise. Today, I look at how powerful You are and I praise You, Lord. **You are in complete control**. El Elyon, You are the sovereign God, the ruler of the universe. All I need is You, Lord. There is <u>nothing</u> **I can't accomplish with You**, Father. Lord, **You open up doors for me, no man can shut**. Father, You part the sea for me to cross, **no man can even imagine Your power**. All I need is You, my Father. Lord, You work through man, getting me to where You have me to reside. Lord, **You are my High Tower**; You sit high and look low. **You own all of me, every man, and yes, the entire universe is completely Yours**. I submit my all and want to live with...More of You God.

(Genesis 14:1-24, Genesis 1:1-31, Isaiah 7:14, Deuteronomy 6:4, Exodus 6:2-3, Genesis 21:33, Genesis 2:4, Hebrews 6:20, Psalm 91, Psalm 83:18)

Year One:

_____
_____
_____
_____
_____
_____
_____
_____
_____

Year Two:

_____
_____
_____
_____
_____
_____
_____
_____

July 17

You are **my Lord**. The translation of Your name Lord in Greek, is "Kurios", a word meaning **master**. Today, Lord, Jesus, I show reverence to You and Your great Name. Lord, You are King of Kings, God of Gods, and Lord of Lords. You are **the ruler of this world**. There is **no one who ranks higher than You**, Lord. Lord, Jesus, You are my King. You have **complete dominion over me**. I cannot even begin to grasp or even imagine, how powerful You are, Lord. While the earth is spinning 1,000 miles per hour at the equator and moving over 60,000 miles an hour around the sun, I do not even feel any of this motion, because You are the Creator. How could I not serve a great, God, like You! Lord, **Your power is limitless**, and your creation demonstrates it daily. How grateful I am being able to tap into Your power, Lord, Jesus. Lord, I will be obedient to Your Word and seek Your face. Father, I just want...More of You God...I just got to have...More of You God.
(Acts 17:10-11, Revelation 4:8, Revelation 11:17, Revelation 15:3, Revelation 16:7, Revelation 21:22)

Year One:

_____
_____
_____
_____
_____
_____
_____
_____

Year Two:

_____
_____
_____
_____
_____
_____

July 18

God, El Roi, my God, who **sees everything**. Today, I appreciate You for being a God, who lives and sees my all. Father, I am glad to know no matter what I am facing or how I am feeling, **You are all knowing**. You do not miss, not, one intricate detail of my life or my situation. **You are Omniscient**. My eyes are open to Your great work within my life. I see Your manifestation of goodness keeping me daily. As I walk with You, Lord, God, my faith continues to grow. When it comes to my future, my vision is usually somewhat obscured; but I know a God who tells me to keep looking to the hills. Lord, You, **Jesus, can do all things and through You, I can**. Lord, I'm trusting You to **direct my future**, watching over me each and every day. My **vision is getting clearer** as I walk with...More of You God.

(Isaiah 61:3, Genesis 16:7-16, Hebrews 4:13, Matthew 10:30, Psalm 147:4, Deuteronomy 29:29, Daniel 2:22, Acts 1:7, Job 34:21)

Year One:

_____
_____
_____
_____
_____
_____
_____
_____

Year Two:

_____
_____
_____
_____
_____
_____
_____

July 19

Everlasting God, EL Olam, today, I'm honoring the God who is the, First and the Last, the Beginning and the End. Lord, God, You are a sovereign, eternal ruler of the entire universe. **You are beyond time or space.** El Olam, You are my God, who has no beginning or ending. God, **You are unchangeable,** for Your plans and purposes are timeless. They shall be done, because **You fail at nothing.** EL Olam, You created time, so You are not limited in time in any way. **Before there was a universe and before there was time, Lord, God, You existed.** Nothing about You will ever change! Your character, Your Word, Your promises, and Your kingdom will never end. I thank You, God, for every area of my life. You are faithful, dependable, constant, and reliable. God, my Father, **I marvel at Your greatness;** You are eternal for **You are never in a hurry, nor are You ever late.** The **past, the present, and the future, are all the same to You,** my Lord. Therefore, my Savior, I will wait on You with patience, knowing You are a good, good, God; my life couldn't be in better hands. EL Olam as I wait on You, I am mesmerized by...More of You God.
(Deuteronomy 33:27, Revelation 1:8, Psalm 90:2-4, Isaiah 41:4, Hebrews 13:8, 2 Peter 3:8, Revelation 11:17, Proverbs 8:23)

Year One:

_____
_____
_____
_____
_____
_____

Year Two:

_____
_____
_____
_____
_____

July 20

Mighty God, El Gibhor, today, I praise You for being **the Messiah, who came back to redeem me.** You are so gracious, You gave me the choice to willingly accept You as my Lord. El Gibhor, You are my Master. You are **my Prince of Peace. You have all the <u>authority</u> and the <u>weight of responsibility</u> in Your hands.** Lord, God, You are my Counselor. You **bring completeness to every area of my life.** Father, guide my path, my Mighty Warrior. You keep me away from all harm and danger. You show Your unwarranted lovingkindness to me, daily. You repaid all of my iniquities. Father, God, I thank You for being my Shield and my Horn of Salvation. Lord, You are my Hero; You **prevail in everything.** You are an all-inspiring God, who keeps all of Your covenants. Lord, I thank You, and I trust You with my life. My life depends on trusting in...More of You God.
(Isaiah 61:1-3, Luke 4:18-21, Nehemiah 10:4, John 1:41, John 4:25-26, Isaiah 7:14, Psalm 22:16-18, Isaiah 11:1)

Year One:

_____
_____
_____
_____
_____
_____
_____

Year Two:

_____
_____
_____
_____
_____
_____
_____

July 21

Mighty God, EL Berith, **the God of Covenants**. Today, I thank You for not giving up on me and agreeing to **deal with mankind through a binding contract.** Thank You for the precious gift, **the eternal covenant the covenant of grace.** It is through Your salvation, Your, Son, Jesus Christ, dying on the cross for my sins, I can count on life everlasting with You, Lord. As long as I have faith in You, Lord, I know what direction my life will go. Father, You took all of my failures. By Your grace You have lifted me up, so I am able to live forever. Lord, I look forward to going to heaven and praising You 24/7. I just want to sit at Your feet and let You know how much I love You, Lord, Jesus. You say in Your Word, **You will let me experience heaven, right down here on earth.** Hallelujah! Father, You left me here with the Holy Spirit, and it comforts me, leads me, guides me, and protects me. I thank You, Lord, **Your covenant is simple and direct.** Lord, Jesus, You continue to reward me, by pouring down Your blessings on me. Father, fill me up with a heart of obedience and a selflessness spirit. Lord, **do a new thing in me.** I will only have the desires in my heart to do what is only of Your will. My heart is seeking after...More of You God.

(Psalm 105:8-11, Jeremiah 31:31-34, Matthew 26:28, Jeremiah 33:21, Hebrews 6:18, Romans 9:7-13, Psalm 74:20, Nehemiah 9:38)

Year One:

_____

_____

_____

_____

_____

Year Two:

_____

_____

_____

_____

_____

July 22

God, my God, Theos. Father, You are the **only true and living God.** You are very unique in all of Your ways. You are transcendent; You are my Savior. Today, Lord, I want to honor You for being a special divine gift to me. I thank You, the **God and owner of everything.** You created and left me in charge, having dominion over this land and everything on it. Father, I feel so special because You made me out of Your own image. Therefore, I know, what type of power resides inside of me. **Father, You are the only, Judge.** I will refrain from judging my neighbors. I will work at sharing Your Word to my neighbors, and letting You cleanse/renew their souls. **Father, You have all the authority.** I honor You today, as You sit on Your throne. All the glory belongs to You, Lord, God! All the glory is Yours, Lord, Jesus! It gives me great pleasure to dig deeper, getting to know...More of You God. (Isaiah 44:6, 1 Timothy 2:5, Isaiah 43:11, 1 Corinthians 8:6, James 2:19, Deuteronomy 6:4, Isaiah 43:10, Jude 1:25, Isaiah 42:8, Mark 12:29)

Year One:

_____
_____
_____
_____
_____
_____
_____

Year Two:

_____
_____
_____
_____
_____
_____

July 23

Holy Spirit, today, I'm happy I have a relationship with You. You are all powerful, Holy Spirit. You have an external will, and You distribute spiritual gifts to me. Holy Spirit, **You have a mind searching the deep things of God and You know them**, oh, so well. You also have emotions because I can grieve You. I promise to be sensitive to You, Lord, Jesus, and to obey you. Thank You, Holy Spirit, for communing and having fellowship with me. **When I do not know what to say, and/or how to say it, You speak on my behalf to the Father.** Holy Spirit, You are so awesome; **You guide me and make awesome decisions for me.** Inside and out, You take me and clean me up. I respect You, Holy Spirit, and I'm going to be still and quiet; so I can hear Your voice for the directions You have for me to move forward. Holy Spirit, You are welcome here...I open my mind, body, and soul, to...More of You God. (Matthew 12:31-33, Luke 24:45-49, Acts 2:1-5, 1 John 2:19-27, Micah 3:8-10, 2 Corinthians 5:16-18, Romans 8:2-6)

Year One:

_____

_____

_____

_____

_____

_____

_____

Year Two:

_____

_____

_____

_____

_____

_____

July 24

Wonderful Savior, I'm so grateful today, You have done so many great things for me. As people look at me, they all call me blessed; that's why I humble myself to You, the Powerful One, my Savior. My spirit rejoices in You, Lord, Jesus, for **You have delivered me out of the darkness into the light**. My soul says, "Yes to You, Lord, I'm available to You." Lord, God, I know, there is no Savior, besides You. **You were sent to preserve my life**. Hallelujah, Lord, Jesus! You came to this earth to preserve and deliver a remnant like me. Before You, Lord, my life was a catastrophe, but **now, I have Your oil on me; I have been found**. My hope is in You, Lord, Jesus, my Savior. Lord, anoint me with…More of You God.

(John 3:16, Romans 6:23, Acts 4:12, John 14:6, John 3:36, John 1:14, 1 John 5:1-21, Romans 10:9, Luke 1:35, Isaiah 9:6)

Year One:

_____
_____
_____
_____
_____
_____
_____
_____
_____

Year Two:

_____
_____
_____
_____
_____
_____
_____
_____
_____

July 25

Emmanuel, Emmanuel, today, Lord, God, I know, **You are my God-with me**. Thank You, Emmanuel, no matter what situation I'm in or going through, You hold me with Your right hand, and walk with me; **sometimes, while leading the way You carry me, just as a loving Father would do**. Oh, how grateful I am to You, my Father. You do not wait for me to be cleansed, fixed, scrubbed, or primped. **You take me, just, as I am; You meet me at whatever level I'm currently on**. I always know I can depend on You. Emmanuel, **You love me just as I am**. You keep on loving me as You work on taking me to a higher level in You, Lord, Jesus. **I'm going higher, my level is advancing**, as I enter into...More of You God.

(Isaiah 7:14, Matthew 1:22-23, Isaiah 9:6, Joshua 1:9, Isaiah 41:10, 1 Corinthians 3:16, Revelation 3:20, Psalm 23:4)

Year One:

_____
_____
_____
_____
_____
_____
_____
_____

Year Two:

_____
_____
_____
_____
_____
_____
_____
_____

213

July 26

King Jesus, Lord, **You were born my King**. Today, I honor You, King Jesus, because You are my everything. You are the King of Israel. You are the King of righteousness. **Your name is Love for You love unconditionally.** Lord, You are the highest King, who is unique in all Your ways. You are **the Way Maker, and the King of miracles.** King Jesus, **You supply all my needs.** You watch over me day and night. You are the **King of blessings overflowing, supernatural, and divine.** You are the King of heaven; all the angels are bowing down to You, and singing glorious praises, unto You. You are **my King, who forgives me of my sins, and heals me of all diseases.** What an honor it is for me to join in with the angels praising Your Holy Name and bowing at Your feet. King Jesus, I'm at Your door knocking to get in, to have...More of You God.

(Psalm 145:1, Isaiah 9:6, Isaiah 11:10, Acts 2:30, John 12:15, 1 Timothy 6:15, Revelation 17:14, Revelation 19:16, John 18:37)

Year One:

_____
_____
_____
_____
_____
_____
_____
_____
_____

Year Two:

_____
_____
_____
_____
_____
_____

July 27

God the Creator. My God, who **created the heavens and the earth.** Father, today, I acknowledge the act of Your creation, for it is merely a mystery to me. Because You created me by faith, I can't grasp it; yet, You can because You are the Almighty God. You, Lord, my Creator, are not bound by any space or time; You are an all self-sustaining, God. **The universe depends on Your constant divine upholding, and without it, we would cease to exist.** My God, the Creator, You give life to all men and everything on this earth. **In You, I move, I live, and have my being.** Lord, You created things we cannot explain in our own terms. **You are so magnificent, words cannot describe Your creativity or Your power.** All of Your creation is beyond my comprehension. It is simply marvelous and beautiful. I grab a hold of You moment by moment, depending on...More of You God.
(Nehemiah 9:6, Genesis 1:1, Isaiah 45:7-18, Isaiah 66:2, Ephesians 3:9, Revelation 4:11, Isaiah 37:16, Colossians 1:16, Psalm 8:3-8, Genesis 1:26-28, Genesis 5:1, Isaiah 42:5)

Year One:

_____
_____
_____
_____
_____
_____
_____
_____

Year Two:

_____
_____
_____
_____
_____
_____

July 28

God, El Qanna, my God, **is a jealous God**. Today, I am thankful for how You watch over me faithfully, lovingly, and passionately. Lord, God, I know, **You love me too much to be without me.** Your passion, Father, vibrates in my spirit; it ignites my fuel all through my limbs, empowering me to pick up my cross and to follow You, my Savior, my King. Lord, God, I'm here to worship You, for I know, **You desire my love.** I will not worship no other god, **I will not get consumed with money, cars, houses, clothes, or even people.** You are my God and there is none other. **Your name is the name above all names.** I know, You are a jealous God (**jealousy means someone is afraid of losing something**), I am always Yours, Father. God, here I am to bow down to You. Here I am to worship You. Lord, You are my God. Dear Precious Savior, my joy comes from worshiping You, and getting filled with...More of You God.

(Exodus 20:5, Exodus 34:14, Deuteronomy 6:15, Nahum 1:2, Exodus 34:6-14, Deuteronomy 4:24, Isaiah 42:8, 2 Peter 3:10, Hebrews 12:29, 2 Corinthians 11:2, Matthew 10:28)

Year One:

_____
_____
_____
_____
_____
_____
_____
_____

Year Two:

_____
_____
_____
_____
_____
_____

July 29

Jesus Christ, when You came to this earth and laid aside Your heavenly power, You did not lay aside **all** of Your power, Lord, Jesus. Today, Jesus, I thank You for **laying Your life down on the cross for me and the rest of this world.** You came down fully human, for You suffered weariness, pain, and You were tested. However, **You never ceased to be the Creator of the universe.** Jesus, I am grateful for all of Your miracles, signs, and wonders I read in Your Word. **Your miracles are manifesting amongst me, now, every day.** I truly appreciate who You are and who You are to me (my everything). **Jesus Christ, You are the truth, for no one can get to the Father, unless they go through You.** I'm delighted You sit at the right hand of the Father, interceding on my behalf. Hallelujah! I will continue to get on my knees in prayer, seeking after...More of You God.

(John 14:6, 1 Timothy 2:5, Proverbs 8:35-36, Hebrews 4:10, John 1:1, John 8:18, John 17:24, Colossians 1:15-17, John 1:15, Revelation 1:17-18)

Year One:

_____

_____

_____

_____

_____

_____

_____

_____

Year Two:

_____

_____

_____

_____

_____

July 30

The Holy One, my Savior, who is **without blemish**. Today, Holy One, I'm ecstatic my sins are forgiven; I have been clothed with divine righteousness. Jesus, I commit myself unto You. I want to live a better life and ask You to remove all selfishness, bitterness, immorality, dishonesty, and greediness. I want to be more like You, Lord, Jesus. **My purpose on this earth is to be Your servant**; therefore, my highest priority is to do Your will, Your way, because all the glory belongs to You, Holy One, Jesus, my Savior. Yes, You are the separate one, which means, **You are separate from all of Your creatures**. You are the light of the world. You are radiant, brilliant, beautiful, infinite, pure, and spotless. Holy, Holy, Holy is my Savior. I want to stay in Your brightness with...More of You God.

(1 John 2:20, Isaiah 43:3-15, 1 Peter 1:16, Psalm 22:3, Isaiah 57:15, Isaiah 6:3, Revelation 4:8, Job 6:10, Psalm 71:22, 1 Samuel 2:2, Isaiah 40:25, Psalm 77:13)

Year One:

_____
_____
_____
_____
_____
_____
_____
_____
_____

Year Two:

_____
_____
_____
_____
_____
_____
_____

218

July 31

God, You are the one and only, God Almighty. Lord, today, I'm **here to praise You forevermore**; it's the reason why You created me. I now have the pleasure of getting to know You. **You created me for Your pleasure, for everything You do is perfect**. You make no mistakes. If I never did exist You would still be the same God. God, You amaze me, You took me, a man and crowned me with glory, and honor, thank You, God. Lord, God, You are completely sovereign and holy. **There is not anyone before You and not anyone after You.** God, You are worthy to be praised! **You are all powerfully and totally, awesome**. Here I am, to worship You. I love You so much; I desire to get closer to...More of You God.
(Psalm 62:11, Job 26:14, 1 Corinthians 6:14, Psalm 8:5, Psalm 135:6, Isaiah 46:10, John 4:24, Isaiah 43:7, Genesis 1:26, Ephesians 3:9-10, Revelation 4:11)

Year One:

_____
_____
_____
_____
_____
_____
_____
_____

Year Two:

_____
_____
_____
_____
_____
_____
_____
_____

August

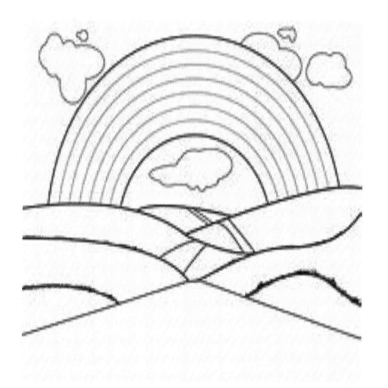

August 1

Lord, God, You are **so faithful**. Today, I'm not going to look at what my circumstances currently, represent. Father, I'm going to tap into the **supernatural which only comes from believing**. You are doing a **miracle**, in my life. I must **first believe in order to receive**. As I look around, it looks like craziness is happening all over me. However, I realize I am **getting closer to my breakthrough**. The devil doesn't want me to keep believing. He is trying to break me down, hoping I will give up, and miss out on my glorious victory. You have greatness waiting for me, right around the corner. My faith is getting stronger and stronger, as I hold on to Your hand. I see a slow progression of something great about to happen in my life. I know, in the morning a change is coming, and You will blow my mind. Thank You, Lord. You are so amazing, Your love is constant. I love to reach up for...More of You God.

(Deuteronomy 7:9, Psalm 36:5, Psalm 89:8, Psalm 119:90, Lamentations 3:22-23, Romans 3:3, 1 Corinthians 1:9, 1 Corinthians 10:13, 2 Thessalonians 3:3, Hebrews 10:23)

Year One:

_____
_____
_____
_____
_____
_____
_____
_____

Year Two:

_____
_____
_____
_____
_____
_____

August 2

God, Your **grace is sufficient**. Today, I'm reflecting on my life, looking at situations I thought were so horrific. Most people I know thought I was losing my way and getting further away from You. However, I serve an awesome God, who **takes** these very **situations/obstacles and uses them to get me even closer** to Him. As a matter of fact, You **use these events to help me and to help someone else, all at the same time.** Yes, You are a **BIG, BIG, God**, and there is <u>nothing</u> **impossible for You.** You take my mess, turning it into a blessing for myself and for others. How awesome is my God! Again, You are the Master of turning the bad, into the good, all for Your glory. I praise You, Lord, God; I cannot make it without You. You are so worthy of all praises. I sing and rejoice with...More of You God.
(2 Corinthians 12:9-12, Ephesians 2:8, Romans 5:1-21, Romans 11:6, Hebrews 4:16, 2 Timothy 2:1-2, Acts 20:24)

Year One:

_____
_____
_____
_____
_____
_____
_____
_____

Year Two:

_____
_____
_____
_____
_____
_____

August 3

Jesus, the **God, of miracles**. You turned water into wine. You fed over 5000 men and women with five loaves of bread and two fishes. My Savior, You healed the woman with the issue of blood. You gave sight to the blind. You raised the dead man from the grave. You healed folks with all kind of diseases, and casted out demons. Your list goes on and on. The **greatest miracle, was when You died on the cross for my sins, and on the third day You rose from the grave. You ascended into heaven, and are seated at the right hand of the Father.** Oh, how great You are my Lord, my Savior. Today, when I look at what You have already done, I know, I'm in great hands. Lord, as long as I walk with You, I will have an amazing life on this earth. I'm so grateful You are my Father, and I know You, Lord. I welcome You in my life, thanking You for...More of You God.
(John 2: 1-11, Matthew 14:13-21, Mark 6:30-44, Mark 10:46-52, John 11, Mark 16)

Year One:

_____

_____

_____

_____

_____

_____

_____

_____

Year Two:

_____

_____

_____

_____

_____

_____

223

August 4

The Great I Am, is in the room with me, today! You are my way when I am feeling lost. You hold and keep me comfortable when I am weary. Lord, when I am weak, You are my strength, making me strong. Father, when my life looks chaotic, when it seems I do not know where to turn, You are my hope and my direction. You are, who You are, Lord, Jesus. When I go through difficult situations, when I am sad, You are my joy, and You bring me peace. As I'm on the battle field; You are my army. **You are my armor always protecting me, and You give me the victory. Yes, You are who You are, my Father.** When my body is feeble, and I'm feeling ill and down, You lift me up and heal me. Oh! Hallelujah! You are the **GREAT I AM!** I am unstoppable with...More of You God.

(Exodus 20:7, 2 Corinthians 1:3-5, Psalm 23:4-6, Psalm 30:5, Psalm 147:3, Isaiah 40:1, Matthew 11:28, Romans 15:4, Isaiah 26:3, John 16:33, 2 Corinthians 4:8-9, Psalm 37:39, Psalm 138:3)

Year One:

_____

_____

_____

_____

_____

_____

_____

Year Two:

_____

_____

_____

_____

_____

_____

_____

August 5

A life worth living is a life loving, my neighbor. Today, I'm **tapping into Your love, Lord, Jesus. You loved me first; Jesus is love, and You command me to love my neighbor as I love myself**. I'm not jealous or envious of myself, so how can I exhibit these feelings toward my neighbor. I must be giving and loving to all people, regardless if they love me or not. I am to be a witness for You, my Lord, my God. I must love my neighbor enough to desire them to be saved and to receive salvation, just as You do, Lord. I will respect my neighbor in regards to their needs, as well as, their desires, as I do my own. Lord, this is not easy for me. I need Your help, please. Father, assist me with this commandment. I know, You can and I know, You will. **I will continue to see my neighbor's worth by giving my love**, as I grow in...More of You God.

(1 John 4:7-8, Romans 8:37-39, 1 John 4:16, Ephesians 3:17-19, Romans 8:38-39, John 15:12)

Year One:

_____
_____
_____
_____
_____
_____
_____
_____

Year Two:

_____
_____
_____
_____
_____
_____

August 6

Lord, Jesus, I know, You have a purpose and a plan for my life. The very fact You woke me up, today, I can walk into my new blessings. Father, I thank You. Along my journey, I will have new lessons, allowing me to grow and prosper. Lord, these lessons will take me to a higher level in You, Father. I will not relinquish. I will not turn around, because, right now, I am unstoppable with You, my King. Thank You, Lord, for holding me by Your right hand, assuring me I'm going to a-chieve greatness. Yes, Lord, **I will stay the course; I cannot stop**, for what You have waiting for me is **indescribable, unimaginable, and more than what, I can ever ask of You. I am walking into my new season**. Thank You, Father, for doing a new thing in my life and mind. Oh, how grateful and privileged I am to have You as my Father. I can now persevere with...More of You God.
(Ephesians 3:20-21, Psalm 62:8, Isaiah 41:13, Isaiah 48:13, Psalm 89:13-15, Isaiah 43:19, Psalm 103:5, 1 Corinthians 2:9, Isaiah 35:1, Revelation 21:5)

Year One:

_____
_____
_____
_____
_____
_____
_____
_____

Year Two:

_____
_____
_____
_____
_____
_____
_____

August 7

Today, I'm **tapping into love**. Father, first, teach me to love You, and then to love my neighbor, as myself. The big question, is **how do I love my neighbor so much?** Well, in order for me to even love myself, I must first know how to love You, Abba, Father. As I'm getting closer to You, really getting to know who You are, and loving on You; I can now love myself, because I know, who I am in You. Yes, I'm made wonderfully and divinely through You, my Savior. Ok now, I can love my neighbor, just as I love myself, but **it all boils down to loving You first, Father. I realize I must love all three (You, my neighbor, and myself) to function in a balanced life.** From this day forward, I will embrace my feelings with compassion, gentleness, tenderness, and caring, tapping into only what my positive feelings are telling me. I must make sure I am loving myself. God, You created me this way. I will walk with the authority You have given me, to do Your work on this earth. Abba, Father, I love You, Lord. I will continue to tap into loving on...More of You God.

(Matthew 22:37-38, Deuteronomy 11:13-15, John 14:21, Proverbs 8:17, Psalm 145:20, Psalm 91:14, Psalm 37:4, 1 Corinthians 2:9, Ephesians 6:24)

Year One:

_____
_____
_____
_____
_____
_____

Year Two:

_____
_____
_____
_____
_____
_____

227

August 8

Lord, with You, I can **live a complete life**. Today, I'm aiming to live a life full of joy, hope, love, and peace. With You, God, I can live with serenity, divinely, joyously, and drunkenly, in You. Father, I know, by walking with You, I can do what is right, and love others. Lord, I want to live my life, **so I am pleasing unto You**. Therefore, I want **to be loving, walk humbly, and act justly**. Father, You know what is best for me. You will protect, provide, and lead me, to the destination You have designed for me. Father, do a great work through me, all for Your glory. I just want to go a little bit deeper and a little higher in You, Lord. As I climb Your ladder, Father, all of the glory belongs to You, Lord, Jesus. From this day forth, I'm **expecting** to see **great miracles** occurring **in my life**. Thank You, Lord, Jesus. You are so beautiful to me. Lord, as I search and seek after You, I see...More of You God.

(Romans 12:1, Ephesians 5:8-10, 2 Corinthians 5:9, Galatians 6:8, Colossians 3:20, 1 Thessalonians 4:1, 1 Timothy 2:1-3, Psalm 149:4, Haggai 1:7, Hebrews 11:6)

Year One:

_____
_____
_____
_____
_____
_____
_____

Year Two:

_____
_____
_____
_____
_____
_____

August 9

Today, an **explosion** is occurring in my life. It is **developing me** and taking me to **another level in You**, Lord, Jesus. This awakening is opening my eyes and the world, to who You really are, Lord, God. It is showing us how powerful You are and letting us know, **You have all control in Your hands**. Yes, all the glory belongs to You, Father. I see Your overflow and prosperity coming to me. You say, all I have to do is **ask and it shall be given to me**. Therefore, it is **imperative, I open my mouth**. I now, realize in order to receive something from You, Lord, I must always do something first (believe). Right now, I speak blessings and more than enough in my life. I will not lack anything; I will have enough to share with others. Father, thank You for being **the God of plenty**. I can't stop praising You, Lord, Jesus. My store house must be filled with...More of You God.

(Isaiah 42:12, Habakkuk 2:14, Psalm 29:1-2, Psalm 115:1, Psalm 86:8-12, John 14:13, Matthew 7:7-21, Luke 11:9, Mark 11:22-24, Matthew 21:22, Psalm 23:1)

Year One:

_____
_____
_____
_____
_____
_____
_____

Year Two:

_____
_____
_____
_____
_____
_____

August 10

Father, I thank You, today, You are **turning all things around all to my good**. Lord, You are the God, who takes a situation bad/horrible, and You turn it into my good. All the glory is Yours, Father. **You take my mishap and turn it into a must-have**. Lord, Jesus, You know, my yesterday, today, and tomorrow. Therefore, as long as I seek You in all I do, throughout my life, You will guide me each and every step. Today, I surrender unto You, Father. I want what You have for me, not what the world wants me to believe is mine. **I rebuke what looks good to the eye and the flesh**, because it is poisonous to my life and growth. Now, I'm walking into a fresh season, where the crops will be plentiful. It is now, harvest time; I'm ready for my miracles to manifest in my life. Thank You, Lord, Jesus, for **changing my life into a life of possibilities. I'm speaking to all situations/things and putting a demand on them, in the mighty Name of Jesus.** I move forward and win with...More of You God.
(Romans 8:28-32, Acts 16:16-34, Psalm 25:4-5, Psalm 5:8, Psalm 27:11, Psalm 31:3, Psalm 61:1-2, Job 22:28)

Year One:

_____
_____
_____
_____
_____
_____
_____

Year Two:

_____
_____
_____
_____
_____
_____

August 11

My Savior, today, I'm **releasing my past** and all things, trying to strip me and take me out. It's time to forgive everyone who came against me, trying to hurt, betray, or destroy me. I let them all go. As I release all of this garbage, I am now, opening myself up for restoration and provisions. Father, You say, **You will give me back seven times what the enemy has taken from me.** I declare and decree, it is now, my time! Lord, Your divine favor is resting on me, waiting to manifest. Hallelujah! Hallelujah! I am filled with joy all down in my bones. Your favor comes to those waiting on You, Lord, Jesus. I must not try to control my situation, but give it to You, God. I now know, it is done in the Name of Jesus. As I'm waiting on You, Lord, I will seek after...More of You God.

(Psalm 51:10, Matthew 5:44, Luke 6:27, Matthew 6:14-15, Matthew 18:21-22, Colossians 3:12-14, Hosea 12:6, Psalm 27:14, Psalm 37:7, Psalm 25:5, James 5:7-8)

Year One:

_____

_____

_____

_____

_____

_____

_____

Year Two:

_____

_____

_____

_____

_____

August 12

Today, Lord, Jesus, I'm **setting my atmosphere for You to do something grand in my life**. Jesus, I'm not looking to the natural; I'm **looking to the supernatural, the Spirit**. I put You first, Father; no matter what tries to come up against me, today, I will continue to press into You. Have Your way, Lord, do what You want to do in me and through me. Holy Spirit, come now, Lord, Jesus, I open myself completely up to You. Come now, Lord, God, and make changes in my life to take me a little higher. These adjustments will move me a little closer to You, Lord. Have Your way in me, now, Jesus. **I want to get closer to Your heart. I want all You have for me…I'm going deeper in You, Lord, pressing** into…More of You God.
(Romans 12:2, Daniel 4:16, 1 John 3:2, Revelation 21:1, 2 Corinthians 3:18, Zephaniah 3:9-19, 2 Samuel 14:20, Acts 22:10, 1 Samuel 21:13, Hebrews 7:12, Philippians 3:21)

Year One:

_____
_____
_____
_____
_____
_____
_____
_____

Year Two:

_____
_____
_____
_____
_____
_____
_____

August 13

God, today, I'm **not taking my eyes off of You**, Lord, Jesus. I'm keeping my eyes and mind **on the prize of the high calling.** I am seeking provision, all over my life. I know, I have the victory through You, Lord, God. There isn't any stopping me now. **I will have what You say I will have, and I will live as You say I shall live.** Today, no matter what the world brings my way, I will not let it drag me down. I have overcome the works of the enemy, in the Name of Jesus. I **rebuke all negativity; I hold onto Your thoughts and Your ways, Father.** I know, You are the Great All Mighty and Your Name is the Name, above all names. Everything You do, Father, is great and good. I'm welcoming every blessing You have for me on this day. Blessings are surrounding me, as I seek after...More of You God.

(Philippians 3:14, Hebrews 12:1-2, Isaiah 55:8-9, Romans 12:2, Philippians 2:8-11, John 16:33, 2 Peter 3:9, Ephesians 6:10, 1 John 5:4, Zechariah 9:15)

Year One:

_____
_____
_____
_____
_____
_____
_____
_____
_____

Year Two:

_____
_____
_____
_____
_____
_____
_____

August 14

Jesus, You came down here on this earth, so I could be victorious. Today, I'm walking in my victory; I am lost without You, Lord. **What is impossible for man is ALL possible for You, Lord, God.** I put all of my trust in You, Lord. No weapons formed against me will be able to overtake me. As the fiery darts of hurt and pain come flying my way, they will bounce off of me. I have **Your mighty shield of protection covering me. I am able to rest in Your peace.** You have sent Your angels down here, to surround me and protect me from all danger. Thank You, Lord, for the assigned angels watching over me. You think so much of me, and love me so much, I am so grateful for Your love. Lord, Jesus, I am desperate for...More of You God.
(Deuteronomy 20:4, 1 Corinthians 15:55-57, Proverbs 21:31, Matthew 19:26, Luke 18:27, Isaiah 54:17, Hebrews 1:14, Psalm 91:11)

Year One:

_____
_____
_____
_____
_____
_____
_____
_____

Year Two:

_____
_____
_____
_____
_____
_____
_____
_____

August 15

On this day, and moving forward, **I am blessed exuberantly, exceedingly, and more than what I can even ask**. I am blessed coming and going. I have, because **I open my mouth and speak it into existence**. Right now, I am turning my situation around. **I shall ask and speak it (declare and decree a thing).** Lord, God, here I am, knocking at Your door, seeking and asking. You say unto me, I have not because I ask not. Right now, I'm speaking prosperity in every area and every situation in my life, in the Name of Jesus. Whatever I need, I have it in You, my Savior, my Father. My victory comes with getting closer to You, Lord, Jesus. My knowledge of who You are and who I am in You, Lord, is increasing. I have the victory through You, Christ Jesus. My victory comes with tapping into...More of You God.

(James 1:25, Revelation, 1:3, Luke 11:28, John 1:16, Ephesians 1:3-5, Matthew 7:7-12, Jeremiah 29:11-13, John 15:7, Romans 8:28, 1 John 5:4)

Year One:

_____
_____
_____
_____
_____
_____
_____
_____

Year Two:

_____
_____
_____
_____
_____

August 16

Father, today, I am rejoicing because I am **still standing**. My back was up against the wall, but **You** still **made a way for me**. Lord, thank You for **never giving up on me**. I have found out **prayer is the answer**; it **changes everything**. Prayer is **one of the most powerful tools and weapons** You have given me. I will continue to tap into my prayer life with You, Lord, Jesus. The more time I spend on my knees, I get to know You just a little bit deeper, and our relationship gets closer. My heart yearns to be where You are, my Savior. As I get to know You, Lord, my faith gets stronger and stronger. Right now, I refuse to look at what is in front of me, appearing to be a giant. As I look to You, my Heavenly Father, I know, **I win with You**. My will to win is greater than my desire to give up on my life, Father. I press on and persevere with…More of You God.

(James 5:16, 1 Thessalonians 5:17, 2 Chronicles 7:14, Philippians 4:6, Hebrews 11:6, Matthew 21:22, Mark 11:22-24, Ephesians 2:8-9, Proverbs 3:5-6)

Year One:

_____

_____

_____

_____

_____

_____

_____

Year Two:

_____

_____

_____

_____

_____

_____

_____

August 17

Jehovah, I thank You for always **providing and sustaining a way** for me. Today, I'm going to continue to have an **unwavering faith and blindly walk with You**, Lord, Jesus. All of my trust is in You, Father; this journey I'm on shall be led by You. I will continue, daily, getting on my knees, seeking after seeing Your face, asking for Your complete guidance for my life. Lord, I want to do what is pleasing in Your sight. I know, my ways and thoughts are not like Yours; but, Lord, I want to be more like You, Jesus. As the world sees me, I want them to see **I'm a living testimony for You**, Lord, Jesus. Let my light shine so brightly, all people coming in contact with me will feel Your healing powers through me, Lord, Jesus. I surrender completely to You, Father. **I want to be used completely for Your glory**. Now, my life is all about the purpose and plan You have for me to accomplish. I love You, Lord, Jesus! Use me! Lord, use me! This place I'm in is rewarding, with having...More of You God.
(Matthew 6:26, Luke 12:24, Acts 14:17, 1 Corinthians 13:2, 2 Corinthians 5:6-7, Ephesians 6:16, 1 Chronicles 16:11, Psalm 105:4, Psalm 102:2, Exodus 33:20-23, Revelation 22:4)

Year One:

_____
_____
_____
_____
_____
_____
_____

Year Two:

_____
_____
_____
_____
_____
_____

August 18

King, Jesus, today and forevermore, I humble myself before Your throne. Throughout my life's journey, **I will sit at Your feet**. As I travel through ups and downs, I will remain at Your feet. When doors open up and my life is on a high, I know, it was only You, God. **You opened the door, and made it possible for my life to blossom.** Many times, when I'm feeling alone and trying hard, but not seeing results as fast as I think I should, I know, **You're there interceding on my behalf.** **Either You are <u>protecting</u> me from something or <u>setting me up</u> for something <u>spectacular</u> to happen.** You are going to work everything out to Your good for my good. In the middle of all of my trials, I praise You, Lord, Jesus. Hallelujah! Hallelujah! Hallelujah! All the more reasons why, it is imperative for me to wait on You, Lord. While I wait, I sit at Your feet, seeking after...More of You God.
(Psalm 110:1, Micah 4:4, Matthew 26:36, Matthew 14:19, Luke 10:39, Judges 21:2, 2 Samuel 7:18, Mark 10:37, Hebrews 12:2, Revelation 3:21, Revelation 4:10)

Year One:

_____
_____
_____
_____
_____
_____
_____

Year Two:

_____
_____
_____
_____
_____
_____

August 19

Father, today, I am having that **now-faith of a mustard seed**. I'm believing the **dreams You have placed in my heart, will come into fruition**. I will have a **more-than-enough** abundant life's journey. **I know, I must have the faith of hoping for something I cannot physically see, but I must mentally put a picture in my head, it is done!** Lord, direct my vision and give me the instructions to fulfill all You desire for me. Father, I put my all into this dream. This passion I have, let all I do be in honor of You, my King. From this day forward, I will keep a positive mindset. I will speak positivity over my life and all who I come in contact. Blessings are following me all the days of my life. I praise Your Holy Name! My faith grows while seeking after...More of You God.

(Matthew 17:20, Luke 17:5-6, Hebrews 11:1-6, John 14:1-31, Matthew 13:1-58, Matthew 21:22, Mark 11:22-24, Luke 1:37)

Year One:

_____
_____
_____
_____
_____
_____
_____
_____

Year Two:

_____
_____
_____
_____
_____
_____

August 20

Lord, today, I am standing on the bible verse stating, You will renew my mind. Father, I know, if I think well, it will reflect in my life, and I will live better. Lord, I'm **praying to be spiritly minded.** I want to have a mindset of You, God. I'll keep all garbage out of my thinking pattern. Father, let me be open and willing to receive Your thoughts and ways for my direction. **Even when it appears all odds are against me, I trust You, Lord, Jesus.** Holy Spirit, expose unto me, what You want inside of me, allowing it to manifest out to others. Lord, search and fill my heart making it pure, with Your goodness, and Your grace. Right now, **I deny myself, so I can do Your will.** I know, this will take some sacrificing on my part, but, Holy Spirit, what You have for me is much greater. I can't even bring my mind to imagine what You have in store for me. Lord, Jesus, **my mind is fixed on You.** I'm open and available for...More of You God.

(Romans 12:1-2, Philippians 4:6-8, 2 Corinthians 4:16, Ephesians 4:23, 1 Peter 1:13, Colossians 3:2, Colossians 3:16, Joshua 1:8-9, Philippians 2:5, Jeremiah 29:11, 1 Corinthians 2:16)

Year One:

_____
_____
_____
_____
_____
_____

Year Two:

_____
_____
_____
_____
_____
_____

August 21

Jesus, Jesus, Jesus, today, as well as, every day, **You are all I need.**
You are my motivation for my life to thrive. I know, as long as I have
You in the forefront of my life, I have the victory in every situation and
condition, coming my way. No weapon formed against me will
prosper. Lord, I look back where I came from, it was only by Your
divine design, I am moving forward towards, more of Your glory.
When pitfalls were in my way, waiting for me to fall in, trying to snatch
and grab me, Oh, Heavenly Father, You were there to block and intervene on my behalf. **Lord, You are always here to open up the doors
in front of me. You're taking me to a higher level in You.** So the rest
of the world may be overcome by my testimony, Yes, You make my
situation and victory public for the entire world. Jesus! Jesus! Jesus!
How grateful I am to have a Father, like You. You are so good. My
heart cries out with joy, just as long as I have...More of You God.
(John 14:6-8, John 12:46, 2 Timothy 1:7, John 15:5, John 15:16, Psalm
124:7-8, Philippians 4:19-20, Romans 8:32, Psalm 40:17, Psalm 37:4,
Psalm 27:5)

Year One:

_____
_____
_____
_____
_____
_____
_____

Year Two:

_____
_____
_____
_____
_____
_____

August 22

Father, today, I'm crying out for You to **comfort my heart**. Right now, Lord, Jesus, my heart is broken; it needs repairing. For years, so many family and friends have passed away. I'm praying they are resting comfortably with You now, Lord. I'm just missing so many love ones. But now, I'm looking for You, Father, **to heal my heart and mind, putting me back together**. This empty space in my heart, Father, please fill it up with Your love, Lord, Jesus. I need You now, Father, to close this gap of grieving, losses, emptiness, pain, sorrow, loneliness, and weariness. These feelings are trying to bound and hold me in captivity. Right now, I release all of these feelings, in the Name of Jesus. **Manifest Yourself within me now...Holy Spirit Come...You are welcome here...I need You.** My life is nothing without...More of You God. (Psalm 34:18, Proverbs 3:5-6, Revelation 21:4, Psalm 73:26, Isaiah 41:10, 1 Corinthians 13:7, John 14:27, Psalm 55:22, 2 Corinthians 12:9, Matthew 11:28-30)

Year One:

_____

_____

_____

_____

_____

_____

_____

Year Two:

_____

_____

_____

_____

_____

_____

August 23

King, Jesus, today, I am so happy to say You are my King; You are my everything. I have the breath of life and Oh, how happy I am to say, thank You, Lord. **You keep me functioning, by pouring Your spirit into me daily. You speak life in me on a day-by-day, moment-by-moment basis. I realize the hardest thing about my life, is life itself.** In order to get to the mountain top, I have to walk through this unknown valley. Therefore, as I walk through this journey, I must not waver. Now, I'm walking with a spirit of consistency and persistency. I will not relent; I will continue to persevere with Your strength, Lord, and with Your confidence, Father. As long as I have You on my side, the battle is already won. **This is a year of victory for me.** Many situations and obstacles were trying to hold me back; they are now unfolding and getting out of my path. I'm on the road to a new season in my life. I shall win, as long as I keep reaching towards...More of You God.

(Matthew 10:16-22, Hebrews 6:11-15, Colossians 1:11-12, Romans 12:12, Psalm 27:14, Galatians 6:9, Ephesians 6:16-19, 2 Timothy 4:1-5, Romans 5:2-5)

Year One:

_____

_____

_____

_____

_____

_____

_____

Year Two:

_____

_____

_____

_____

_____

_____

August 24

Lord, today, there is an **awakening occurring in my house**. My house meaning: my body, mind, spirit, and household. Father, speak to me, speak to me. I have a **hunger inside of me yearning for more of You, God**. Continue to **open my eyes**, so they are **fixed on You**. **Open my ears**, so I can **hear You speak to me, clearly and precisely**. I feel victory in my life. There were things I had problems with, and stumbled through, now, I trample over them. Now is my time to shout out, I have victory manifesting in my camp! Things are about to happen so fast, it's making my head swim. But, Yes, Lord, I know, it is because of Your mercy, grace, and promises, You have covering me. I'm a child of the Most High God; therefore, I will rejoice and be glad in this thing called life. The more I look to You, God, the more I have life with...More of You God.

(Proverbs 30:5, John 10:27, Romans 1:20, James 3:17, Numbers 22:28, 2 Chronicles 20:21, John 14:17, 1 Corinthians 3:16, Romans 8:26-27)

Year One:

_____
_____
_____
_____
_____
_____
_____

Year Two:

_____
_____
_____
_____
_____
_____
_____

244

August 25

Today, I declare the will of God over my life, my family, every situation, or condition. Father, make me more like You, Father. Lord, cleanse, renew, and restore me. **Align all of my desires, wishes, and dreams with You, Lord, Jesus.** Impart in me a vision to create an awesome vision board. **I will put my goals on paper**, and then, I will **walk them out with You, Father.** I know, You say, a person without a vision will perish. Lord, I want to flourish and accomplish all You have for me to complete. Lord, at the end of my time here on earth, **I want to enter into Your gates, hearing, "*Well done my faithful servant, I am well pleased with you.*"** So, Lord, create in me a new heart, filled with Your joy, peace, and love. The first piece of my puzzle (my life) must start with love. **My love shall conquer all I endeavor.** I love You, Lord, Jesus. My world must revolve around loving, praising, and having...More of You God.

(John 7:17, Romans 12:2, 1 Thessalonians 5:16-19, Mark 3:34-35, Romans 8:27-29, 1 Peter 2:13-16, 1 Peter 3:17, 1 Peter 4:19, 1 John 2:16-17, 1 Timothy 2:4)

Year One:

_____

_____

_____

_____

_____

_____

Year Two:

_____

_____

_____

_____

_____

_____

August 26

Savior, today, I realize **the pain I have been going through is necessary for my growth and new season.** Father, You have been preparing and molding me, getting me ready for where You are about to take me. However, it seems like the closer I get to this new season, I feel farther and farther away from it. Everywhere I look, I'm experiencing more pressure and pain. Lord, You know, I have been working so hard to make compelling and powerful moves, in my life. I'm looking for a return in them, so they are indicative of the work I have put in for this new season. As I look around, it looks pale and dull, appearing as no evidence of any of my hard work materializing. However, **Lord, I know, I have a Father, in heaven, who has made me many promises and lives inside of me. Therefore, I know, yes, I know, I will be victorious and fruitful.** Nothing will stop me from achieving, or entering into this New Season, You have carved out, just for me. My new season all comes with...More of You God.
(2 Corinthians 5:17, Ephesians 4:22-24, John 3:3, Isaiah 43:19, Revelation 21:5, Romans 6:4, Colossians 3:9-10, Jeremiah 29:11, 1 Corinthians 15:51-55, 2 Peter 3:9)

Year One:

_____
_____
_____
_____
_____

Year Two:

_____
_____
_____
_____
_____

August 27

Jehovah, God, I thank You for the breath of life You give me, today and every day. I cannot live off of bread alone. I have to push/press my way through, by seeking after You day in and day out. **Father, You are my food and drink.** I praise You, Lord, Jesus, for being the **living water, inside of me.** Holy Spirit, have Your way with me, right now. I will live with the purpose and plan You have mandated on my life. Lord, speak to me. Lord, Jesus, I just want to get closer to You; I want to walk with You every day of my life. Father, **I'm positioning, preparing, and pressing into the new provisions, You are about to release over me. My waiting season is over; I have planted the necessary seeds. I have watered them and now I'm waiting on You, Lord, to multiple them.** I need Your strength, because I do not want to get weary, Father. Give me the patience and the faith, to wait on You, Lord. I know, **Your timing is impeccable and undeniable.** As I'm waiting, Lord, I will continue to seek after...More of You God.
(Job 33:4, 2 Peter 1:20-21, Ezekiel 37:4-14, Galatians 6:9, Psalm 126:6, James 5:7-11, 1 Corinthians 3:6-9, Jeremiah 17:8, Matthew 13:30, Luke 10:2, John 4:35, Isaiah 60:21)

Year One:

_____
_____
_____
_____
_____
_____

Year Two:

_____
_____
_____
_____
_____

247

August 28

Today, Lord, Jesus, I recognize, I must now **face my enemy**. Right before I receive my new season from You, the enemy is waiting to steal it. I know, **no man can take what You have for me**. However, the devil doesn't want me to believe, I am worthy of the blessing You are about to bestow upon me. **The glory of the Lord is here**. It is about to **rain on my territory and what has been dry will, now, start to bloom and blossom to its full potential**. It is <u>limitless</u> with You, Lord, Jesus. I stand up straight, all girded up with my armor on. I fight the enemy with the Word of the Lord. I shield myself with my strong faith in You, Lord, God. I trust You, Lord, if You tell me You are about to do it, it is a done deal, Lord, Jesus.   While my enemy shoots his fiery darts at me, I can hear them bouncing right off of my shield. Lord, thank You for Your divine protection over me. My faith continues to grow. I realize, You're guarding me more and more, as I get to know...More of You God.
(Luke 10:19, Leviticus 26:3, Proverbs 25:21, Psalm 44:5, 2 Chronicles 16:9, Zechariah 4:6, Revelation 14:15, Leviticus 19:9-10, Matthew 13:23, John 15:1-11, Exodus 34:22, Joel 3:13)

Year One:

_____
_____
_____
_____
_____
_____
_____

Year Two:

_____
_____
_____
_____
_____
_____

August 29

God, today, I'm asking You to **keep my mind fresh and not on stupidity**. I **do not** want to be stuck in the process, plan, or past; I don't want to miss out on Your **fresh moves**. Father, I do not want to stay caught up in what is not of You. I plan to keep my eyes on what is important to me; You are my all, Lord, Jesus. My love for You, my faith in You, my belief in You, my in awe and respect for You, is undeniable. Lord, I want to show You how much You mean to me. You are near and dear to my heart. **I am nothing without You, Lord**, but an old filthy rag. **It is all because of Your Son, Jesus, dying on the cross; I have been made righteous.** Oh, what a precious gift from You, God. You didn't have to do it, but You gave Your Son's life, up for little bitty old me. **How powerful You are, Lord, because on the third day, Your Son was raised from the dead; death could not hold Him down.** Lord, now, I know, You are speaking and letting me know, what I though was dead in my dreams and desires, You are about to rain down on them, because of who I am, Your precious child. Thank You, Father, for being so gracious to me...I desire each day, to walk with...More of You God.
(2 Corinthians 5:17, Ephesians 4:22-24, John 5:24, Revelation 21:5, Ezekiel 11:19, Romans 6:23, Romans 10:13, Romans 6:4, John 6:40)

Year One:

_____
_____
_____
_____
_____
_____

Year Two:

_____
_____
_____
_____

August 30

Lord, God, **I will not give up**, today. I'm in the right state of mind, and I plan to continue on this journey. Father, **I know, if I make a way for You, You will make a way for me. If I make a way for someone else, You will make a way for me.** As I walk this journey with You, I will not be selfish and foolish. I have the faith of a mustard seed. I will not relinquish or turnaround from the goals and plans You have for me. I'm working on being in that special place You have for me. I know, as I settle in, on Your time, You will make all things work out for Your good and my good. **It is all about me waiting for You to approve, prepare a place, and make provisions for me.** Right now, You are working on my behalf. **I'm <u>expecting</u> to see change.** I'm waiting patiently on You, Lord, Jesus. I'm starting to see change and feel change. I will not give up, for the battle is not mine; it is Yours, Lord, Jesus. I will continue to hold on to Your unchanging hand with...More of You God.

(Micah 6:8, Colossians 1:10-11, Deuteronomy 8:6, Romans 13:13, Ephesians 2:10, 2 Chronicles 7:17-18, John 4:32-34, 1 John 2:6, Hebrews 10:22, Luke 10:27)

Year One:

_____

_____

_____

_____

_____

_____

Year Two:

_____

_____

_____

_____

_____

August 31

Heavenly, Father, today, I can truly say, **I know, everything in life first happens by the transition of my voice (invisible)**. It really seems weird, but it is true; my voice is not seen, therefore, it doesn't belong to the visible world. Now, I'm rising up and having a truthful voice. **A voice for what the Word says, a voice for what God tells me to say, a voice for protecting myself, my family, and all mankind.** No matter what tries to come my way, regardless if I make a mistake, I will always get right back up. I will speak to You, God, and follow the guidelines You have mapped out for me, Lord. **I refuse to let the devil dictate to me who I am, and what I can, or cannot do.** "Devil, you get back, right now, for the voice of the Lord, has spoken to me. Satan, I know, You do not like God's voice." I have my ear open to You, Father. I'm one of Your sheep, and I have my ear tuned into You, Lord. I get closer to You and wait on my direction from You with...More of You God. (Mark 11:22-24, Proverbs 18:21, Matthew 21:22, Isaiah 55:11, 2 Corinthians 4:13, Romans 4:17, Matthew 12:34-36, Genesis 1:1-31, Joshua 1:8)

Year One:

_____
_____
_____
_____
_____
_____

Year Two:

_____
_____
_____
_____
_____
_____

September

September 1

Today, I'm getting ready for **my new season**. A new month is here, and it's going to **bring blessings**. It will **be very fruitful and divinely spiritual**. I have the door open, Lord, Jesus, for You to step right in, conveying and exposing a new season in my life. It is time for Your new beginnings to manifest all over me. As this door opens, I need You, Lord, to **prepare my mind, so I will not be closed minded to the opportunities You present unto me**. Father, as You present this vision, let me remain focused on You and the provisions. **I'm ready and I'm able, because You said so, Father**. **You are about to do a new thing in me, through me, and for You**. I will walk with a different walk, and I will start receiving new results. I'm now a changed person. **I'm now kingdom-minded, with kingdom-vision, and kingdom-purpose**. Nothing can stop me now, with...More of You God.
(Ecclesiastes 3:1-8, Acts 1:7, Genesis 1:14, Genesis 8:22, Luke 21:25-27, 2 Timothy 4:2-4, Jeremiah 8:7, Acts 1:8, Psalm 31:14-15)

Year One:

_____
_____
_____
_____
_____
_____
_____

Year Two:

_____
_____
_____
_____
_____
_____
_____

253

September 2

Lord, as I walk this life, I want it to be all about You; I want the world to see I am Your child. Therefore, today, I want to convey a **spirit of love** to all who I encounter. As a Christian, Father, I must show love and not judge my fellow mankind. **Jesus is love. Because God lives inside of me, I have love within.** In order for me to do Your work, to go out and work on getting lost souls to You, Lord, **I must show love.** When I walk into a room, I want the individuals to say, "You are a-nointed. I can feel and sense there is something different about you." **I know, love isn't visible; however, it is beautiful. Love is an action, it is what others will feel, making it visible to them.** My love is what will help to change a person, a city, a state, a country, and a nation. Love is kind; it's not envious; it does not boast; it isn't proud; it isn't rude, self-seeking, or easily angered. Love doesn't keep records of wrongs, nor does it delight in evil, but it rejoices in the truth. With this spirit of love, I will protect, trust, have hope, and always perse-vere, because love never fails. I love growing with...More of You God. (Matthew 22:37-39, John 13:34-35, Romans 12:8-10, John 4:7-8, Matthew 5:44-45, John 15:12-13, Luke 6:31-35, Mark 12:31, Romans 13:10, 1 Corinthians 13:4-8)

Year One:

_____
_____
_____
_____
_____

Year Two:

_____
_____
_____
_____
_____

September 3

Today, all in my soul, I have the **spirit of joy**. I'm bubbling up and overflowing with the strength of the Lord. You are my joy, Father. I have my eyes set on You, Lord, Jesus. You are the Author and the Finisher. You know my beginning and my end. You are the First and the Last. I thank You, Lord, for all You have done for me and what You continue to do for me. **I have so much gratitude for Your exceedingly great and precious promises.** Father, I'm so thankful for my relationship with You, Lord, Jesus. **You are pure joy.** Lord, **I know, where the spirit of the Lord resides: there is liberty (freedom) and I'm free indeed.** I have a **joy inside of me which is unspeakable and untouchable.** This joy now causes me to give unto You and to serve You more and more each day. This joy I have inside of me, comes with having...More of You God.

(1 Thessalonians 5:16-18, Zephaniah 3:17, Philippians 4:4, Romans 12:12, Psalm 94:19, Psalm 118:24, Habakkuk 3:17-18, 1 Peter 1:8-9, Psalm 16:11, Isaiah 61:10, John 16:24)

Year One:

_____
_____
_____
_____
_____
_____
_____
_____

Year Two:

_____
_____
_____
_____
_____
_____

255

September 4

God, today, I'm speaking about the **spirit of peace**. I need the kind of peace that only comes with and through You, Lord, Jesus. Your peace that surpasses all understanding. Yes, I **have gone through many trials, but I have peace.** Everyone around me cannot understand why I'm full of peace, but it comes from You, Lord, God. I will continue to hold onto Your unchanging hand and have faith; I can do all things through You, who strengthens me. **No weapon formed against me shall prosper.** Everything I'm going through/have gone through, I know, You are going to turn it into my good, Lord, Jesus. **When doubt tries to creep into my spirit, I rebuke it and stand firm on Your Word, Lord.** Father, as I mature in my walk with You, I see peace manifesting daily in my life. **Lord, it is by Your grace I'm able to weather life's storms.** Father, I surrender my all to You; my peace comes with fellowshipping and experiencing...More of You God. (Colossians 3:15, Galatians 5:22, Hebrews 12:14, 1 Peter 5:7, James 3:18, Philippians 4:7, Proverbs 12:20, Proverbs 16:7, Psalm 29:11, Romans 12:18, Romans 14:9, 1 Peter 3:9-11)

Year One:

_____
_____
_____
_____
_____
_____
_____

Year Two:

_____
_____
_____
_____
_____
_____
_____

September 5

My Savior, today, is a day to tap into the **spirit of patience**. As I look at myself, Lord, I am putting on the heart of patience. According to Your will, I will deliberately and willingly have an attitude of determination to overcome the negative things I'm confronted with, today. I pray without ceasing for Your strength, as well as, the power to be patience and strongly stand on Your Word. Lord, Jesus, guide me, led me, and keep all harm and danger, away from me. Lord, let me have a heart for Your people, so I'm able to work with Your people. I want to be able to fulfill the purpose and plan You have for me on this earth. **Father, I want to be an example to Your people, so they will see my obedience to Your Word, and they will want to be more like me, to be more like You, Lord, Jesus**. Lastly, Lord, I will endure trials and tribulations here on earth. But Father, give me the patience to be able to stand. **I know, You have the final word, regarding everything in my life**. Therefore, I know, I have the victory, and I shall win with...More of You God.

(1 Corinthians 13:3-5, Proverbs 14:29, Ephesians 4:2, Romans 12:12, Galatians 6:9, Proverbs 16:32, Psalm 37:7, Romans 8:25, Psalm 27:14, Exodus 14:14, Colossians 3:12, Psalm 5:3)

Year One:

_____
_____
_____
_____
_____
_____

Year Two:

_____
_____
_____
_____
_____
_____

September 6

Father, I'm longing to be better, to live better, and to lead by example. Today, Lord, I'm asking for the **spirit of kindness**, in all I do and all that I am. I am coming humbly before Your throne, Lord; **I want to be a reflection of You**. With all whom I encounter, let me be compassionate, tender, and sweet. Father, I'm committed to showing Your love by being gracious and pleasant. Right now, in the Mighty Name of Jesus, I'm rebuking all bitterness, rage, anger, brawling, slander, and all malice. I will have an **attitude and spirit of servitude, serving in Your kingdom and serving Your people**. Let my heart be pure. I need You to cleanse, renew, and restore me from my old ways. Father, **let my heart be tuned into Yours**, so when people look at me, they will see You and only You, Lord, Jesus. I love You, Lord, Jesus. I can only display outwards actions of love with...More of You God. (Ephesians 4:32, Luke 6:35, Proverbs 11:17, Colossians 3:12-14, Proverbs 31:26, 1 Corinthians 13:4-7, Proverbs 19:17, Galatians 6:10, 1 Peter 3:9, 1 John 3:18, Philippians 2:1-30)

Year One:

_____
_____
_____
_____
_____
_____
_____

Year Two:

_____
_____
_____
_____
_____
_____
_____

September 7

Jesus, today, I'm dealing with the **spirit of goodness**. God, pour Your spirit in me now, so I will be more like You and a doer of Your Word. Savior, I want to **obey Your law, abiding by You, Holy Spirit**. Father, help me to do well by everyone, even my enemies. I want clean hands and a pure heart, Lord. Jesus, I want to be a part of the light of the world. All the good I do on this earth, is **only for the glory of You, Father**. Lord, I know, living a life close to You, allows for me to reap all of the great and good benefits, You have for me. Father, I just want to **be pleasing to You**, Lord, Jesus. Father, guide me in all I do, let me **be an encouragement to someone through Your Word**, drawing them closer to You, Jesus. Lord, I can only have a character of excellence, integrity, truth, and an appreciation for beauty with...More of You God.

(Galatians 6:10, Romans 12:9, Romans 12:21, Psalm 37:3, Matthew 5:15-16, Nahum 1:7, Galatians 5:22-23, Jeremiah 6:16, Ephesians 4:29, 2 Peter 1:5-7, Luke 6:36, Titus 2:14)

Year One:

_____
_____
_____
_____
_____
_____
_____

Year Two:

_____
_____
_____
_____
_____
_____

September 8

Faithful, faithful, faithful, is our Savior, Jesus Christ, the King. Today, I'm holding onto the **spirit of faith**. I believe God is who He says He is; I will continue to believe in Him, and only Him no matter what the world is throwing my way. I trust You, Lord, for **Your Word is true**; I will stand on it, day and night. Father, I know, You will **work everything in my life for my good**. Let Your will be done, Father. Holy Spirit, have Your way in me, now. **My faith comes through Your influence in and on me.** Lord, I have the kind of faith to speak to any mountain and it will be removed. Father, I believe You will do what You say You will do. I'm **standing on Your Word, the truth, and Your promises.** Lord, You have **never failed me, and I know, You never will.** God, my Savior, Your Word does not lie, and I will hold on without fainting. My strength is in You, Lord, Jesus. My faith gets deeper, stronger, and everlasting with...More of You God.
(Romans 10:17, James 2:19, Hebrews 11:6, Matthew 21:22, Ephesians 2:8-9, Luke 1:37, Hebrews 11:1, 1 Corinthians 2:5, Proverbs 3:5-6, James 2:14-26, 2 Corinthians 5:7, Psalm 46:10)

Year One:

_____
_____
_____
_____
_____
_____
_____

Year Two:

_____
_____
_____
_____
_____
_____
_____

September 9

Lord, Jesus, today, I'm working on having a better **spirit of meekness/gentleness**. Father, let all of **my actions be very gentle** to all who comes near, so **they will see Your love in me**. Futhermore, this action of gentleness, will produce an attitude of meekness. Lord, with this mighty power You provide to me, let me not misuse it in anyway. Holy Spirit, enter and work through me, enabling the spirit of meekness, to manifest throughout my life. Lord, I need You now; Father, I cannot do it without You. My flesh is weak, but with You, I am strong. **Your Word tells me to live a peaceful life. If someone hurts me, I should take it and love on them, rather than causing them pain.** I am **an overcomer and with You**, Lord, Jesus, I can do all things. My life is not the same, as long as I have…More of You God.
(Titus 3:2, 1 Peter 3:15, Psalm 18:35, 2 Timothy 2:24-26, James 3:17, Galatians 5:22-23, Galatians 6:1, Proverbs 15:1, Matthew 11:29, James 1:19-20, 2 Samuel 22:26, 1 Corinthians 13:4-5)

Year One:

_____
_____
_____
_____
_____
_____
_____
_____

Year Two:

_____
_____
_____
_____
_____
_____
_____

261

September 10

Lord, God, today, I'm going to work on the <u>spirit of self-control (temperance)</u>. I know, there are so many things I need to restrain from. Your Word says, I should flee from sin; I realize not only do I need to flee from evil things, but too much of a good thing, is not good for me either. Lord, **I need Your power instilled in me**, so I can truly have self-control. I'm a work-in-progress; I work daily to have the self-discipline of obedience to the call, and purpose You have on my life. I must **take up my cross and follow You. I must deny myself and live my life for You, Lord, Jesus**. I will seek You day and night. As I'm seeking You, You **are working to empower me to do Your will and to act according to Your purpose**, You have for me on this earth. I **lay down my old ways and surrender unto to You**, Father. I can only gain selflessness control, by seeking after...More of You God.
(Proverbs 25-28, 1 Corinthians 10:13, Galatians 5:22-23, 2 Peter 1:5-7, 1 Corinthians 9:24-27, 2 Timothy 1:7, Proverbs 16:32, 1 Peter 4:7, Titus 2:11-14, Titus 1:8, 1 Peter 5:8, 1 Corinthians 13:4-5)

Year One:

_____
_____
_____
_____
_____
_____
_____
_____

Year Two:

_____
_____
_____
_____
_____
_____

September 11

Lord, You are so beautiful to me. I thank You for the **Holy Spirit**, residing in me, working in and through me. Today, Father, I'm so grateful for all the **gifts of the spirit** You make available to me. I will continue to seek Your face and cry out to You to impart these gifts to me. You tell me **all I have to do is ask and it shall be given to me**. I know, Lord, **I must have the fruit of being patience, because it is not on my time, but it is on Yours**. These gifts are not about me, they are all about You. **They are to be used for Your glory and Your divine purpose**. Lord, Jesus, I take this day forward to learn more about Your gifts and to tap into these gifts wholeheartedly, so that You can use me like I have never been used. I open myself up unto You, Father, clean my heart and my mind, so it will be more like Yours, Lord, God. I can only receive these gifts by the power of Your Spirit, which is why I am crying out now for...More of You God.
(1 Peter 4:10, Romans 12:6-8, 1 Corinthians 12:1-31, 1 Timothy 4:1-40, 1 Corinthians 12:7-11, Acts 2:1-47, Ephesians 4:11, 1 Corinthians 13:8)

Year One:

_____
_____
_____
_____
_____
_____
_____

Year Two:

_____
_____
_____
_____
_____
_____
_____

September 12

Holy Spirit, today, I'm asking You to work within me, now, Father. I'm seeking for the **gift of wisdom**. Lord impart in me a new vision of You, Lord, Jesus, and of Your glory. Lord, I'm overly joyful with Your love, for who You are and who You are in me. God, I want to have **the kind of wisdom You gave Solomon**. Father, give me the kind of a-nointing when an issue manifests or an important decision needs to be made; it is **through Your Spirit I hear the answer and make good decisions**. Father, I want to have Your hand on me at all times. Lead me, Lord, Jesus. Lord, let Your supernatural power flow through me naturally; let me use it according to Your Word. Let me speak wisdom that is well beyond me. It shall be unknown to me, because it is coming directly from You, my Father. Lord, it is only up to You to give me the gift of wisdom. I understand I can ask, You tell me to, but I know, **the final answer is Yours**. I know, if I ask, I will definitely receive at least one of Your gifts. This gift will only come with me seeking after...More of You God.
(Proverbs 2:6, Ephesians 5:15-16, James 1:5, James 3:13-17, Proverbs 16:16, Ecclesiastes 7:10, Colossians 4:5-6, Proverbs 19:8, Proverbs 11:2, Psalm 90:12, Matthew 7:24, Isaiah 55:8)

Year One:

_____
_____
_____
_____
_____
_____

Year Two:

_____
_____
_____
_____
_____
_____

September 13

Father, today, if it is Your will, I'm seeking to have more **knowledge in the Spirit**. Lord, God, I only want this gift to help me **be insightful and more helpful in edifying Your church**, Lord. Jesus, I have a desire to seek out and personally experience Your Word. Father, use me as a vessel for this generation at hand. We need You, Lord. Lord, I'm yearning to be more like You, Father. I want to be used for Your glory. To give to Your people, impress upon me a relevant message, or an insight. I realize I **must stay close to You; I must seek Your face.** In **order for this spiritual gift to manifest** for any given situation, I **must stay in Your Word.** Father, this kind of knowledge I'm asking for is to help direct and take Your people, to another level in You. Lord, God, I have a heart for You. Father, purify me and make me whole. I'm praying now, to stay humble, and keep a heart of sensitivity for Your people. Father, impart in me a new thing, knowledge. Lord, God, I want...More of You God.

(Proverbs 18:15, Proverbs 2:10, Proverbs 1:7, Hosea 4:6-7, Proverbs 8:10, Proverbs 24:5, Proverbs 15:14, Proverbs 12:1, Proverbs 3:1-35, Proverbs 2:1-22, Hosea 4:6, 1 Corinthians 12:8)

Year One:

_____

_____

_____

_____

_____

_____

_____

Year Two:

_____

_____

_____

_____

_____

September 14

God, I want to see things that have yet to occur. Today, Lord, Jesus, I'm asking for the **spirit of faith**. Father, I trust in Your Word and in Your promises. You are a God who does not lie. Hallelujah, Lord, Jesus! I believe, if You said it, it shall be done. Right now, I **may not see it in the natural, but I see it in the supernatural**. I'm rejoicing in Your promises. Throughout my life's experiences, Father, my **faith grows as I walk with You**. Also, **it grows through hearing and studying Your Word**. Every day I walk with You, I see and feel Your faithfullness manifest in my life. I yearn for You as my faith grows. Lord, You are my rock! I will not let worldly things disturb me; You have my life in the palm of Your hand. I know, that I know, You are going to take care of all things in my life, and You are going to work them out to my good. My faith keeps on growing with having and hearing of...More of You God.

(Ephesians 2:8, Galatians 3:11-13, Mark 11:22-24, 1 John 4:7-12, 1 John 5:4, 2 Corinthians 10:3-5, Deuteronomy 28:2-8, Ephesians 3:20-21, Ephesians 4:29, Ephesians 6:10-18)

Year One:

_____
_____
_____
_____
_____
_____
_____

Year Two:

_____
_____
_____
_____
_____
_____
_____

September 15

Lord, My Savior, today, I am crying out for the spiritual gift of healing. It is only **through Your supernatural miraculous power, it brings healing and deliverance from disease, and all infirmities.** Father, only You can destroy the work of sin/the devil in the human body, giving me the gift to heal. Lord, God, I'm asking You now, to **anoint my hands, pour Your holy oil all over me.** All to edify Your church, other believers, and to glorify You, Lord, Jesus. There are so many of us crying out unto You, we need You, Father. We are suffering with physical, mental, and emotional problems. Lord, use me as a vessel to show Your people, You are the same God who we read of in Your Word. The same God, who healed the woman with the issue of blood, healed the blind man, brought back man from the dead, and much more. You did it then, and You are still doing it, now. With healing hands, let me walk this day forward, in the Name of Jesus. There is healing, in the Name of Jesus! I cry out Your Name now, Jesus! Jesus! Jesus! I can only have Your healing power through You. If it is Your will, I can only function in healing with...More of You God.
(James 5:14-15, 1 Peter 2:24, 1 Corinthians 12:1-31, 1 Timothy 5:23, Acts 28:27, Proverbs 12:18, Exodus 15:26, Revelation 22:2, 1 Corinthians 14:2, Acts 3:6, Mark 11:24)

Year One:

_____
_____
_____
_____
_____
_____

Year Two:

_____
_____
_____
_____

September 16

Abba, Father, today, I'm asking for a supernatural power to **intervene against earthly and evil forces**. Lord, God, exhort me to **work within Your power**, doing something abnormal or natural for me. I'm asking for the **spiritual gift of miracles**. I will use this gift to edify Your church and Your people. It shall be **used to combat unbelief and deliver non-believers**. Through believing in Your, Son, Jesus Christ, who died for them and rose in three days, they will repent and will have the gift of eternal life. This gift and all of Your gifts are a blessing from You, Father. Lord, God, **You choose who shall receive which gifts and they are only for Your glory. I must seek Your face day-in and day-out, by keeping Your Word in me**. Let me operate in what is pleasing to You, Father. It is a fact, miracles come from You, and only You. Therefore, I must keep my eye on the sparrow, and chase after...More of You God.

(Acts 4:30, John 4:48, Acts 3:16, 2 Thessalonians 2:9, John 14:12, Acts 19:11, Mark 16:17, Mark 10:27, Luke 18:27, Mark 9:23, Jeremiah 32:27, Luke 9:16-17, Matthew 17:20)

Year One:

_____
_____
_____
_____
_____
_____
_____
_____

Year Two:

_____
_____
_____
_____
_____
_____

September 17

Heavenly, Father, if it is Your will, speak through me. Today, I'm seeking and praying to have the **gift of publicly speaking forth the Word of God**; the <u>spiritual gift of prophecy</u>. Lord, let me teach unto Your people, Father. God, I need You to motivate my actions, my words, and shape my perspective on life; all for Your glory, Jesus. Lord, before I have the ability to call sin, wrong doings, and compromises being made, I need You to make me a new creature within You, Holy Spirit. From this day forward, have Your way and do a new thing inside of me. **I must stay focused and stay faithful in Your Word**. Father, put a boldness on me, so I will be outspoken. Only to be used to edify Your church, as well as, Your people. Lord, God, **I can only have this discerning spirit, with staying in You**. Father, I'm always seeking after...More of You God.
(Acts 2:16-21, Amos 3:7, 1 Corinthians 13:2, 1 John 4:1, Matthew 7:15, Matthew 24:25, Mark 13:23, 2 Peter 1:19-21, Revelation 1:3)

Year One:

_____
_____
_____
_____
_____
_____
_____
_____

Year Two:

_____
_____
_____
_____
_____
_____
_____
_____

September 18

Dear God, have Your way with me. Today, I'm praying to have the **spiritual gift of discernment**. Lord, open me up to **be able to discern if someone is a false prophet or has impure motives**. Let me feel and **sense whether deception or corruption is taking place**, in an individual in the church. Yes, Father, I want to know if the teacher or the prophet is really from You, God. This gut feeling You give will be a warning from You, God. Now, I'm asking for You to allow me to walk with this gift; I will use it to Your glory. Oh, Father, God, fill up my heart with Your heavenly discernment. I want to pick up quickly, what type of individual I'm dealing with, making sure they are an authentic man or woman of You, God. Lord, this life I live is all about, You, edifying Your church, and Your Word. Father, **I want to walk in the fullness of the Holy Spirit**; therefore, I will seek after Your face. I want ...More of You God.

(1 John 4:1, Philippians 1:9-10, Hebrews 5:14, Hebrews 4:12, Proverbs 3:1, John 7:24, Proverbs 2:1-5, 1 Corinthians 14:33, 2 Corinthians 11:13-15, Colossians 2:8, 1 Kings 3:9, Matthew 24:24)

Year One:

_____
_____
_____
_____
_____
_____
_____
_____

Year Two:

_____
_____
_____
_____
_____
_____
_____

September 19

Holy Spirit, enter into me, now. Refresh, restore, and renew me. Lord, my heart is wholeheartedly, seeking after You. Today, I'm asking You to **fill me or refresh me** with the <u>**gift of speaking in tongue**</u>. For example, like in the book of Acts, where the disciples and the 120 people in the upper room were filled with the Holy Spirit. Lord, fill me, **so I will get closer to You and have a closer relationship with You**, Lord, Jesus. Father, this gift is paramount to me, I want to use it for Your glory. I'm going to use it in my private devotional time with You, Holy Spirit. Lord, it is also to **unite the church with You**, Christ, Jesus. You are not a God who hides Yourself. You always make Yourself known to all of us who seek You with our entire hearts. As I give my all to You, You show up and show out, in a supernatural miraculous way. Oh, Lord, Jesus, how grateful I am for the Holy Ghost to enter in, and manifest through me. I offer up unto You all I have, just to have...More of You God.

(1 Corinthians 14:1-40, Mark 16:15-18, Acts 2:1-11, 1 Corinthians 13:1-13, Acts 19:1-41, Acts 10:44-46, 1 Corinthians 1:5, Galatians 5:22, 1 Corinthians 12:8-11)

Year One:

_____
_____
_____
_____
_____
_____
_____

Year Two:

_____
_____
_____
_____
_____
_____

September 20

Father, today, I'm asking You to do a miraculous work in me. I'm seeking and praying for the **gift of interpreting tongues**. Even though I do not know the language being spoken, Lord, I want to have the **ability to understand what a tongues speaker is saying**. Father, I want this gift, so I can edify Your church. When someone speaks in tongue in the church, I will **be able to share with Your children, the Word You have for us**. Holy Spirit, I want all You have for me. I want to abide by Your scripture lifting up Your Holy Name. Father, You are so worthy to be praised! I honor You, and I adore You. You are the Great I Am. Lord, You are, Sovereign. You are Holy. There is none like You, my King. I lift up holy hands to You. Speaking in tongue, my soul cries out for...More of You God.
(1 Corinthians 14:27-30, 1 Corinthians 12:10, 1 Corinthians 14:2-5, 1 Corinthians 14:13, Acts 2:4, Acts 19:6)

Year One:

_____
_____
_____
_____
_____
_____
_____
_____

Year Two:

_____
_____
_____
_____
_____
_____
_____
_____

September 21

My Lord, my Savior, You come so I may have life more abundantly. Therefore, I will serve You all the days of my life. Today, I just want to have a **spirit of serving**. **I know, I will not receive every spiritual gift. We were made to help each other, and to depend on each other.** Father, I want to willingly and diligently sacrifice my energy and time unto You. All for Your glory. Lord, I am available to You; use me as You please. I was placed on this earth for Your purpose and plan, not mine. To edify Your church and Your people, Father, **I am here to fulfill the work and task You have set for me to accomplish.** Lord, whatever You ask or require of me, I will see to it being completely accomplished, to Your satisfaction. Father, **I am Your servant.** I learn daily, as I seek Your face, to be more like, Jesus. Jesus, You are the greatest example of a servant. That's why I desire to tap into...More of You God.

(1 Samuel 12:24, Colossians 3:23-24, 2 Corinthians 9:7, Romans 12:1, 1 Corinthians 15:58, 1 Peter 2:9, Malachi 3:18, Deuteronomy 13:4, Matthew 6:24, Colossians 3:7, Joshua 1:8, 1 Chronicles 28:9)

Year One:

_____
_____
_____
_____
_____
_____
_____

Year Two:

_____
_____
_____
_____
_____
_____

September 22

Savior, You are the Lord of Lords, God of Gods, and King of Kings. **If it is Your will**, today, impart in me the **spiritual gift of teaching**. **How You will use me, is all up to You.** Maybe it is writing a book or article, touching the world. All for Your glory. Father, maybe You will choose me as a Sunday school teacher or a teacher of teachers. Lord, show me how to keep Your Word clear, concise, and simple, so my students will be able to understand, no matter what their intellectual level. I just want to have the capacity to make Your Word clear to all near and far. **Impart in me the doctrine of Your Word.** Give me the qualification and insight on how to break it down, in a form fitting to whatever audience You provide for me. Father, I want to teach whatever You have me teach, all to edify Your church. I'm seeking after pleasing only You, Lord. I have so much joy and pleasure doing what You call me to do. I can only smile with gratitude, as I hold onto...More of You God.

(Matthew 28:19-20, 2 Timothy 3:16, Hebrews 4:12, Romans 10:17, John 16:13, 2 Timothy 2:15, John 17:17, Colossians 3:16, John 14:26, Matthew 4:4, 1 Peter 4:10, 1 Timothy 5:17)

Year One:

_____
_____
_____
_____
_____
_____
_____

Year Two:

_____
_____
_____
_____
_____
_____

September 23

Lord, today, I'm asking You to empower me with a stronger **gift of encouragement or exhortation**. I want to be a light shining, so other believers can mature in You and grow spiritually. I know, the trials and tribulation I go through, You are with me. Therefore, let me walk gracefully through all of them, letting Your glory shine, to all who see me. Let me radiate with Your kindness, Your goodness, Your mercy, and Your grace. **As Your people are going through a test, give me the words from Your Word to empower them, giving them hope and Your perfect peace, surpassing all understanding**. God, I want them to see Your power, Your faithfulness, and most of all, Your love. You love us so much, You gave up Your Son's life for us, so we can have eternal live. What an awesome God You are to all of us! I praise You, Lord! I magnify Your Holy Name! You are so worthy to be praised! My strength is in having...More of You God.
(Mark 11:24, Joshua 1:9, 2 Timothy 1:7, Psalm 121:1-8, Psalm 37:4, 1 Thessalonians 5:9-11, Psalm 55:22, Romans 15:13, Psalm 126:5, Hebrews 10:25, Ephesians 4:29)

Year One:

_____
_____
_____
_____
_____
_____
_____

Year Two:

_____
_____
_____
_____
_____
_____
_____

September 24

God, give me a **heart of giving**. Today, I humble myself, I will make it a point to love my neighbor as myself and Your house (church) with my finances. Father, **I want to give sacrificially; I want to give to where it hurts**. I want to bring joy to those less fortunate than me. I want to make someone's life happier and see joy streaming from their face. Lord, God, use me in a mighty way. Let Your glory reign through me, so lives will be saved. Father, it is all about You, I give because You make me happy, and You have set me free. Now, I want the rest of the world to know of Your goodness; so they can be set free and have the joy of You, Lord, Jesus. All the glory belongs to You, and the edification of Your church. I'm filled with joy and happy to be in Your presence with...More of You God.
(2 Corinthians 9:6-7, Acts 20:35, Luke 6:38, Luke 12:33-34, John 3:16-17, Proverbs 3:27, Galatians 6:6-10, Proverbs 19:17)

Year One:

_____
_____
_____
_____
_____
_____
_____
_____

Year Two:

_____
_____
_____
_____
_____
_____
_____
_____

September 25

Father, today, I want to work on my **spiritual gift of leadership**. I know, everything will rise or fall, depending on the effectiveness of leadership. Therefore, I'm coming to You asking You to **develop my leadership skills**. I will use them all for Your glory, Lord, Jesus. I want to edify Your church. I know, I am the church (the church is not a building), so, whatever, I do and no matter where I do it, I am a reflection of You. You live inside of me and You walk with me day-in and day-out. **Lord, You will only appoint me to what You have for me to do**. It will only be under Your divine direction for me to lead in whatever capacity You have. Maybe, it will be with my friends or it will be at my church. Maybe, it will be at my job or it will be nationally. Father, do it now, **do a great work through me for You**, Lord, God. I want to **be able to discern pure spiritual needs**, helping to take Your people to another level in You. Lord, God, my spiritual growth comes with having...More of You God.
(Deuteronomy 1:15, Mark 10:42-45, 1 Timothy 4:12, Philippians 2:3-8, Matthew 20:25-28, 1 Corinthians 12:12, John 13:12-15, 1 Timothy 3:1-7, Isaiah 6:8)

Year One:

_____
_____
_____
_____
_____
_____

Year Two:

_____
_____
_____
_____
_____
_____

277

September 26

My Savior, thank You for showing mercy on me, daily. Today, I'm asking You to show me how to be a **better Christian, who shows unconditional mercy** upon Your people. Lord, God, allow me to build beautiful relationships with others, and be loyal to them. Let me have a heart to share the pain others are going through, showing them compassion. **This life You have given me is not about me, it is all about You, showing love to Your people.** It is about me caring for others, as I care for myself. It's the second greatest command You have given me. Lord, let me be empathetic with those people who are in need or afflicted. Father, I want to walk with them until You, Lord, Jesus, lift their burden off of them. Strengthen me, Lord, God, so I will be able to sustain, and endure the obstacles coming forth, as I open up myself to do Your work. Father, my heart cries! My heart cries! To those sick and shut in, my heart cries for the lost souls. Lord, God, my heart cries with a cheerful sound of joy, because I have...More of You God.
(Luke 6:36-37, Matthew 5:7, Matthew 9:13, 1 Peter 1:3, Hebrews 4:16, Colossians 3:12, James 2:1-13, Jude 1:23-25, 1 Corinthians 10:13, Proverbs 14:21, Micah 6:8)

Year One:

_____
_____
_____
_____
_____
_____

Year Two:

_____
_____
_____
_____
_____
_____

September 27

Jesus, Jesus, Jesus, You had mercy on me. You came down to earth and died on the cross, so I can now live forever, through Your forgiveness of sin. I come humbly, today, before Your throne, asking for the **gift of forgiveness**. Lord, I want a pure heart. I do not want to **hold any grudges** against Your people. I want a **heart not easily provoked or full of evil thinking**. I will leave the judging up to You, just as Your Word tells us to do, Father. Lord, God, I realize this gift of forgiveness is to be courageous. It doesn't mean I am weak or harsh. I will look at life from a different perspective, a wider view. Father, take me by Your hand, and guide me through Your Word. I know, You have a purpose and plan for me here on this earth. It is to love Your people, and show them how to get to Your Kingdom. I have much assurance and Your great protection over me. I am ready to proceed on the road You have set for me to travel. I look forward to traveling this journey with...More of You God.
(Ephesians 4:32, Mark 11:25, 1 John 1:9, Matthew 18:21-22, Matthew 6:14-15, James 5:16, Luke 6:27, Colossians 3:13, 1 Corinthians 10:13, Psalm 103:10-14, Romans 3:23)

Year One:

_____

_____

_____

_____

_____

_____

_____

Year Two:

_____

_____

_____

_____

_____

September 28

Jesus, my King, today, I'm asking for the **spirit of evangelizing**, **sharing Your gospel with those who are lost**. Lord, God, put a boldness on me, so I will have no fear to teach, and speak Your Word, to all who comes in my presence. **I will not force Your life-changing Word on anyone. I want to do as You, Lord; You never forced Yourself on anyone. You give us all the freewill to accept You or not.** Lord, Jesus, fill me up with Your goodness, Your grace, and Your mercy. Let me go now, with great compassion and commitment, spreading the love of You, Jesus, to all whom I encounter. Lord, give me the ability to effectively and clearly communicate Your gospel. Let me be able to engage Your people in meaningful conversations and help them to overcome the fear of rejection. I want to love freely and for others to see Your love in me. I want them to know who You are, so they will accept You as their Savior. Lord, my love gets stronger and deeper with...More of You God.
(Matthew 28:19-20, Mark 16:15, Matthew 5:14-16, Philemon 1:6, Psalm 66:16, 2 Timothy 3:16, Ezekiel 33:8, Acts 20:24, Acts 13:47, Romans 1:16, Psalm 105:1, 1 Peter 3:15, 1 Corinthians 15:1-2)

Year One:

_____
_____
_____
_____
_____
_____

Year Two:

_____
_____
_____
_____
_____
_____

September 29

Father, throughout this month, I have come asking You for the fruits of the spirit to manifest in and through me. Also, **I'm asking for whatever spiritual gifts You have particularly designed for me.** It could be just one or it could be most of them. Today, I come before You knowing it is Your will being done within me. Lord, God, this is truly all I am asking of You. **When Your will is done, it is something extra ordinary, it is awesome, it is great, and it is supernatural.** Oh! Hallelujah! Hallelujah! Hallelujah! I'm so grateful I can come to You and ask for anything in Your Name. I know, You will consider giving it to me, if it is of You. Lord, I want to be used for Your glory. **I must be equipped, with Your tools, in order to move in a way, I have never done.** Father...You are a wonder...You are a wonder! Let everything having breath praise Ye the Lord! I praise You and I worship You, Lord! I just want to keep my spirit in tuned with...More of You God.
(1 John 5:14, John 14:13, John 16:24, Matthew 21:22, Matthew 7:7, James 1:6-8, 1 John 1:9)

Year One:

_____
_____
_____
_____
_____
_____
_____
_____

Year Two:

_____
_____
_____
_____
_____

September 30

Lord, Jesus, today, I just want You to strip me of all things not of You, allowing the gifts You have to manifest within me. Father, I'm opening myself up unto You, so You can have Your way with me. Use me now, Lord, like You have never used me before. I'm available to You. I'm Your willing servant. I'm excited about the fruits of the spirit and the gifts of the spirit. **I realize in order to use any of these gifts as You command of me, I must stay in Your Word, staying close to You, living the life You require of me.** It is so awesome to know what You have available to me. **I just have to tap in and seek Your face in order to receive.** I believe what Your Word says, I know, it is the truth, and You are a God who does not lie. Therefore, I will love You, and trust You, for all the days of my life. I got joy, joy, joy, down in my soul. I love this place I'm in now. A place learning of...More of You God. (Deuteronomy 11:1, John 15:9-15, 2 Corinthians 10:5, Revelation 14:12, Romans 1:5, John 1:6, Luke 11:28, James 1:25)

Year One:

_____
_____
_____
_____
_____
_____
_____

Year Two:

_____
_____
_____
_____
_____
_____

October

October 1

Hallelujah! Hallelujah! Lord, Jesus, today, I am thanking You for this month, a **month to celebrate Atonement.** Oh! Hallelujah! Father, I thank You for sending Your Son, Jesus, making me whole. **You sent Him to set me free and to make me righteous.** You didn't have to do it, but You did it anyway, Lord, Jesus. Oh, how grateful I am to know how much You love me, Lord. **Atonement is a celebration about You shedding Your blood to cleanse me of all of my sins, "It is finished",** says **the Lord.** This means You have completely set me free. All I have to do is, receive it, open up my heart, and let You, Holy Spirit, change my ways. Father, thank You for having mercy on me. Thank You for reconciliation. I thank You for **allowing me to become one with You, Lord**. My soul cries out to You, Lord, Jesus. Now, I am at peace with You, my Lord, my Savior. I'm coming this month with a new action plan, getting ready to be in Your presence. All I want, Lord, God, is to rest in You. I just want to love on...More of You God.
(1 John 2:2, Galatians 3:13, Isaiah 53:5-6, John 3:16, John 1:29, Romans 3:25, John 10:11, Exodus 24:3, Hebrews 7:27)

Year One:

_____
_____
_____
_____
_____
_____
_____

Year Two:

_____
_____
_____
_____
_____

October 2

Father, God, today, I honor You. **Atonement is a time when I will remember what You have done for me.** I want to show my appreciation for what You have totally finished for me. **Lord, what You have done is complete, and it is perfect.** All You do, God, is good and very good, Hallelujah! Father, You washed away my sins, so I can be clean, white as snow. **God, at the cross an exchange took place. This act was divinely ordained by You. All evil due to come my way, it came to You, Jesus, my Savior.** I was made righteous in honor of You, my Lord. This is such a special gift to me; I want to take this entire month of October to show my gratitude. I want to show You how much I love You. Lord, Jesus, I want to do what is right, in Your sight. Father, I want to do what is pleasing to You, Jesus. You have made eternal life available to me, Hallelujah! I have been set free. My heart is full with Your love. I just want to get ready to bask in Your presence. I am seeking after...More of You God.
(Romans 5:10, 1 Timothy 2:6, 2 Corinthians 5:15, Genesis 4:4, Leviticus 23:26-27, Leviticus 16:1-34)

Year One:

_____

_____

_____

_____

_____

_____

_____

Year Two:

_____

_____

_____

_____

October 3

God, today, I come with a humble spirit. I'm entering into another magnitude of expressions unto You-for all You have done for me. This is the month where **I will to take my prayer, worship, and thanksgiving to another level.** I want to go higher and deeper with You, Lord, Jesus, because of who You are and what You have done for me. Father, now, **I align myself to Your desires, Lord, God.** As I align myself with You, Lord, I know, I enter into many blessings and benefits, You graciously give me. You are a God of freedom, abundancy, overflow, and love. **I'm positioning myself for a time to reap, from what I have sown.** I will be ready. It doesn't matter what hell I might be going through now, Your grace is sufficient. Lord, Jesus, I repent for all the wrong I have done. Now, I'm getting ready for the glory of God, to shine in my life. This will be a time of restoration through Your Son, Jesus the Christ. Who wouldn't serve a God like this! Father, I dedicate my life unto You. I press towards...More of You God.
(Acts 27:9, Leviticus 23:29, Luke 13:3, Hebrews 9:11-12, Leviticus 16:10, Leviticus 16:21-22, Revelation 20:10, James 2:17)

Year One:

_____
_____
_____
_____
_____
_____

Year Two:

_____
_____
_____
_____
_____
_____

October 4

Today, Father, **I'm celebrating because an exchange took place at the cross, just for me.** Now, I am a new creature. All the bad due me, You bared it on the cross. Thank You, Lord, Jesus. **Through Your blood, I am healed, completely.** I am forgiven, whole heartedly, and I was made righteous. Hallelujah! Hallelujah! Hallelujah! I'm continually receiving Your blessings, day-in, and day-out. I have life more a-bundantly. You have shined down on me; You are sharing Your almighty glory with me. I'm so grateful, You created me. **You love me so much, You sacrificed Your, Son, Jesus Christ, on the cross.** This affords me an eternal life with You, Lord, God. Jesus, You are the most precious gift I can ever have. I'm sharing Your Son's life; Holy Spirit, You live inside of me. Now, I'm able to operate in the supernatural, by speaking things as though they are so and seeing them come to pass. Oh Father! How Great You Are! I love You so much, Lord, Jesus! I just want to get closer and closer to You..........I have joy and peace with...More of You God.

(1 Peter 2:24, John 1:29, Romans 5:11, Leviticus 17:11, Romans 3:25, Mark 10:45, 2 Corinthians 5:21)

Year One:

_____
_____
_____
_____
_____
_____
_____

Year Two:

_____
_____
_____
_____
_____

October 5

Lord, today, I just want to thank You for allowing me to get closer and closer to You, Lord, God. Daily, I'm changing more and more into Your image, Lord, Jesus. I come, humbly, before Your throne, asking for forgiveness for all of the wrongs I have done, Father. I repent, right now, Lord, Jesus. Father, I know, my ways and thoughts are not Yours. You say, You will do a new thing, and I'm a willing vessel, so I'm asking You to **do a new work in me**. Lord, Jesus, use me to Your glory; have Your way with me. Holy Spirit, guide me, direct me, and use me. Remove all not pure and holy; cleanse me Lord, Jesus. Oh Father! **I'm redeemed by the blood of Jesus Christ**. Hallelujah! Hallelujah! Hallelujah! I come now, **activating my faith, through my actions**. Your Word is true. I'm holding on, believing in every promise, and knowing, it is done, in the Name of Jesus. Thank You, Lord, for Your sacrifice, and Your new covenant (grace) with me. Lord, Jesus, I'm longing for...More of You God.
(Ephesians 5:2, 1 John 1:7, Leviticus 23:26-32, Mark 12:35-37, Ephesians 1:7, Romans 3:23, Isaiah 53:4-6)

Year One:

_____
_____
_____
_____
_____
_____
_____

Year Two:

_____
_____
_____
_____
_____
_____
_____

October 6

Precious Savior, today, I get down on bended knees, bowing down unto You, my King. This month is a **representation of Your Holy Days**. I come to honor You. I lift up holy hands to You, and only You, Lord, God. You are King of Kings, Lord of Lords, and God of Gods; there is no one like You, Lord, Jesus. Right now, I hear the trumpet sounding. I'm giving You all of the glory. Father, cleanse my heart, so You can reside in it; I want to be more like You, Lord, Jesus. Holy is the Lamb of God. **I will not let the world distract me from getting into Your presence and spending quality time with You, Lord, God**. I know, as I take this time to celebrate You, You always do more for me, than I can possibly do by honoring You. During this special appointed time, as I repent and worship You, with my all, You release blessings, upon blessings, on me. You say, **You will give me an increase, a fresh anointing, miracles, restorations, deliverance, revelation, financial abundance, and Your sweet presence**. This life I have, is all about having, more and...More of You God.
(Joel 2:23, Ezekiel 34:26, 2 Chronicles 5:3, Psalm 126, Isaiah 65:18-19, Hosea 6:1-3, Hebrews 4:1-9, 1 Samuel 4:21, Acts 3:19-21)

Year One:

_____
_____
_____
_____
_____
_____

Year Two:

_____
_____
_____
_____
_____
_____

October 7

Lord, God, this life I'm living is not about me; it is all about You. Today, I'm re-evaluating my life and making it a point to make room for You. I want You to have Your way with me and all who are connected to me. Jesus, during this season, You are about to do something so great in my life, eyes haven't seen nor ears have heard, what You are about to do. **I will be in position for You to show up and show out in my life.** During these Holy days, I'm repositioning myself. **I'm releasing all negativity, bad ways, and attitudes.** Father, I'm looking to Your Word, to direct my path. I am standing on Your Word, the truth, 100 percent, with no turning back. **I am returning to the position when I was so hungry to get into Your presence, when nothing else seemed to matter.** I knew as I sought after You, You would take care of me. As long as I'm chasing after You, I do not have to worry about anything. Whatever, I need it is already done, in the Name of Jesus. Hallelujah! Hallelujah! Hallelujah! My victory is in having...More of You God.

(2 Corinthians 5:14-15, Romans 8:32-35, 1 John 3:16, Deuteronomy 28:15, Hebrews 9:14, Matthew 6:16)

Year One:

_____
_____
_____
_____
_____
_____
_____

Year Two:

_____
_____
_____
_____
_____
_____

October 8

Heavenly Father, I'm seeking after You, in a way I have never done before, I have a beautiful and motivating zeal. It's a fire burning inside of me, making me want to be with You, like never before. **I open up my heart and mind, to be available unto You.** I want You to use me in a magnificent way; a way I have never been used for Your glory and Your glory alone. **Lord, God, I want to see the harvest You desire to bring in.** Father, You say, the road is narrow; but, I'm asking You to straighten my paths. This day forward, I want to be obedient unto You, totally. **Lord, it is only through the atonement, I will receive Your anointing. I must have a heart of repentance. I must speak it, as well as, live a life reflecting You, my Savior, who lives inside of me.** Holy Spirit, come now, refresh, restore, and renew me. To all I encounter, I want to be empowered by You, enabling me to go out and share You, Lord, Jesus. With some, I will have to speak of You to them, and with others, they will see You in me, because of my actions. Empower me, Lord, Jesus. My anointing comes with getting...More of You God.
(Matthew 13:17, Luke 13:24, Matthew 22:14, Matthew 7:13, Romans 5:15, Mark 10:45, 1 Corinthians 6:20, Revelation 5:9)

Year One:

_____
_____
_____
_____
_____
_____

Year Two:

_____
_____
_____
_____
_____
_____

October 9

God, today, I'm working on **changing my ways**. I have a tremendous role to play in excelling to higher levels within Your kingdom. Lord, God, You are a God who never lies; what Your Word says is the truth. **Through activating my faith, I'm going to stand on and tap into it.** A great opportunity You have made available to me; I will not turn back. Now, I will step in on my faith. Lord, there is power in Your blood. I plead the blood of Jesus, over my life. I realize I must have patience. **As I tap into Your Word, it is all about Your time, which is always on time.** However, I must not grow weary as I wait. I will tap in even deeper to hear a Word from You, Lord. Speak to my heart. Speak to my soul. Take me a little higher. Take me a little deeper. I'm thirsty for more of You, Father. Have mercy on me Lord! I will go where You say go, just send me. **This is my time for preparation, positioning for the manifestation of miracles, signs, and wonders to occur in my life.** Right now, this place I'm sitting in, Your presence, is so beautiful. It's a wonder just to have...More of You God.
(Matthew 21:22, Romans 10:17, Hebrews 11:6, Mark 11:22-24, James 2:19, Hebrews 11:1, Luke 1:37, Ephesians 2:8-9, Proverbs 3:5-6)

Year One:

_____
_____
_____
_____
_____
_____
_____

Year Two:

_____
_____
_____
_____
_____

October 10

Atonement **means to "Reconcile" or "To amend."** Today, Lord, Jesus, I'm so grateful You reconciled me back to You. By means of Your accomplishments in life, and in death, Jesus, You came down to earth and showed me how to live. You were faultless throughout Your life on earth; all You have done and said is perfect. **You came and paid my sin's penalties, by dying on the cross, so I can have e-ternal life. Father, You rose from the dead, on the third day, You ascended into heaven with Your Father.** Now, Lord, Jesus, You sit on the right hand of the Father, interceding on my behalf. How can I not be grateful unto You, my Savior, my Lord, and my King? **You have given me salvation.** I did not deserve it. However, You loved me so much, You sacrificed Your Son's life to give me this precious, precious, gift. What a Mighty God, I serve! Lord, Jesus, what You have done is completely finished. **It never has to be repeated, and <u>no one can</u> re-peat it.** No other sacrifice is needed; You paid the price for me. Ole, how You love little bitty oh me. You have now washed away my guilt and shame. Hallelujah, Lord, Jesus! I am now free, living with...More of You God.

(1 Peter 2:24, Leviticus 17:11, 1 John 2:2, Hebrews 9:12, Revelation 5:9, Romans 5:2-11, Hebrews 13:12, Isaiah 53:5, Hebrews 9:22)

Year One:

_____
_____
_____
_____
_____
_____

Year Two:

_____
_____
_____
_____
_____

October 11

Hallelujah! Today, God, I want to thank You. I am free, and I do not have to worry about ever being bounded again. Here I am to worship You, for who You are, Lord, God. Father, I exalt You! I'm so glad You shed Your blood for me. Now, I have eternal salvation; You have made me righteous in Christ. I celebrate You, Father; there is nobody like You, Lord, Jesus. Lord, I'm chasing after You. My desire is to have a heart of obedience unto You, Lord. Father, **I have a desire to have a deeper intimate relationship with You**. I can never have enough of You, Lord, Jesus; You are a Big, Big, Big, God. **Through my praise, prayer, fasting, and giving, now, I will center my life around You, Lord, Jesus**. You are the Beginning and the End; the First and the Last; the Author and the Finisher; You are God, alone. I worship You because of who You are, Lord, God. Father, I am here to remember who You are to me and what You have done for me. Your love is the greatest love of all. **It is time for reconciliation and rebuilding**. I get to have all of this with...More of You God.

(Isaiah 42:6-7, Colossians 1:13-14, Luke 4:18-19, John 8:32-36, Romans 8:1-2, Hebrews 9:15, Romans 6:11-23, 2 Peter 1:2-4)

Year One:

_____
_____
_____
_____
_____
_____

Year Two:

_____
_____
_____
_____
_____
_____

October 12

Father, today, I thank You for sending Your Son, Jesus, to pay a debt, He did not owe. Lord, thank You for paying the ultimate price for me. Now, I can live; I have life everlasting. My sins have been washed away. During these Holy of Holy days, I celebrate You with my complete heart, soul, and mind. I have a spirit of gratitude and love for my Creator, my Lord, and my King. Father, I'm standing on Your Word. To receive all You have for me, You unlocked Your promises, and You bring me into Your presence. Lord, God, You are my High Priest! I have a joy, down deep in my soul. It is time to celebrate all of Your blessings, You bestow upon me daily. This is a time I will unite with other believers. It is time for us to come together to praise You, our Savior. It is a time I will rest in You; You are my peace and joy. I will praise You with my whole being. It is my time to go from glory to glory. I know, You will show up in a mighty way, Lord, Jesus. The glory of the Lord is here. This means, it's my time and season, to have what was taken from me, restored. My abundancy and blessings are in reach. I'm rejoicing in...More of You God.
(Exodus 12:1-50, Leviticus 23:5, Matthew 26:17-30, Mark 14:22-24, 1 Corinthians 11:23-28)

Year One:

_____
_____
_____
_____
_____
_____

Year Two:

_____
_____
_____
_____
_____

October 13

Today, Sweet Jesus, I thank You for the increase and double portion coming my way. Lord, I know, You are already working behind the scenes on setting me up for an increase. I'm getting ready for my blessings to multiply, turning into many blessings. It is now harvest time. I have planted seeds; I have put my seeds in fertile ground; now, it is time for these seeds to blossom everywhere I look, or turn. God, this is the season You will increase me spiritually, emotionally, and physically. I thank You for taking what was once broken in me and putting me back together. Oh, my Heavenly Father, You never fail me. You are always giving me more and more. My life just gets bigger and better. Now, at this time I will seek and obey You like never before. I must position myself, aligning my heart and desires, with You, Lord, Jesus. Father, Your grace is sufficient. It is up to me to prepare accordingly with what Your Word tells me to do, so I may receive all You have for me. My capacity to receive all of Your promises, blessings, and abundant grace, is in seeking after...More of You God.

(Joel 2:25-26, Ezekiel 47:13, 1 Samuel 1:5, 2 Kings 2:9, Job 42:10, Exodus 16:5, Exodus 16:22, Isaiah 61:7, Zechariah 9:12)

Year One:

_____
_____
_____
_____
_____
_____

Year Two:

_____
_____
_____
_____
_____
_____

October 14

Celebrate! Celebrate! Today, **I celebrate the provision You have for me to live forever, through eternal life.** You made this gift available so I can live with You, after I leave this life, here on earth. How awesome! I can live with You forever. What a precious, precious gift! Father, I choose to follow in Your path and be obedient unto You. I have no fear, because **my safeguard is in Your hands.** I want to be more like You, Lord, Jesus. **There is power in aligning myself with Your desires.** I realize, it allows spiritual doors and opportunities to open up. A great outpouring of Your blessings and benefits are given to me-just as You promise in Your Word. Now, I'm in deep prayer, seeking for Your guidance, and repenting. Lord, cleanse, renew, and restore me. Everything I need has been provided to me through, just one sacrifice; Jesus the Christ, the greatest of all, the death of Your Son. These Holy days, I just want to let You know how much I love You, Lord, Jesus. **You have paved the way for me.** I'm hungry and thirsty for…More of You God.
(John 6:53-54, 1 Peter 1:18-19, 1 Corinthians 5:7, Hebrews 11:31, Hebrews 9:7, Hebrews 9:25, Ephesians 1:7, Colossians 1:14-20, Revelation 1:5, 1 John 1:7)

Year One:

_____
_____
_____
_____
_____

Year Two:

_____
_____
_____
_____
_____

October 15

Father, today, is a time for me to come together in unity with other believers, celebrating Your goodness and grace. It is a time for us to be in harmony, because there is power in coming together in numbers, to praise Your Name. It is during these times You show up in a mighty way. This is when the temple is filled with the train of Your robe, and Your glory is manifested amongst us. Hallelujah! When this occurs, there isn't room for anything else. No room for negativity, fear, shame, hurt, disease, financial problems, etc. This is because we are honoring and giving You all the praises due You. This is a time when You shower us with blessings, God. You are so awesome! When we obey and praise You (through You, Holy Spirit), I see promotion, You bless us, and You release the many benefits You speak of in Your Word. You do not have to do it, but it is Your nature. ALrighty now! Who wouldn't serve a God like You? I must have You as the center of my life. I cannot live this life without having...More of You God.

(1 Corinthians 1:10, Ephesians 4:3-13, Colossians 3:13-14, John 17:23, Psalm 133:1, 1 Peter 3:8, 1 John 4:12, Philippians 2:1)

Year One:

_____

_____

_____

_____

_____

Year Two:

_____

_____

_____

_____

_____

October 16

Today, Lord, God, **I am here to be the church.** One common purpose in mind, celebrating my King. It is about **humbling myself and not judging others.** I will congregate with others, fellowshipping with Your children, to honor You, our Savior. Lord, Jesus, the atoning work You did on the Cross is perfect, in all of its ways. **What You have done has set me free.** I'm free to enjoy life. Free to be blessed. Free to be a blessing to others. Free to spread Your Word to the world. Free to have faith of a mustard seed. Free to forgive others. Free to walk in the authority You have given me and not have fear. Free to live an incredible victorious life, and free to be whom I am. Your Word says, I am the head and not the tail; I am above and not beneath. Now, I take this time to declare and decree, all of these things over my life, and all those I fellowship with, in the Name of Jesus. How great You are, Lord, Jesus! You're a Wonder! You're a Wonder! What a pleasure it is to have this precious time, to get to know...More of You God. (Matthew 18:20, 1 Corinthians 11:23-26, Ephesians 5:18-21, Hebrews 10:25, Colossians 3:16, Acts 2:42, Romans 10:17, James 1:22, Ephesians 4:12, 2 Timothy 4:2, Matthew 28:19-20)

Year One:

_____
_____
_____
_____
_____
_____

Year Two:

_____
_____
_____
_____
_____
_____

October 17

Wonderful Counselor, today, **I worship You because of who You are**, and **I honor You for what You have done for me**. Your sacrifice allows me to have everything I need.   I am setup emotionally, spiritually, physically, financially, and relationship-wise.   All material things I need and want, are available to me. **It is the time to align myself with Your spiritual truths**.   I will pray and set myself up for victory. I am repositioning myself by repenting unto You, Lord, God.   I'm getting ready for an almighty powerful breakthrough, overflow, and for abundancy to occur, in my life. I will unite with the saints.   It is time to celebrate my Lord, my Savior, and my King. Today, I will sacrifice from doing those things not of You, Lord, Jesus. I will be obedient to Your Word. My heart is renewed in You, Father. Now, let my ears open up and be sensitive to Your voice, receiving Your divine direction. This is the day the Lord has made, I shall rejoice, and bask in...More of You God.
(2 Peter 3:17, Proverbs 31:25, Genesis 40:13-21, Genesis 41:13, Joel 2:25, Job 42:10, 2 Samuel 3-7, Isaiah 61:3)

Year One:

_____
_____
_____
_____
_____
_____
_____

Year Two:

_____
_____
_____
_____
_____
_____

October 18

Holy is the Lamb of God! **Through activating my faith, this holy day, I will honor You.** Lord, God, You are, Holy! Holy! Holy! **It is time for the earth to stand at attention.** It is time for us to honor You because of who You are, the God of Gods, the Lord of Lords, and the King of Kings. Now, I start by **making You a priority in my life.** I will not fit You in; I will fit everything else in my life after I give You all of my attention. I give You all the praise, honor, and glory. Yes, Father, I come confessing unto You, all of my sins. I'm asking You to forgive me, and give me a heart of you. Allow me not to repeat those sins, Jesus. I worship You, Lord, like never before. I know, **worshiping You is deeper than praising You. It is me coming to You with a heart of giving, offering a sacrifice. Father, I realize my sacrifice is giving up what is not easy for me; it must hurt me in the natural.** Oh, Hallelujah! Hallelujah! Hallelujah! I know, the supernatural is going to be simply more than amazing. **I will be overtaken as Your Word promises.** Lord, Jesus, I am able and ready, to see You manifest in my life, like never before. As I embrace worshipping ...More of You God. (Matthew 6:19-33, Proverbs 16:3, Galatians 2:20, John 3:30, Colossians 3:1-4)

Year One:

_____

_____

_____

_____

_____

_____

Year Two:

_____

_____

_____

_____

October 19

This is a season of double portion and increase. On this day, I come humbly before my Savior, preparing for all You have for me, Lord, God. **Ever since I accepted You as the head of my life, my life has never been the same.** Yes, I have had trials and tribulations, but You have been right here with me, getting me through them victoriously. **I'm preparing my life for increase**; my capacity to receive all of Your abiding and abundant grace. I realize I cannot work for it, **it is a gift from You.** I know, when I praise You, You inhabit my praise. Lord, You are calling me to be more of an **intentional worshipper.** Father, I'm here to worship You in spirit and in truth. I come to glorify, honor, praise, exalt, and please You, God. Because of Your grace and mercy, I have great adoration and loyalty to You. **You've provided a way to escape the bondage of sin, and You give me the gift of salvation.** My soul says, yes to You, Lord, God. My soul says, "I have to have You as the center of my life." I'm tapping into...More of You God.
(John 4:23-24, Colossians 3:14-17, Isaiah 12:5, Hebrews 13:15, Luke 4:8, Hebrews 12:28, Psalm 95:1-6)

Year One:

_____
_____
_____
_____
_____
_____
_____
_____

Year Two:

_____
_____
_____
_____
_____

October 20

Oh, Father, God, today, is a **day to rejoice.** I have joy all deep down in my soul. **This special time of Atonement is a time for me to be very serious about my prayer and consecration.** I'm getting myself in position for the victory You have in store for me. I'm sitting at Your feet, bowing down humbly before You, Father. First, I come to You, giving You the praise belonging to You. I come lifting up Your, Son, Jesus Christ, for sacrificing His life on the cross for me. Now, I repent asking for forgiveness of my sins. Lord, God, I come together with Your people in one room, on one accord, sharing everything in common. I put You first, and celebrate Your Holy Name. This is a time I will rejoice; I am protected by Your blood. I will not have any fear; victory is mine. Father, **I'm thanking You for Your presence, the provisions You make for me, and all the situations You are interceding on**, right now, Lord, God. Lord, Jesus, I celebrate You for all the blessings You give me. Father, my spirit craves for, and my heart cries out for...More of You God.

(John 3:16, 2 Peter 3:9, 1 Thessalonians 5:18, Ephesians 5:20, Psalm 136:26, Philippians 4:4-13, Psalm 106:1-2, Matthew 7:7)

Year One:

_____
_____
_____
_____
_____
_____
_____

Year Two:

_____
_____
_____
_____
_____
_____

October 21

This is a time, Lord, **You'll lift all bondage off of me; I am set free.** Today, I give honor to You, Lord, for releasing the shackles, trying to overcome me. Now, I have deliverance in my mind, my body, my spirit, my relationships, and my finances. **No more bondage, no more shame.** You, Father, have provided miraculous provision and care for me. It's a party! It's a party! **It is time for a Holy Ghost party!** Lord, I sing before You. I dance before You. I lift up holy hands unto You. I bow down before You. I clap unto You. I release a shout of joy unto You. Rain on me, Lord, Jesus! Pour out Your blessings on me, Father. **Your Word says, You will pour out a blessing on me, so much I will not have room enough to store it.** Only You, God, can set a bush on fire, where water cannot put it out. Please, Lord, **Jesus, set me on Your kind of fire. Father, I want to see Your glory.** As I enter into Your presence, as I go deeper and deeper, I see...More of You God. (Exodus 6:6, 2 Timothy 1:7, Romans 4:25, Daniel 9:24, Hebrews 10-14, 1 John 2:2, Isaiah 10:27, James 4:7, Romans 12:2)

Year One:

_____
_____
_____
_____
_____
_____
_____
_____

Year Two:

_____
_____
_____
_____
_____
_____

October 22

It is the time and the season to blow my trumpet. Today, I rejoice in You, knowing **You have already put all things in motion. You have a set time for me. This is the season, as I sow a seed, I will get double portions. I will not have to wait for my season to change; it is going to be harvest time right away.** Hallelujah! Hallelujah! Hallelujah! Lord, God, You have Your own calendar; You move on Your time, not on mine. Father, **You have a sovereign plan for me**, it's only for me. I will be prosperous and live in good health. I'm not worrying about anything; You have already done everything. Your Word says, if the flowers and the birds do not have to worry, then why should I, Lord, Jesus? You have come, so I may have life more abundantly. **This is a season of more than enough.** It's time to praise You for all I have and all still to come. Father, now, as I see how You are working out my life, my plans, and my destiny, it is my honor to continue to seek after...More of You God.

(Galatians 6:7, 2 Corinthians 9:6-8, Luke 6:38, 2 Corinthians 9:10-11, Malachi 3:10, Ecclesiastes 3:1-9, Proverbs 28:20)

Year One:

_____
_____
_____
_____
_____
_____
_____

Year Two:

_____
_____
_____
_____
_____
_____
_____

October 23

Jesus, the Messiah, today, I want to thank You for coming to earth, in the flesh, to wash and cleanse me, from all of my sins. Oh, Lord, Jesus, how great Thou art. Now, You are seated at the right hand of the, Father, interceding on my behalf. Savior, **when You ascended back into heaven, You left the Holy Spirit, with me.** So now, the temple of You, Father, resides within me. Hallelujah! I'm rejoicing, because I believe in Your Word and all You have done. Yes, Father, I have the faith of a mustard seed. **My faith gives me access into You.** Now, You, Jesus Christ, dwell in me. You are a Big, Big, God! No tabernacle, temple, or building, can contain You. Father, You are majestic. You are all powerful. You are all mighty. There is no one greater. **It gives me so much joy, because You desire to dwell in me. I am Your habitation.** Lord, God, I will be obedient unto Your calling on my life. Continue to fill me with...More of You God.
(Psalm 51:2, Acts 7:55-56, Romans 8:34, Ephesians 1:20, Colossians 3:1 Hebrews 1:3)

Year One:

_____
_____
_____
_____
_____
_____
_____
_____

Year Two:

_____
_____
_____
_____
_____
_____
_____

October 24

Today, I'm so grateful I can come to You with confidence and enthusiasm. It's pure relief to know I can cast my cares and desires on You. Now, is the time to come together in unity, with Your people and celebrate, the Great I Am, my Father. Lord, God, I realize You have already done everything I need. However, **I must tap in through meeting the conditions of Your Word. It is called tapping into my faith.** I know, **faith without actions is dead.** I will now activate my faith in You, Jesus, my Savior. Jesus, I recognize You are my Passover. **Through Your death on the cross, I have been saved by Your blood.** Glory! Hallelujah! You saved me, Lord, Jesus. Now, I have Your divine salvation. I have been made whole and complete. Nothing but the blood of Jesus, has come and rescued me. Thank You, Father, for loving me so much! I love You, Lord, God. My spirit says "Yes" to...More of You God.

(Luke 8:25, Mark 2:5, Luke 5:20, Matthew 15:28, Luke 17:5, Acts 6:5-8, Acts 11:24, Revelation 2:19, Romans 1:8)

Year One:

_____
_____
_____
_____
_____
_____
_____
_____

Year Two:

_____
_____
_____
_____
_____
_____

October 25

Father, today, I will **meet You at Your Throne**. I am entering in with faith to be completely reconciled and redeemed. Your Throne is a holy place and I can get everything I need right here; Your glory resides there. Lord, Jesus, I am coming to You, in the Name of Jesus, asking You to take my life, renew, and restore it. King of Kings, take my heart and mold it. I want to have a heart of You, Jesus, a heart of love. It is the greatest spiritual gift of all. Lord, God, take my mind and transform it; let it be fixed on You, Lord. **This special holy time at Your Throne, is a time of righteousness, justice, renewal, and holiness**. While I'm at Your Throne, I am kneeling down on holy ground. What a place of comfort and peace! It's totally sacred at this place. **Father, You sent Your precious, Son, Jesus, to bring me back from Satan and death**. Now, I can be in Your presence. I have been saved by Your blood. You have given me eternal life. Lord, Jesus, You are the greatest gift of all. I praise You! I worship You! I adore You! I love being in this holy place with ...More of You God.
(Hebrews 4:16, 1 Kings 22:19, Isaiah 6:1, Isaiah 63:15, Acts 7:49, Hebrews 8:1, Revelation 4:1-6, Psalm 45:6, Psalm 103:19)

Year One:

_____
_____
_____
_____
_____
_____

Year Two:

_____
_____
_____
_____
_____

October 26

As Your child, today, I am going to **let my light shine**. The light of You, Lord, Jesus, is beaming and glowing through me. I am Your vessel; **Your Spirit lives in me, giving me holy power**. So now, I'm able to share Your life with others, hoping and praying they will receive You. I'm praying all who come near me will grab a hold of Your Word. Let them believe in You and tap into the access You have given us. The access to be free, and live eternally, through, the blood of Jesus. It is only through me sharing what You have done for me and others, it will give lost souls access to true restoration, and they will receive all the promises You have for them. **I must teach, it is all about becoming one with God. Through faith in Jesus Christ, this is the only way to access You, God,** and to receive all of Your promises. Lord, You greatly desire to pour out Your blessings on me and all others. We must tap into repenting, receiving, and acting with obedience to please You, our Savior. I want to do what is pleasing in Your sight, Father, and tap into...More of You God.
(Matthew 5:13-16, John 8:12, Romans 13:11-14, Ephesians 5:7-14 Colossians 1:9-14, 2 Corinthians 4:3-6, John 12:35, Isaiah 60:1)

Year One:

_____
_____
_____
_____
_____
_____

Year Two:

_____
_____
_____
_____
_____
_____

October 27

Lord, today, is a day to **look back over my life**. I'm reflecting over my behavior. "Have I been doing what You have called me to do?" You created me to love You. I am to spread Your love to others, throughout the entire world. "Am I fulfilling my purpose and the plan You have for me?" I can only do what is pleasing to You by having Your Spirit live inside of me and manifesting on the outside of me. **Everything is possible, as long as I love You.** Moreover, **if I love You, I will have a desire to have an intimate relationship with You and only You.** Lord, Jesus, I say, "Yes to You", because I love You so much. Sometimes my actions do not line up with this heart full of love, I have for You. Please, Father, forgive me; sometimes my flesh is weak, but Lord, God, You are strong. I am leaning on Your understanding, not mine. Therefore, I am now strong in You. Hallelujah! I repent of all of my wrong doings. I have a heart to walk on the straight and narrow road with You, Lord. I want to live for You, God. My faith is in You, Father. My faith is growing by hearing about...More of You God. (Jeremiah 29:11, Romans 8:28, Ephesians 3:8-12, 1 Corinthians 6:19-20, Psalm 20:4, Ephesians 2:10, Exodus 9:16, Mark 16:15-16)

Year One:

_____
_____
_____
_____
_____
_____
_____

Year Two:

_____
_____
_____
_____
_____

October 28

Atonement is a **day to experience repentance bringing me to the next level of glory in You, Lord, Jesus**. Today, I give it all to You, Father. I give: my love, my life, and my all. I am **putting myself into position, to get back what the devil has stolen from me**. All those possessions and things You have given me, Father; it is time in Your time, Lord, God, for **full restoration**. Your time is the right time. It is perfect timing, **You know my today, tomorrow, and my end**. I trust You, Lord, Jesus! Lord, **this now-season, is a move of You. It is going to allow me to reap, at the same time I sow**. Glory! Hallelujah to the Most High! I have a praise, I must get out. I have an overwhelming sensation bubbling up inside of me. I feel greatness overflowing, and I know, it is the glory of God. A fresh anointing all in my soul. As I praise You, I feel You coming near. In Your presence nothing stays the same. It is all about healing in any area I need or desire. No doubt, it can and will take place. I thank You, Lord. Your presence is divine. I'm rejoicing in, and I'm in awe with...More of You God.
(Psalm 23:3, Psalm 51:12, Amos 9:14, 2 Corinthians 13:9-11, Galatians 6:1, Exodus 21:34, Acts 20:21)

Year One:

_____
_____
_____
_____
_____
_____
_____

Year Two:

_____
_____
_____
_____
_____

October 29

God, today, I'm **tapping into miracles, signs, and wonders**. Lord, You said in Your Word, all I have to do is speak it and it shall manifest. Once I speak it, I hold onto faith. With my faith, I can speak to a mountain and tell it to move, "Bye, bye, mountain." Hallelujah! I rejoice in You, Lord, God! **I have a new revelation over my life**. I have received deliverance. <u>**Now,**</u> **I live and move by the power of the Holy Spirit**. My obedience adheres to Your Word, Father. I am free indeed. The glory of the, Lord, is here. I receive You. Yes, Lord, I believe in You, Father. Yes, Lord, Your Word is true! Father, **I am believing You will restore the years taken from me**. This includes: my health, finances, relationships, etc. I'm speaking of all things holding me captive. You have removed them and set me free. Now, it is time to walk into my new season. A season of prosperity and growth. A time to live and not die. A time to pray and not be weary. A time to consecrate and not grow faint. A time to give and not hold a tight hand. Oh, Father, God, I love You so much. I'm always wanting...More of You God.

(John 8:32, Isaiah 61:1, James 2:20, 1 Corinthians 14:1, Matthew 17:14-21, John 5:19, Galatians 5:6, Acts 2:22, Hebrews 2:4, Acts 5:12, 2 Corinthians 12:12, Acts 4:30, Acts 6:8)

Year One:

_____
_____
_____
_____
_____
_____

Year Two:

_____
_____
_____
_____
_____

October 30

Lord, You are a God, **all of my firsts belongs to You.** Today, Father, **I honor You with my first fruits.** Lord, I am so thankful favor is upon my house. You are a God who takes pleasure in my success. Father, **my barns will be filled with plenty and my vat will overflow.** Lord, Jesus, **You are setting me up for reaping.** My Father, You are pouring out unlimited blessings to me. Thank You Jesus! No, I will not hesitate. I will sow my seed. Your divine harvest is on the way. I will do what is right and what You request of me, to give with an open heart and open hands. I must stay focused, in Your will, Father. Holy Spirit, **I cannot deny You of what belongs to You.** You are so worthy! I honor You Lord! You bless me with miracles and favor. Hallelujah to Your Holy Name! You're Worthy! You're Worthy! I love this intimate relationship I have with You. I'm getting closer and closer to...More of You God.

(Proverbs 3:9-10, Nehemiah 10:35, Ezekiel 44:30, Romans 11:16, 2 Chronicles 31:5, Exodus 22:29, James 1:18, 1 Corinthians 15:23)

Year One:

_____
_____
_____
_____
_____
_____

Year Two:

_____
_____
_____
_____
_____
_____
_____

313

October 31

As the bible speaks, I stand, firmly, remaining **a Remnant for You,** Lord. Today, I confirm, I will remain faithful to Your truth, despite of any and all apostasy or opposition. I truly realized, it is only by Your Grace, Lord, Jesus, I have been saved. **It is not and never will be, by my own merit**. Lord, God, I appreciate all You have done for me. Your mercy and forgiveness is such an amazing precious gift. I rejoice in Your salvation and truth. By Your stripes, I am totally healed and restored. **Now, I will tap into the benefits and promises, You have awaiting me**. My integrity is unshakeable. Satan, you have no power. I rebuke you in the Mighty Name of Jesus, my Savior. Yes, Lord, I will remain loyal to, my King. **Now, I go walking in the boldness of the Lord**. My King, whom is seated on the high throne, I'm going to spread Your goodness, grace, and mercy. Yes, Father, You are the God, who sits high, and looks low. Thank You, Lord, Jesus, for making me righteous, by Your stripes. This is the day the Lord has made. I will rejoice and be glad in it. I will continue to seek after...More of You God.

(Matthew 7:13-14, Romans 9:27-28, Romans 11:5, Micah 2:12, Colossians 2:8, Titus 2:12, Colossians 3:1-25)

Year One:

_____
_____
_____
_____
_____
_____

Year Two:

_____
_____
_____
_____
_____

November

November 1

Hallelujah! I just can't get enough of You, Lord, Jesus! **This month is a month to just tell You thank You, Lord.** Today, Father, I thank You because of who You are, Lord. You are the One who is, and was, and is to come. The Lord of Lords. The King of Kings. The God of Gods. Yes! You are the Great I Am. Lord, Jesus, You are the First and the Last. The beginning and the End. You are Alpha and Omega. I call You, Emanuel. Abba, Father, You are so beautiful to me. Everything about You is amazing. You are Awesome. I love You, Lord, God! My heart is filled with You, now. I can't get enough of, Your joy, love, and peace. I want more of You, Father. My soul cries out to You, Jesus. I can't get enough! I just got to have more and more of You, Jesus. You're Sovereign. You're Holy. You are Wonderful to me, Jesus. I can't get enough of You, Lord. I just want to say thank You, Lord. Thank You! Thank You! Thank You, Lord, Jesus! Hallelujah! Hallelujah! Hallelujah! My Savior! My Lord! My King! I can't get enough of You; I got to have...More of You God.
(1 Thessalonians 5:18, Psalm 107:1, Ephesians 5:20, Colossians 3:15-17, James 1:17, Psalm 106:1, Psalm 105:1, Psalm 118:1-18)

Year One:

_____
_____
_____
_____
_____
_____
_____

Year Two:

_____
_____
_____
_____
_____
_____

November 2

Lord, God, today, I thank You, because, **the veil of separation has been torn**. Now, **through prayer**, I have direct access to You, the God of the heavens and earth. I'm so thankful, I can communicate with You any time of the day, and I'm so grateful there isn't any limit to how long I can talk to You. I thank You because Your Word says, I can look up to the hills and cry out to You for Your help. You tell me, to release my burdens and let You carry them. Who wouldn't serve a God like You! I thank You I can come and talk to You about all things going on with me in my life. Of course, there is nothing in the world You do not know is happening or has happened. Yes, Lord, You already know the first and last of my life. You knew me before I was in my mother's womb. You already knew then what mistakes I would make. Also, You knew what great things I would accomplish. You knew how at this very moment I would look at myself and ask these following questions. **"Father, what plans do You have for me, now?"** **"Where are You taking me, next, Father, in Your kingdom?"** Father, I'm so grateful to have this intimate relationship with You, getting to know...More of You God.
(Matthew 27:51, Mark 15:38, Luke 23:45, Hebrews 10:19-22, Hosea 6:1-2, Acts 17:27, 2 Corinthians 4:14, James 4:8, Romans 5:1-2)

Year One:

_____
_____
_____
_____
_____
_____

Year Two:

_____
_____
_____
_____
_____
_____

November 3

Father, today, I am so grateful for this beautiful day, You have made. Thank You, Lord, for **this opportunity to see another day**. I know, tomorrow is not guaranteed, but I'm here now, and I'm excited. Lord, You woke me up this morning with the breath of life. You made me out of Your own image; You breathe into my lungs. You breathed into Adam's nostrils to give him life; just as You gave him life, I have life. Each and every breath I take, is only because of Your goodness, Your grace, and Your mercy. I welcome this day, yes, a brand new day. **A day for more hope for my future**. Yes, another day, to work on living my life, with the purpose and plan, You mandated, Lord, Jesus. This is the Day the Lord has made, I shall rejoice and be glad in it. Yes, Father, I will enter into Your gates with thanksgiving and into Your courts with praise. It's a beautiful day. I know, **everything is just going to get better and better**. With You, Lord, Jesus, I have the victory! Every precious day You give me is amazing, with having...More of You God.

(Genesis 2:7, Acts 17:25, Job 33:4, Isaiah 42:5, Psalm 33:6, Psalm 92:1-2, 1 Chronicles 16:8, Psalm 100:4, Colossians 3:15, 1 Timothy 1:12)

Year One:

_____
_____
_____
_____
_____
_____
_____

Year Two:

_____
_____
_____
_____
_____

November 4

Savior, today, I thank You for **the gift of faith**. Oh, what a blessing not having to earn eternal life. I have been given immediate access to this everlasting life by believing in Your Son, Jesus Christ and in His life's sacrifice, paying the price for my sins. Lord, now, I have been made whole; my salvation is secure. I'm so glad You tell me in Your Word, how to tap into my faith in You, Father. **In Your Name Jesus, You tell me I have been given the power and authority**, to lay hands on the sick and to cast out demons. Also, You tell me, to **speak as though it is so**, have patience, and it will come to past. I must wait on You. Lord, I am so glad, I can speak to the mountain (the problem, the situation, the opportunity), and tell it to move. **With my faith in You, it shall move, on my behalf**. Because I am a child of the Most High, I'm so grateful, nothing is impossible for me. **Through my faith, everything I need or want is within my reach**. Lord, Jesus, You are so great and amazing. It is powerful getting to know...More of You God.

(Colossians 2:7, 1 Chronicles 16:34, 1 John 5:5-13, Galatians 3:22, James 1:6, John 7:38, Mark 10:52, Mark 11:24, Romans 1:17, Romans 10:10, Matthew 17:20)

Year One:

_____

_____

_____

_____

_____

_____

Year Two:

_____

_____

_____

_____

_____

November 5

Praising, praising, praising, my way through. Lord, today, I thank You, because, **I can praise You, even in the middle of all of my mess**. Father, no matter what I'm going through, You promise, You will be with me and see me through. Hallelujah! I thank You for my trials; **they draw me closer to You**. They remind me this is only a temporary place here on earth. I will one day have an eternal home made possible, through Your Son, Jesus the Christ. I thank You, **as I'm going through trials and tribulations You hide me in Your secret place, wrapping me in Your wings**. Hallelujah! I have no fear; I know, Your Word is true, and nothing can separate me from Your love, Lord, God. I realize, **there isn't a problem in the world bigger than the God, I serve**. Yes, Father, You have created even the blacksmith (enemy) whom wants to come to kill, steal, and destroy, my joy. The enemy cannot overpower me, because I am made in Your own image, and the Holy Spirit resides inside of me. Using **Your Name, all I have to do is open my mouth and speak to the problem/the situation, telling it what to do and where it needs to go**. Thank You, Lord, for empowering me. My faith and strength, gets stronger with...More of You God.
(Psalm 103:1-5, Hebrews 13:15, Psalm 104:33, Psalm 51:14, Jeremiah 20:13, Psalm 145:3, Psalm 28:7, 2 Samuel 22:4, Psalm 68:32, Psalm 47:7, Isaiah 4:23-24)

Year One:

_____
_____
_____
_____

Year Two:

_____
_____
_____
_____

November 6

Dear gracious Savior, today, I thank You for **the gift of the Holy Spirit.** Jesus, when You left this earth to sit next to Your Father in heaven, You left a precious, precious gift with me **the Holy Spirit, who lives inside of me. The Holy Spirit gives me great comfort, guidance, and direction.** There are times I don't even know how to pray, however, You are so awesome, **the Holy Ghost, will speak on my behalf.** The Holy Spirit, knows what I need and understands my weaknesses. According to Your perfect will, He prays for me, over me, and my life. Father, I thank You for the supernatural power which comes from You, God. It strengthens and keeps me encouraged. Your Holy Spirit, builds me up and takes me to a maturity level with You, Father. Holy Spirit, take me a little deeper and take me a little higher. Your supernatural power, Lord, God, can accomplish much more than what I could ever dream. I'm going higher and deeper with...More of You God.

(John 4:23-24, Philippians 3:3, Luke 1:67-68, Luke 10:21, Acts 11:15-18, Ephesians 5:18-20, Acts 10:44-46, Colossians 3:16-17)

Year One:

_____
_____
_____
_____
_____
_____
_____

Year Two:

_____
_____
_____
_____
_____
_____
_____

November 7

Lord, I'm so blessed You see the big picture of my entire life. Today, I'm grateful unto You, **You are my banner.** **You are the God, who goes before me.** Sometimes, I pray for things I want a certain answer for; however, You answer them completely different than what I had hoped. Lord, You intercede on my behalf. You either say, *"Yes"*, *"Wait"*, *"Not quite yet"*, or You say, *"No."* There are times when Your *"Yes"* is quick, and there are times it takes a while. No matter what, **every time You answer me (because You are a Big God), You always accomplish and deliver much more than the one thing I'm praying.** You answer multiple things in my life and in the lives of others. Father, You are so good, You always answer my prayers way better than what I could ever imagine. Lord, You're Sovereign Ruler over all. **I thank You for being totally in control.** I'm learning how to submit, let go, trust, and let You, Lord. God, all of this patience comes while I'm submitting to...More of You God.
(Deuteronomy 31:8, Isaiah 45:2, Exodus 13:21, Numbers 14:14, 2 Samuel 5:24, Psalm 77:20, Psalm 136:16, Exodus 32:1, Deuteronomy 1:30)

Year One:

_____
_____
_____
_____
_____
_____

Year Two:

_____
_____
_____
_____
_____
_____

November 8

God, today, I thank You for **Your Word, the truth**. In Your Word, You provide everything I need to know to live through this life and to obtain eternal life with You. Lord, Jesus, I am so glad You are a God, who does not lie. I can count on every Word in Your Word to be right, to be honest, and to be perfect. You are perfect in all of Your ways. **You are my Rock**. You are faithful and just. You are fair, and You do no wrong. You are my hope, and You are my inheritance. I thank You for caring enough about my welfare; You spell out what I need to know to be successful throughout this life. Lord, God, You are so tender and merciful unto me. I adore You, I love You, and I give You the upmost respect. Jesus, Jesus, Jesus, I can't live without You. **Your Word is the living Word. Heaven and earth will pass away, but I will always have Your Word to stand on**. My hope and prayer is in You, Father. I must hold onto Your unchanging hand. I'm in awe and so happy to experience...More of You God.

(Romans 15:4, Isaiah 40:8, Matthew 7:24, Hebrews 4:12, Proverbs 30:5, Psalm 119:105, 1 Peter 2:2, 2 Timothy 3:16-17, James 1:22)

Year One:

_____

_____

_____

_____

_____

_____

Year Two:

_____

_____

_____

_____

_____

_____

November 9

This place I'm in, right now, is so beautiful. I have no fear, and I cannot be shaken. Father, this place I'm in is called *in Your presence*. Today, I want to tell You how much **I love to bask in Your presence**; it is truly a privilege to rest in You.   This fellowship I have with You is sweet. I have so much joy, walking in obedience and having faith in You, Lord, Jesus. **There is nothing I cannot persevere or obtain, when I'm in Your presence.** As long as I tap into, You, Lord, You make the opportunity of victory manifest unto me. In Your presence I find joy, peace, love, happiness, patience, comfort, healing, and whatever I need. Victory! Victory! Victory! It's mine! It's mine! It's mine! Father, I am determined to keep You before me continually. I trust You, Lord, Jesus, with everything I have and everything I am. I get into my secret place (my prayer closet), getting down on my knees, seeking You, first.   Lord, I will be patience and wait on You to direct, and guide my path. I sing because I'm happy. Father, I have so much joy with...More of You God.
(Isaiah 57:15, Acts 17:28, Exodus 33:14, Psalm 16:11, Jeremiah 29:13, 1 John 4:12, 1 Kings 8:27, Psalm 139:18, Matthew 28:20, John 14:16, Exodus 25:8)

Year One:

_____
_____
_____
_____
_____

Year Two:

_____
_____
_____
_____
_____

November 10

God Almighty, today, I thank You because <u>I have been redeemed</u>. I have been delivered and set free. All bondage has been removed off me; the shackles and the chains have been broken. I feel a sense of relief; my heart is no longer heavy (*"Baggage be gone!"* says the Lord). **Now, I feel like a bird or a butterfly; free.** I'm enjoying the beauty of You, Lord. **I am empowered by Your blood**, Lord, Jesus. You have cleansed me and made me all new. My conscience is clear; I have been restored from all guilt. I know, all of my sins have been forgiven by You, Lord, Jesus. **God, You loved the world so much, You gave Your only Son, Jesus Christ's life on the cross for all transgressions. So, as long I believe in You, I should not perish, but I now have eternal life**. Yes, without this most precious gift from You, God, I, totally, fall short from Your glory. Now, I can go from glory to glory. I am renewed, refreshed, and restored with...More of You God.

(Psalm 116, Isaiah 6:7, Leviticus 4:27-31, Proverbs 16:6, Romans 3:25, Hebrews 2:17, Micah 7:18, Acts 13:38, Matthew 26:27-28, Luke 24:46-47)

Year One:

_____

_____

_____

_____

_____

_____

Year Two:

_____

_____

_____

_____

_____

325

November 11

Abba Father, today, I give You all honor for my health and my strength. Thank You, Lord, Jesus, for **my five senses**. When one is not working affectively, one of the other senses will work twice as hard. It's all because of Your glory. As I press forward, spiritually, physically, mentally, and socially, I thank You for making the way for me, Father. Lord, God, **as my flesh must die, my inner-self has to be renewed, keeping me spiritually healthy**. I thank You, Lord, for **imparting wisdom into me**. Your wisdom allows me to live a healthier life, for the rest of my days. **Father, with Your Word inside of me, I'm able to endure anything coming my way**. I will put on my armor of the Lord, to fight the battles trying to destroy me. *"You shall win"*, thus says the Lord. I stand on all of Your promises. I will speak to the illness, the problem, the situation, and it shall be removed, in the Name of Jesus. I thank You, Lord, as I keep pressing forward, I can persevere with...More of You God.

(1 Corinthians 6:19-20, Romans 12:1-2, 1 Timothy 4:7-9, Proverbs 14:30, Proverbs 3:7-8, Matthew 11:28-29, Isaiah 40:29-31, Psalm 145:15-16)

Year One:

_____
_____
_____
_____
_____
_____

Year Two:

_____
_____
_____
_____
_____

November 12

Yes Lord, today, I glorify and thank You for all of the **love ones You have placed into my life**. How grateful I am to have friends and/or family loving me. They help me in my time of need, by showing me the love of Jesus inside of them. I appreciate the care and love I receive, only by Your grace and Your mercy. Each day, I am thankful for **friends who have turned into family**. **My family is a circle of strength**. I have a life surpassing what I truly deserve. But, through Your blood, Lord, Jesus, I have been made righteous. I'm blessed with blessings on top of blessings. We are centered by Your faith, Lord; it is only by Your love, Father, we are kept. Lord, continue to keep us safe; keeping our relationships, pure, honest, and gratifying, for all the goodness, You most graciously supply us. Let us learn from one another, growing and praying unto You, our King. I'm so grateful to live with and grow closer to...More of You God.
(Jeremiah 30:19, Psalm 9:1, Psalm 107:8-9, Colossians 3:23-24, Genesis 2:24, Exodus 20:12, Psalm 127:3-5, Psalm 128:3, Mark 3:23-25, Ephesians 3:14-15)

Year One:

_____
_____
_____
_____
_____
_____

Year Two:

_____
_____
_____
_____
_____

November 13

Today, Lord, Jesus, I thank You, **because I know, nothing can sep-arate me from Your love**. I am so grateful I have been adopted into the Royal family. By the stripes of Jesus, Your, Son, I have been made righteous, Hallelujah! I am a child of the Most High; You are con-tinuously watching over me. No matter how I may feel, alone, de-pressed, abandoned, etc., I must keep my mind on You, Father. You will never leave me or forsake me. You are the way, the truth, and the life. Lord, I trust You; I will lean on You for the rest of my life. Father, I surrender unto You. **You are my strong tower; mighty in power**. Your love is tender. Father, **You are my Rock in the middle of any suffering or overwhelming situations, I may encounter**. Lord, I can always count on You. You never leave me by myself; You carry me through. Oh, what a joy it is to have this intimate relationship with...More of You God.
(Romans 8:31-39, Ephesians 1:5, Galatians 4:7-9, John 14:6, Philippians 3:14, 1 Corinthians 8:11, Psalm 18:2, Zephaniah 3:17)

Year One:

_____
_____
_____
_____
_____
_____
_____

Year Two:

_____
_____
_____
_____
_____
_____
_____
_____

November 14

Father, today, I thank You for **all of the tools You have provided me with to win this battle called life**. You have given me everything I need, right in Your Word. **Your Word is a road map** to guide me throughout my life. It gives me the victory in all occurrences here on earth. Right now, I stand on Your Word; it is true, and it is alive. Father, You tell me to tap into You; I will continue to work on using Your tools. This-way, I will perfect my walk with You. I will never be perfect. However, I want the world to see You in me, Father. **I want to be a reflection of You**. Therefore, I must read Your Word; then I will know what You ask and require of me. Also, I'll know how I am to live daily, using the equipment You have given me to persevere, grow, and live an abundant life. Yes, Lord, I am a changed child. I once was lost; but now, I have been found in You, Lord. My focus is on staying in tune and tapping into...More of You God.
(Colossians 3:16, James 1:18-21, 1 Thessalonians 2:13, 2 Timothy 2:15, Philippians 2:16, 1 John 2:14, Revelation 6:9, Deuteronomy 8:3, Jeremiah 15:16, 2 Samuel 23:2)

Year One:

_____
_____
_____
_____
_____
_____
_____

Year Two:

_____
_____
_____
_____
_____
_____

November 15

Prayer is powerful! Lord, today, I give You all the honor and the glory, for <u>allowing direct communication, the ability to access You, 24/7</u>. Father, I'm so thankful the veil was broken. Now, **Jesus is sitting on Your right side interceding on my behalf**. Whenever I come before Your throne, I have a humble heart and spirit. **I must come clean, first, by asking for Your forgiveness**. My prayer availeth much; for now, I'm righteous through the blood of Jesus. I rest assure, confidently, You will answer my prayers, as long as they are in Your will. I will pray fervently without ceasing. I know, there is nothing too hard for You, God. Lord, You tell me I have not because I ask not; I have to knock and seek. Heavenly Father, I have a prayer of thanksgiving unto You, and I have a prayer of gratitude for You, Father, because You sent Your Son, to die on the cross cleansing, my sins. I come praying on behalf of others, as well as for myself. My prayer life gets stronger and stronger while tapping into...More of You God.

(1 John 5:14-16, 1 Chronicles 16:11, 2 Chronicles 6:21, 2 Chronicles 7:14, Ephesians 1:18, Jeremiah 29:12, John 17:15, James 5:13, Matthew 26:41, Romans 12:12, Psalm 4:1, Luke 11:2-4)

Year One:

_____
_____
_____
_____
_____
_____

Year Two:

_____
_____
_____
_____
_____
_____

November 16

Father, today, I thank You for the **power and authority, You give me**. A power and authority to speak healing and casting out demons, in the Name of Jesus, and it is done. **I am so grateful You're in me, and You're greater than the world.** **Your power is greater than the enemy,** because You are the creator of the enemy. Lord, I realize, now, **my life needs to be characterized by Your power, Father**. I shall tap into the supernatural power of You, my Savior. It shall manifest in the natural. What a mighty, God, I serve! I thank You, Lord, for the **wisdom and revelation You impart in me**. I am now going from glory, to glory, to glory. My faith in You is all I need, to open my mouth to speak it, as though it is so. **For faith is something I cannot see in the natural; but in the supernatural, It Is Real**. I get more powerful, and my faith grows with...More of You God.

(Luke 10:19, Matthew 10:8, Ephesians 6:11, Mark 16:17, Matthew 28:18-20, Psalm 8:6, 2 Corinthians 3:16-18)

Year One:

_____
_____
_____
_____
_____
_____
_____
_____

Year Two:

_____
_____
_____
_____
_____
_____

November 17

Thank You Father! Today, I thank You for this **beautiful life You have given me**. You make a way for me each and every day. Lord, You give me a more abundant life, **my life is fulfilled because You are the center of my life**. Jesus, because of You I have a blessed life, and it is more than what I could ever imagine. My life is exceedingly, overflowing with Your goodness and Your grace. Because of You, Father, I glow with the light of the Holy Spirit, who resides inside of me. Lord, I am overwhelmed, and I have so much gratitude for You, because You love me so much. With You, Lord, Jesus, I have peace, joy, comfort, love, and a purpose. Lord, as I go through this beautiful day You have made, let me share these precious gifts You have bestowed upon me. I'm grateful! I'm grateful! I have the best life now, living with having...More of You God.

(Job 33:4, Acts 17:25, Nehemiah 9:6, Malachi 2:5, Revelation 11:11, Ezekiel 47:9, John 10:10, Matthew 6:33, Galatians 2:20, Deuteronomy 8:18, Jeremiah 29:11, 3 John 1:2, Psalm 1:3)

Year One:

_____
_____
_____
_____
_____
_____
_____

Year Two:

_____
_____
_____
_____
_____
_____
_____

November 18

Jesus, Jesus, Jesus, today, I thank You for **my life's purpose**. Lord, my life is all about You; it is not about me. I thank You because of Your grace and mercy on me; I can now go around and share Your Word, with the world. Now, I can let all near and far, those East, West, North, and South, know about You. You are a God who is a good, good, God; who is a big, big, God. Lord, I will tell them of Your sufficient grace; You will never leave them or forsake them. I will go and tell of my Savior, who died on the cross for us all, giving us eternal life. Yes, Hallelujah! **I will spread the good news about You, God. There is nothing impossible for me, or for all those near or far, as long as we hold onto Your unchanging hand.** Your hand can knockout our enemies without us even doing anything, except believing in You. I'm giving all things to You, Lord, Jesus. My purpose is to spread the Word of You, Father. I will always seek after...More of You God.

(Job 42:2, Proverbs 19:21, Proverbs 20:5, Philippians 2:12-13, Romans 8:28, 2 Timothy 1:9, 1 John 5:20, John 14:6, Romans 5:10, Romans 6:23)

Year One:

_____
_____
_____
_____
_____
_____
_____

Year Two:

_____
_____
_____
_____
_____

November 19

Savior of the world, today, I thank You for **Your protection**. I thank You I can put on the armor of the Lord, knowing I will be okay. My battle is won. Father, I'm grateful no weapon formed against me will be able to prosper. Without a doubt, I am the head and not the tail; I'm above and not beneath. Hallelujah! Hallelujah! **My struggle is not against flesh and blood, but against principalities and powers in high places.** So, I cannot win my battles alone; I must have the power of You, Jesus. I must come in Your Name, standing on the truth, accepting You as my Savior, and being made righteous. I will go in peace because of Your gospel; I will shield myself with faith. I will wear the helmet of salvation and the sword of the Holy Spirit. Yes, Lord, I will pray without ceasing, and I will be watchful. I can only tap into this armor with having...More of You God.
(Exodus 14:13-14, Psalm 91:7, Nahum 1:7, 2 Corinthians 4:8-9, Psalm 34:19, 2 Samuel 22:3-4, Deuteronomy 28:13, Ephesians 6:10-18)

Year One:

_____
_____
_____
_____
_____
_____
_____

Year Two:

_____
_____
_____
_____
_____
_____
_____

November 20

Lord, I thank You today, for the **adversities I have encountered thus far in my life**. Father, all of these trials and tribulations I have endured and I'm still facing, but pressing through; these things have gotten me closer to You. I'm grateful because it was only through Your loving kindness and Your mercy, I have made it this far. **During these deserted moments, my faith has increased.** I truly see You in a mighty big way. Lord, **I know, You are real; there is no doubt in my mind, You are real**. I have learned during these tough and seemingly lonely times, I am not alone. **With Your strength, Lord, Jesus, I can move mountains**. Father, You are all knowing, You know what it takes to build our relationship, to get me to seek after You. You're moving our intimate relationship closer. Father, I just find myself wanting more and more, of You. I just got to have...More of You God.
(Jeremiah 32:27, 1 Peter 4:12-13, Deuteronomy 31:6, Proverbs 3:5-6, Isaiah 41:10, John 14:26-27, Psalm 55:22, Psalm 91:14-16)

Year One:

_____

_____

_____

_____

_____

_____

_____

Year Two:

_____

_____

_____

_____

_____

_____

November 21

Jesus, today, I give You the honor and the glory! I'm so thankful for **Your forgiveness**. Father, it is great to be forgiven for the evil and vindictive things, I have done. You wash me white as snow. Again, I can walk with a free spirit and mind. My, my, my, how amazing are You, Father! Your love runs deep and wide. No one can love me the way You love me, Lord, Jesus. Additionally, **it is true joy to experience the ability to be able to forgive**, by releasing what was wrongfully done unto me, loving You unconditionally, and let You, Father, handle the situation. God, You say in Your Word, to give all of our burdens unto You; **vengeance is Yours**. Yes, it cleans my mind, my heart, and my soul; it gives me a sense of feeling free. **Yes, Lord, it is well!** Lord, You have Your way, releasing a cleansing upon me. Oh! How grateful, I am for freedom. Nothing or no one can separate me from the greatest love of all-Yours, Lord, God. Oh, how humble I am unto You. I serve the only God, my Father in heaven. Yes, Lord, I find pleasure in...More of You God.

(Romans 12:19, Mark 11:25, Proverbs 17:9, Matthew 6:14-15, Colossians 3:13, Ephesians 4:32, Matthew 5:23-24, 1 John 1:9, 2 Chronicles 7:14, Acts 13:38, Daniel 9:9, Psalm 86:5)

Year One:

_____
_____
_____
_____
_____
_____

Year Two:

_____
_____
_____
_____
_____
_____

November 22

Holy Spirit, today, I'm thanking You for the **ability to have essential and core values, in my life**. Lord, **You have given me purpose**. I'm grateful I can discern how to make right decisions, to move forward, and have goals in my life. Father, **You have given me the knowledge and wisdom to create life-changing milestones, in my life, and in others**. Lord, whatever is of You, always creates a ripple effect. Everything You do is huge and amazing. **When You make changes in my life, it is making changes in others' lives**. Further, these changes continue to flow on to others. Only You, God, can do these great works. As long as I stay connected to You, You'll have great blessings for me. All I have to do is be patience and hold on. I must have faith of a mustard seed, without doubting You will ever fail me. All the glory belongs to You, Lord. Lord, Jesus, this is why I cannot live without...More of You God.

(Philippians 3:8, Matthew 13:44-46, 1 Peter 2:4-7, Psalm 8:3-8, Matthew 16:26, Mark 8:37, Matthew 20:28, Acts 20:28, 1 Corinthians 7:23, Proverbs 3:13-15, Proverbs 8:11)

Year One:

_____
_____
_____
_____
_____
_____

Year Two:

_____
_____
_____
_____
_____

November 23

The Great I Am.   Lord, Jesus, today, I thank You for **my quiet time; the time You allow me to spend, just, with You, Lord**. Father, this is the most precious time of my day.   I get to bask in Your presence, alone with You. Lord, I thank You for **my prayer closet**. This is where I can go and hide away with You; **my secret place; my safe place**. This sacred place, I can call on You for all things; most importantly, I thank You for **all You do for me and for who You are**, the Most High King. Lord, God, this quiet place with You, **allows You and me to fellowship together**. I sit quietly and wait to hear from You. Speak to me, Lord; I want to hear from You, Father. This quiet time allows me to pick up a book like this, helping me with my devotional time with You. Lord, You are a good, good, God; I do not have enough tongues to tell You how grateful I am.   **As I tap in during this quiet time, I'm setting up my life for miracles, signs, and wonders**. You are the reason for the season, loving and waiting to hear from...More of You God.
(James 4:8, Matthew 6:6-8, Revelation 3:20, Isaiah 41:1, Lamentations 3:25-28, Philippians 4:7-9, Revelation 2:1-5, Psalm 1:1-4, Proverbs 5:1-2)

Year One:

_____
_____
_____
_____
_____
_____
_____

Year Two:

_____
_____
_____
_____
_____

November 24

Today, Lord, Jesus, I am so grateful and thankful for **Your gift to face fear**. I'm so glad I'm not afraid of my fear; they want to try to stop me, and overtake me; but, Lord, You give me strength to confront it, rebuke it, and demand it, to leave. **This is a time where I stand on Your Word, knowing You have my front, my back, and my sides.** Hallelujah! You say, I should not have fear of anything other than You, alone. I gain so much strength, confidence, and courage, from every incident where I encounter fear; **I face it dead on**. Lord, You give me the ability to say, "I am not afraid; I can conquer all things through Christ who lives inside of me." There is not a weapon forming against me prospering. **Yes, Lord, if You did it before, You can, and will, do it again.** I have the victory through, my Father, in heaven. My faith gets stronger, and my fear decreases, as I get wrapped up in...More of You God.

(Isaiah 35:4, John 14:27, Joshua 1:9, Matthew 6:34, Isaiah 43:1, Psalm 23:4, Psalm 34:4, Psalm 27:1, 1 Peter 5:6-7, Psalm 118:6, 2 Timothy 1:7, Psalm 115:11, Psalm 103:17)

Year One:

_____
_____
_____
_____
_____
_____
_____

Year Two:

_____
_____
_____
_____
_____
_____
_____

November 25

Father, today, I give You all the praise for <u>always providing for me</u>. I'm so thankful for the food, clothing, and shelter, You give me. **The flowers and the birds do not worry where their food comes from; You provide for them, so for me to worry, why should/would I?** I'm grateful I am Your child; You have adopted me into the royal family. Yes, Lord, I am strong and I am rich; I shall have houses and land, Hallelujah! I will lift my eyes up unto the hills from where my help cometh. I'm thankful You are no respecter of person. **What You do for one, You will do for another.** The key for me, is to have faith as small as a mustard seed. To have faith knowing **You are the way maker, the miracle worker, and the promise keeper.** All things are possible with You, Lord. When it appears there is no way for me, I look to You, my Father. I know, You will turn the situation around to my good. Yes, Lord, You are working for my good. **Now, whatever mountain I am facing, You allow me to move the mountain, or walk up the mountain.** Hallelujah! Hallelujah! Hallelujah! I got the victory! I continue to win, as long as I stay with, and trust in...More of You God.

(Psalm 22:26, Psalm 146:7, Proverbs 10:3, Psalm 107:9, Matthew 6:31-32, Luke 12:31, Philippians 4:19, Psalm 34:10, Psalm 84:11-12, Luke 12:24, Psalm 36:6)

Year One:

_____
_____
_____
_____
_____

Year Two:

_____
_____
_____
_____
_____

November 26

Glory, glory to the Master, my King! Today, I'm grateful and thankful, **You are my everything.** I know, **as I put all of my trust, hope, and faith in You, doors open up, my path is laid out for me, and obstacles are removed.** I have faith in Your love and wisdom, working in my life. Lord, You are working on every intricate detail for me; therefore, I'm going to keep my eyes focused on You, my Master, my King, my Lord. Lord, as I release praises unto You, You rebuild my strength, my trust, and You restore my awareness. How great and powerful You are, Lord, God! You're my peace, my joy, my strength, my health, my love; the list just goes on and on. You are my everything. I couldn't make it in is this world without having You, Lord. As I praise You, I realize, I just want more and more of…More of You God.

(Psalm 33:4-6, 1 Peter 2:1-5, Exodus 15:2, Isaiah 41:10, Isaiah 40:28-31, Isaiah 55:8-9, Psalm 147:5, Proverbs 16:7, Isaiah 26:3, John 14:27, John 16:33, Philippians 4:6-7)

Year One:

_____
_____
_____
_____
_____
_____
_____

Year Two:

_____
_____
_____
_____
_____

November 27

Jesus! Jesus! Jesus! There is something about Your Precious Name. Today, I'm filled with joy; I'm so thankful for **Your Powerful Name**. I thank You, Lord, **You have given me the grand authority to call on the Name of Jesus, in any situation**. I can call on Jesus, to thank You, and I can call on You to help me. Jesus, You are always just one call away; **even when You are quiet, You are right here in the midst of my situation, waiting for me to lean on You**. Jesus, when I call on Your Name, I can see a **rainbow** in the sky, beaming down and glowing right over me. **The revelation of Your covenant and all of Your promises, stare me right in my face, as I call the Name of Jesus**. Thank You, Lord, Jesus, I can call on Your Name to get the demons to flee out my life. I can say Your Name and healing takes place. Oh! Lord! Jesus! Jesus! Jesus! There is something so great about Your Name. When I'm down and weary, I can call the Name of Jesus. I'll just sit, be patience, wait, and know You are on Your way, Jesus! **There is all power in the Name of Jesus!** This is why I praise Your Name, Jesus, with joy, just loving on...More of You God.
(John 14:13-14, John 16:23-24, Luke 10:17, Mark 16:17-18, Acts 3:6, Acts 3:16, Acts 4:10-12, Romans 10:13, Matthew 28:19, 1 Corinthians 6:11, Colossians 3:17)

Year One:

_____
_____
_____
_____
_____

Year Two:

_____
_____
_____
_____
_____

November 28

Here to glorify Your Name! Jesus! Thanking You today, Lord, for **Your miracles, signs, and wonders-all wrapped in the Name of Jesus.** Jesus, the God, who saves. There is salvation in Your Name, Jesus! Jesus! Jesus! There is nothing like Your Name, Jesus. I'm here to lift up Your Name, Jesus. **Your Name is more powerful than anything I'm going through, and it's more powerful than anything I can imagine or fathom.** By the Name of Jesus, walls are broken, cell doors are open, and chains loosened. Just as in Your Word, when Paul and Silas were praying, the jailers awakened, and the prison doors were opened, along with their bondage loosened. Hallelujah! Jesus! Jesus! Jesus! I do not know another Name like Your Name, Jesus! My soul is renewed, revived, and restored, when I call on the Name of Jesus. I don't know of any other name matching up with You, Jesus. You are, King of Kings, and Lord of Lords. I have a happiness in my soul, getting closer to...More of You God.

(John 1:3, 1 John 3:8, Hebrews 2:14, John 16:33, Acts 5:31, Luke 10:17, Mark 16:17-18, Matthew 8:27)

Year One:

_____
_____
_____
_____
_____
_____
_____

Year Two:

_____
_____
_____
_____
_____
_____
_____

November 29

I exalt Your Name above all names, Jesus! Today, I get down on bended knees, knowing before it is all said and done, every knee shall bow, and every tongue will confess, You are Lord of Lords, my Sweet Jesus. I'm thankful for **whatever I ask in Your Name, Jesus, it will be given to me**. Yes! Jesus! You are the truth, the way, and the life. Jesus! You are great! Your name is great in might. You are greatly to be praised. There is safety in the Name of Jesus; Your Name is a Great Tower. Jesus! You are my Helper, always here, in my time of need. Jesus! Jesus! Jesus! You are Alpha and Omega. The Beginning and the End. The First and the Last. Hallelujah! Your Name shall be great amongst the nations; there is no one above You, Jesus. Jesus, You are the Word. In the beginning, the Word was with You, because of who You are, the Great I Am. Jesus! Jesus! Jesus! **You are my everlasting Rock. I can keep standing with You, Jesus.** I hold on and keep standing strong with...More of You God.
(Acts 2:33-36, Philippians 2:9, Revelation 19:11-16, Deuteronomy 10-17, Psalm 136:3, 1 Timothy 6:15, Revelation 1:5, Revelation 17:14)

Year One:

_____
_____
_____
_____
_____
_____
_____

Year Two:

_____
_____
_____
_____
_____
_____

November 30

Jesus! Jesus! Jesus! I sacrifice all of my praise up unto You. Today, I'm just so happy and thankful to **know You, Jesus**. There is no breath of life without You, Jesus. Jesus, You are my Teacher. You came down on this earth, showing me what to do and how to live. Jesus, You shed Your blood, so now, I'm free indeed, and my sins have been washed away. Hallelujah! Jesus, You are Love, for You first loved me. You loved me enough to die on the cross for my sins, giving me eternal life. Jesus! Jesus! Jesus! There is just something about Your Name. You're my Master. You're my Savior. You're my Jesus. I'm so grateful. I just have to lift up holy hands unto You. I worship You, Lord! I praise You, Jesus! You are the Jesus who teaches me how to pray. **You are the God Almighty, Jesus, who ascended into the heaven and is seated at the right hand of the Father. You are the Jesus sitting there, interceding on my behalf.** Oh Jesus! I love You so much. My heart is happy as I praise on...More of You God. (Galatians 4:8-9, Ephesians 1:17, Ephesians 3:19, Colossians 2:2, 2 Corinthians 10:5, Philippians 1:9-11, Hebrews 7:25, Luke 22:69, Mark 16:9)

Year One:

_____

_____

_____

_____

_____

_____

Year Two:

_____

_____

_____

_____

December

December 1

Father, God, this month, I **celebrate the coming of my Savior, Jesus Christ.** Today, Lord, God, I thank You. Over 2000,00 years ago, You sent Your Son, Jesus Christ, here on this earth, to save me. He was born of a human father and a human virgin mother, through natural biological process. Father, thank You for sending Him down from heaven. **Jesus, You came sinless, and You remained sinless.** Therefore, You could and did save me from my sins. Hallelujah to the King! I celebrate Your birth. **Without You, I was lost; but now, I am found.** I have hope, love, peace, and all goodness, through the coming of Your Son. Jesus, I was alienated from God, under His righteous judgment, but You came and turned my life around. Now, Jesus, through Your power, You came and rescued me. **Oh, what a happy day, when You entered into this world.** I'm grateful and thankful to have...More of You God.

(Isaiah 9:6, Luke 2:7, John 3:16, Matthew 1:18-25, Isaiah 7:14, Romans 6:23, John 17:3, Colossians 1:15-17)

Year One:

_____
_____
_____
_____
_____
_____

Year Two:

_____
_____
_____
_____
_____
_____

December 2

Jesus, **You are the reason for this Christmas season**. Today, I rejoice; **all the treasures of wisdom and knowledge are hidden in You**. You came to give me life more abundantly. To truly live, I must tap into You. Salvation is only from You, Lord, Jesus. **Your Name Jesus, means You are the anointed one, who certainly saves**. Hallelujah to my Savior! I need You, Jesus; You are the God with me through all of my mistakes, losses, pains, persecutions, tragedies, burdens, disappointments, and all trials. Savior, without a doubt, I cannot handle any of these obstacles alone. I thank You for understanding; You have felt and borne my individual burdens. As I cry out to You, You perfectly know. Through Your infinite and eternal sacrifice, I have Your mercy enduring forever and ever. I'm filled with joy; a child was born, Jesus the Christ. You came to save little bitty ole me. Yes, Jesus, I'm rejoicing in having...More of You God.
(Matthew 1:21, John 10:28-30, Isaiah 53:5, Acts 4:12, 1 John 4:9, 1 Corinthians 15:57, Luke 19:10, Philippians 2:6-8, Psalm 136, Psalm 100:5, 1 Chronicles 16:34)

Year One:

_____
_____
_____
_____
_____
_____
_____

Year Two:

_____
_____
_____
_____
_____
_____

December 3

As this holiday season approaches, today, I celebrate the birth of You, Jesus. Lord, Jesus, You didn't just come to lay in a manger; but **You had a mission, purpose, and plan, on this earth. You came and paid a huge price, just for me. You ransomed me from sin, sickness, and hell.** Who wouldn't serve a God, like You! Jesus, You came to destroy the works of the devil. You came to deliver me from all of my fears. You came to declare the Father to me. You came to give Your life as a ransom for me. You came to call me to repentance. You came to give me eternal life, the most precious gift of all. Hallelujah! Hallelujah! Hallelujah! Jesus, You came and completed a majestic work; **it is finished**. It never needs to take place again. You are the greatest, and there is none above You. The King was born. The only reason for this season. I'm celebrating…More of You God.

(Luke 2:1-20, Isaiah 53:3-7, Zechariah 9:9, Jeremiah 23:5, John 1:9-14, Luke 9:48, Romans 5:6, Galatians 4:4, Revelation 12:1-5)

Year One:

_____
_____
_____
_____
_____
_____
_____
_____

Year Two:

_____
_____
_____
_____
_____

December 4

Jesus, You came down to this world very humble, and laid wrapped in a manger. Your parents were poor from Nazareth, an area not held in high regard. God, I know, You have all the power; You could have chosen anyway for Your Son Jesus, to enter into this world. However, **You chose a very humble entrance.** Jesus, today, I thank You. You came setting an example for me, and to let me know, You came for all. You came showing me how to live my life, to help those in need, to sacrifice, and to share what I have to help others. You came showing me Your heart for the less fortunate. Savior, **You came, not just for the rich man or the poor man, but for all men.** Jesus, You have spoken to me saying, "*A humble spirit will obtain honor*." Just as Your Word, says, You have been given the highest honor. God, **You have a beautiful way of lifting me up and repositioning me.** Even when I am broken and my spirit is crushed, You are here. Father, I shall always come to Your throne, humble and in honor of You. I have a spirit of "Yes", unto You, Lord, God. Always wanting and seeking for...More of You God.

(Matthew 1:18-23, Luke 2:7, Matthew 2:11-12, Psalm 72:11, Micah 5:2, Luke 2:15-20, Luke 6:20-26, Mark 10:21, Matthew 25:40, Proverbs 14:31, Matthew 9:36)

Year One:

_____
_____
_____
_____
_____
_____

Year Two:

_____
_____
_____
_____
_____

December 5

Lord, Jesus, **You came down to this earth to show me the will of God**. Jesus, You came down here, and yes You were and are the will of God. You made it plain and clear, what is God's will, and what is the enemy's will. Today, I thank You, because You totally set me free, Lord, Jesus; **You paid the price**. Hallelujah! Jesus! My Savior, **You went to the Cross and You destroyed every work, put in place by the enemy**. Jesus, Your death and resurrection has made me complete. It took care of my body, soul, and spirit. Glory! You came and put a whipping on the devil. Now, I have the victory. I'm so grateful **You came and gave me the keys to death, hell, and the devil**. Right now, I'm encouraged; I know, how powerful I am. You came and empowered me; I'm strong, free, and a winner. I know, who I am and whose I am. All the reason why I can't stop loving on...More of You God. (Hebrews 1:3, John 1:14, Hebrews 2:9, 2 Peter 1:16-17, John 1:18, Colossians 2:9, Matthew 5:17, Romans 15:8, Ephesians 2:13-15, Luke 19:10, Matthew 20:28)

Year One:

_____

_____

_____

_____

_____

_____

_____

Year Two:

_____

_____

_____

_____

_____

_____

December 6

Father, God, today, I'm reflecting on You, **the God of miracles. Every detail surrounding Christmas is showing Your power, Your might, and Your glory.** I'm reminded of the stories of Elizabeth, Zechariah, and Mary. Lord, You answered their prayers! As stated in Your Word, Elizabeth was very old, well past child bearing age and she became pregnant. However, when the angel came to her husband, Zechariah, to inform him, he did not believe, Elizabeth was pregnant. So, God, You did not allow him to talk (he was mute) anymore until John the Baptist was born, their son (a miracle). But, **when You, God, are in it, there is nothing impossible.** I understand, Lord, **even when I can't see what You are doing or how You are doing it, I must trust You.** As the story continues, at the same time, Elizabeth's sister, Mary, was pregnant with baby Jesus. However, because of the presence of Jesus, when Mary went to see Elizabeth, John the Baptist leaped in her belly, and Elizabeth was filled with the Holy Spirit. Lord, **as Your presence surrounds me, I know, what You're doing to me and for me, is life-changing.** I celebrate the Holy Spirit; You fill me up, especially during this wonderful season. Holy Spirit, come, for I welcome You. I'm lifting up holy hands with…More of You God.
(Luke 1:39-45, Luke 1:56, Luke 1:6-13, Luke 1:67-79, Malachi 3:1-6, John 3:6-8, Acts 2:1-5, 1 John 2:19-17)

Year One:

_____
_____
_____
_____
_____

Year Two:

_____
_____
_____

December 7

Lord, today, as I embrace my thoughts in this Christmas season, I think of Joseph, a true man of God who was getting ready to marry Mary. He was faced with her carrying a child conceived by the Holy Spirit. **"How would I feel if this was happening to me?"** "How would I react when the angel appeared in a dream?" "Would I believe?" "Would I have doubt?" Father, as I look over my life and all of the challenges it brings, I realize, I must truly rely on Your wisdom, grace, and mercy, just like Joseph. Joseph believed, and when he awaken from his dream, he did just as the angel of the Lord directed him to do. He took Mary as his wife, and he kept her as a virgin until she gave birth to a Son. They called this Son, Jesus. Hallelujah! **I ask You, Lord, to allow me to keep on trusting You, in all circumstances**, just like Joseph. **Give me discernment, Lord, to know what is of You and what isn't**. I'm waiting on You, Lord, Jesus. I have Your subtle assurance of peace; it passes all understanding, as I move forward. My life and all decisions, must depend on...More of You God.
(Luke 1:26-38, Matthew 1:18-25, Isaiah 7:14, John 1:14, Ephesians 2:8-9, Isaiah 43:25, Philippians 2:13, Psalm 146:3, Matthew 11:28-30, Jude 1:24)

Year One:

_____
_____
_____
_____
_____
_____

Year Two:

_____
_____
_____
_____
_____

December 8

Savior, today, I thank You, because **I have no more bondage**. Jesus, since You came into my life, delivering me from all fear; I will never be the same. Death is an ugly reality, I must face. But, I must not be troubled; because, Father, **You have a place just waiting for me**. **You died on the cross, sealing the deal, allowing me to have access to eternal life with You**. Now, Jesus, You're in heaven with Your Father. You have prepared a place there, especially for me; **I must believe in order to receive**. Hallelujah! Lord, Jesus, since You are in heaven, You left me with the Holy Spirit, who is dwelling inside of me; the great comforter. Now, I'm filled up with Your hope, joy, and perfect peace. I know, my earthly death will result in my immediate entrance into eternity, with You, Lord, Jesus. My faith increases daily, especially with me continuing to study Your Word and living by it. As I constantly look over my life, to see what You have brought me through, yes, Lord, Jesus, I am encouraged. **I celebrate Your birth, Jesus, throughout this Christmas season**. Lord, Jesus, I'm happy to live with...More of You God.
(Colossians 1:13-14, Romans 11:26, Isaiah 59:20, Matthew 1:21, 1 Thessalonians 1:10, Romans 8:1-2, Hebrews 9:15, Revelation 1:5, Acts 7:55-56, Romans 8:34, Ephesians 1:20, John 14:3)

Year One:

_____
_____
_____
_____
_____

Year Two:

_____
_____
_____
_____
_____

December 9

Jesus, today, I thank You, **You came here making a statement to the entire world**. Lord, Jesus, **You came and declared, the Father of the World is You, God**. You came and let us know of the goodness, kindness, loving spirit, our Father, has towards us. Yes, Jesus, You came and truly showed Yourself unto us. You are the true and only living God, the God of Gods. Lord, Jesus, You, have always been with God from the beginning. But, You came revealing, giving us a duplicate or mirror image of God, through You. You say in Your Word, You have declared God by showing, revealing, demonstrating, and interpreting Him for me. Thank You, Jesus, for showing up and showing out, coming in the flesh, but still having the spirit of God. I'm so grateful. You loved me enough to want me to truly understand who You are, who I am, and whose I am. I celebrate You with all of my heart. This is a joyous, great, and significant time of the year. My heart rejoices. I'm singing with the angels, crying out...More of You God.
(John 1:14, John 13:31-32, John 17:4-5, 2 Peter 1:17, Colossians 1:27, Isaiah 60:19-21, Habakkuk 3:3, John 1:2, Psalm 19:1, John 11:40-44)

Year One:

_____

_____

_____

_____

_____

_____

_____

Year Two:

_____

_____

_____

_____

_____

_____

December 10

King Jesus, **You came and made a way for me**. I celebrate You, today. Now, I can take myself out of all situations, just letting go, and letting You, Jesus, handle all things. You came and shed Your blood for me; **I have access to Your power, like never before**. Jesus, You came and gave Your life as a ransom for many. You came and walked this earth, in the flesh, with Your disciples. Now, You left an imprint for me, showing me: how to live, how to fight, how to spread Your Word, how to treat my fellow man, and how to tap into You, to have eternal life. **Lord, You came not to be served; but You came to serve us**. Hallelujah to my King! Now, I have been redeemed. Lord, Jesus, You came to call me to repentance. **I was sick, but You are my doctor**. Now, I am healed by salvation. Father, I come before You asking for forgiveness of all of my sins. Lord, I trust and have complete faith in You, Jesus. I'm so blessed to be in this place with...More of You God. (Matthew 3:3, Mark 1:3, Luke 3:4, Hebrews 12:13, Colossians 1:14, Romans 6:23, Matthew 20:28, Mark 10:45, 1 Samuel 12:24)

Year One:

_____
_____
_____
_____
_____
_____
_____

Year Two:

_____
_____
_____
_____
_____
_____
_____

December 11

Jesus! Jesus! Jesus! **You are the greatest Christmas gift of all.** Today, I rebuke what the world is trying to do with Your special day of celebration. I rebuke the world trying to turn Christmas into a financial opportunity. The world is totally forgetting why we truly celebrate this special day. <u>Christmas is all about You, Sweet Jesus</u>. It is about Your Father, loving me so much; Lord, You sent Your Son, to this earth, just for me. Jesus, You came to give me Eternal Life, which is the greatest gift I can receive. Yes, Lord, Jesus, I must first believe in order to receive this precious gift. **This gift does not come automatically. I must trust in You, Lord**. Jesus, all of my trust is in You. All of my hope is in my Maker. I could not make it down here on earth without You, Lord, Jesus. I have great joy. Joy to the world for You have come, King Jesus. Lord, I have an everlasting, overwhelming joy with...More of You God.
(Micah 5:2-4, Luke 1:31-33, John 1:14, Luke 2:10, 1 John 5:1, John 3:16, Revelation 3:5-9, 1 John 5:13-14, Romans 8:24-25, Romans 12:12, 2 Samuel 7:28, Psalm 9:10, John 14:1)

Year One:

_____
_____
_____
_____
_____
_____
_____

Year Two:

_____
_____
_____
_____
_____
_____
_____

December 12

Hallelujah! Hallelujah! Today, I give thanks because **a King is born**. Jesus, **You came to restore my relationship with God**, my Father. **Everything about You coming to this earth was about saving my life.** Oh, how thankful I am unto You, Jesus the Christ. Lord, Jesus, You came to glorify Your Father's Name and to accomplish the work which He had given You to do on this earth. You came to fulfill, not to abolish, and to demonstrate Your righteousness. Jesus, You spent time down on earth to teach and to testify the truth. Jesus, You went from city to city preaching to the people. You came to save souls, the lost. I am grateful that I am now, found. Hallelujah! Father, I was a sinner; Jesus, thank You for coming to save me from my sins. Jesus! Jesus! Jesus! You came to serve and to give Your life as a ransom for many. Now, You are giving me life and giving it to me more abundantly. Hallelujah to the King! I sing praises unto You. Rejoicing with having...More of You God.

(Titus 3:5, Lamentations 5:21, John 1:14, John 17:24, Hebrews 2:9, John 12:23, John 13:31-32, Luke 19:10, Romans 3:23, Hebrews 7:25)

Year One:

_____
_____
_____
_____
_____
_____
_____

Year Two:

_____
_____
_____
_____
_____
_____
_____

December 13

Jesus, **You came to teach me how to be a disciple for You**, Lord, God. Today, I celebrate You; You came to this earth in the flesh, **to teach me how to fish**. Your Word speaks, telling me to go out deep into the world, becoming a fisherman of men. Lord, You say, You will help me, lead me, guide me, and be with me, all the way, until I fill up my net. As I have a life impacting others, pushing them to strive for more, Your blessings on top of blessings are coming my way. Jesus, my hope is in You. I will continue to be a disciple for You, Jesus. I will go out into the entire world telling of Your goodness, grace, and mercy. The world must know, You are, God of Gods, Lord of Lords, and King of Kings. Yes, Lord, there is no one like You, Lord, Jesus. You came to save the world. **Now, it is my duty to share what You came and did over 2000,00 years ago.** The King is born. Glory! Hallelujah! I say, "Yes", to Your calling on my life. I'm stepping into...More of You God. (Matthew 4:19-23, Mark 1:16-18, Luke 5:1-11, Matthew 7:29, John 8:2, John 7:16, 2 John 1:9, Matthew 9:37, Matthew 16:24, Deuteronomy 10:17, 1 Timothy 6:15)

Year One:

_____

_____

_____

_____

_____

_____

_____

_____

Year Two:

_____

_____

_____

_____

_____

December 14

Savior of the world! **Remarkable indeed You are**, God, the Father, the Son, and the Holy Spirit. Today, during this special season, I honor and celebrate You. **Because of who You are and what You have come on earth to do, You set me free.** Through Your Name, Jesus, now, I have access to healing, deliverance, protection, redemption, provision, salvation, yet even more. You have come to set me free indeed. Yes, Jesus, You are my helper in all facets of my life. **There is no demon in hell who can stop what You have done for me.** All I have to do is believe and greatness shall manifest. When I'm in trouble, You save me. You are my fortress. You are my very present help. Words cannot describe how much I love and adore You, Your Majesty. You, Lord, Jesus, are the only one I bow down to, in honor of Your greatness. Today, I sing with the angels, rejoicing. I worship You the King. I sing because I'm happy getting...More of You God.
(Revelation 14:7, Philippians 2:9-11, Isaiah 53:4-5, 1 Peter 2:24, Psalm 18:2, 1 John 5:18, Romans 8:1-2, Matthew 19:25-26, Romans 10:9-10)

Year One:

_____
_____
_____
_____
_____
_____
_____

Year Two:

_____
_____
_____
_____
_____

December 15

How should I really celebrate Christmas? Today, I look at this special commemoration and I ask myself a question. **"Am I celebrating You, Jesus, the way I truly should?"** I believe I need to take a few minutes to just ponder over the true meaning of Christmas. **Christmas is an annual Christian festival celebration of Jesus Christ's birth.** I'm amazed by how You, Jesus, were conceived, as well as why You came. You actually accomplished all God instructed You to do. Hallelujah! **Your Word tells me, to go out and tell the world about who You are, what You have done, and how we can obtain salvation.** I glorify and praise You, Lord, Jesus. **Your birth represents what was done on Christmas. This special day, God, is a day You rested Your favor upon me.** You came, Jesus, as the truth, the way, and the life. You came as the truth for a confused world, a way for a lost world, and as life for a dying world. This miraculous news is precious everlasting good news. I will share this news all of the days of my life. I hope and pray others will believe in order to receive Your gift of salvation. I have a heart yearning for others to be saved with...More of You God.

(Mark 1:1-3, Matthew 24:14, Micah 5:2-3, Zechariah 6:12-13, Luke 2:21-35, John 14:6, Mark 16:15, 2 Timothy 4:2, Matthew 10:7)

Year One:

_____
_____
_____
_____
_____
_____

Year Two:

_____
_____
_____
_____

December 16

I'm going to keep my eye on the prize of the high calling. Today, as well as, moving forward, **I will continue to stay focused on You, Lord, Jesus. If it wasn't for You, Jesus, Christmas wouldn't even exist.** God, You came down from heaven as a little baby, in human form, dwelling amongst us. **Your glory was manifested right here on earth.** Thank You, Lord, for going to the cross, just for me. Now, I'm part of the royal family, forever. **Your birth is good news, the reason for us to continue to celebrate, not only annually, but daily.** Hallelujah! A Savior is born! Yes, Lord, Jesus, You are the Messiah! I celebrate You, Lord, Jesus, giving gifts to others, in remembrance of the greatest gift of all. The indescribable, perfect holy gift, my Savior, You, Jesus. I decorate my house with lights; because You are the true light who has come down to earth to light up the entire world and save us. I open my mouth, singing with joy, to extol my living Savior, my King. I decorate my Christmas tree with ornaments and lights, in representtation of the eternal life You bring, Jesus. So much beauty, joy, and love, associated with Your birth, Jesus. Every Christmas season is about me celebrating and honoring...More of You God.

(Philippians 3:14, John 17:4-5, Jeremiah 23:20, Luke 2:1-10, Mark 1:1, 1 Peter 2:9, Matthew 5:14-16, John 10:28, 1 John 2:25, Matthew 1:18-23, John 1:1-14)

Year One:

_____

_____

_____

_____

_____

Year Two:

_____

_____

_____

_____

December 17

Father, I was a sinner, I fall short, and everyone on this earth falls short. Today, **I celebrate Christmas, because You thought enough of me, You knew I was in mortal danger.** So, **You sent Your only Son, Jesus, to rescue me and give my life back.** Now, I can celebrate the gift of eternal life with You, Father. Jesus, You came and laid down Your life for me. Christ, the Son of God, You became a man, willingly sacrificing Yourself for the atonement of my sins. Lord, Jesus, You saved me from a justly, most definitely, deserved eternal punishment. Hallelujah! I will continue to celebrate You, offering up good tidings and great joy. Why? Because, I honor the deliverer who has been born. Lord, Jesus, this is such a glorious time of the year for me; it has an enormous meaning to me. However, it is simple in its place of origin. The tradition/practice is just beautiful; it encompasses rich memories. It is a charitable heartfelt implant in my spirit. **You saved me**. The reason why, I simply cannot get enough of having...More of You God.

(Romans 3:23, Galatians 1:4, John 3:6, Ephesians 2:8-10, Revelation 3:5-9, Psalm 89:1-4, John 1:1-18, Luke 1:14-17)

Year One:

_____
_____
_____
_____
_____
_____

Year Two:

_____
_____
_____
_____
_____

December 18

God, You so loved the world, You sent Your Son, Jesus. Today, Lord, Jesus, I celebrate You for coming to show me the way to live this life, on earth. **You came, Jesus, to direct me on how to guard my heart, giving it, solely to You, Jesus.** Lord, Jesus, **You make me aware of who I should or shouldn't allow, into my space.** So, as I celebrate You, I open myself to giving unto You and those in need. I love all people. This is Your second commandment, to love my neighbor as myself. However, I must guard my heart. I will strive for contentment in all things. I'm trusting You, God, to provide all my needs on Your timetable, Father. Lord, I will have a cultivating spirit of gratitude always. I will refrain from complaining while waiting. I will be kind and compassionate to others. I will forgive others, just as You came to forgive me. Hallelujah! **This is a season of giving and trusting You, my Savior.** I'm reaching up for...More of You God.
(John 3:16, John 14:6, Psalm 25:4-5, James 1:5, John 10:3-4, Proverbs 3:5-6, Psalm 25:9, John 16:13, Psalm 119:105, Proverbs 4:23, Matthew 7:6, 1 Thessalonians 4:1-8)

Year One:

_____
_____
_____
_____
_____
_____

Year Two:

_____
_____
_____
_____
_____
_____

December 19

Jesus, today, **I'm preparing for something beautiful and holy.** I'm celebrating Your birth, Lord, Jesus. It is a time of anticipation, hope, joy, and peace. This is a time for me to humble myself. **I'm preparing my home for what has come, what is to come, and what must become.** Hallelujah! **This now-season, I celebrate Your salvation coming from and through, the most precious gift, the life of the Babe of Bethlehem, Jesus Christ.** Prior to Your birth, Jesus, God, You were silent for 400 years. However, You did not forget Your people. Lord, Jesus, I want to see Your glory all around me, daily. The shepherds were so blessed to be able to see You, Jesus. When the angel appeared to announce Your birth, they got to see Your shekinah glory. This great Gospel brings joy unspeakable joy. It brings salvation for my sins and reconciliation with You, my God. Thank You, Lord, for saving me. Glory to God! I have a praise, and I have got to get it out. Praising on...More of You God.

(Isaiah 7:14, Isaiah 11:1, John 1:14, Romans 6:23, Galatians 4:4-5, Matthew 1:18-25, 1 Timothy 1:15-17, Isaiah 9:6-7, Titus 3:3-7, Malachi 4:5-6)

Year One:

_____
_____
_____
_____
_____
_____

Year Two:

_____
_____
_____
_____
_____
_____

December 20

Heavenly Father, a *(suddenly)* happened, when the angels came and told the shepherds over 2000,00 years ago a Savior was born. Hallelujah! Yes, Father, You are the same God yesterday, today, and forevermore. During this precious Christmas season, I have an expectancy of greatness occurring in my life. I'm celebrating Your greatness entering into this world, just for me. A new season is about to occur in my life. I will not have fear, for the glory of the Lord, is here. This time of the year, I will face fear dead on. It is banished by joyful, unstoppable faith in You, Lord, Jesus, my Savior. Thank You, Lord, Jesus, for blessing me abundantly. You deserve all the honor and praise. Now, I come to bless Your Holy Name; it all belongs to You, Father. You came giving me a spirit of, "I can." Yes, Lord, I can do all things through You, Christ, Who strengthens me. I am nothing without You, Jesus. You're worthy, Lord, Jesus! I praise You! I praise You! Hallelujah! A King is born. My joy is in having...More of You God. (Luke 1:5, Luke 2:20, 1 Kings 8:42, Psalm 47:7, Psalm 136:4, Luke 1:49, Revelation 21:5, 2 Corinthians 5:17, Isaiah 65:17, Isaiah 66:22, Philippians 4:13, 1 John 4:4)

Year One:

_____
_____
_____
_____
_____
_____
_____

Year Two:

_____
_____
_____
_____
_____

December 21

Forever and forever, I come to say thank You, Jesus. Today, Father, **I thank You for sending Your Son, Jesus**. I cannot thank You enough. Now, I can let go of the distractions of this world. **I'm preparing for what You are going to do, in my life**. I, first, want to celebrate Your birth, Jesus. You came to birth in me something new and amazing. You brought me a mighty long way, Lord. I'm letting go of my past; now, looking to the future. I'm looking at what this next hour, day, week, month, and year, will bring. **It will allow me to edify You, my King**. This is my sensational, spirit-filled, outpouring season, looking me straight in my face. **Upgrades and favor are on the way; it is going to be a turnaround season**. What the devil meant for evil, You are already working on turning it around, to my good. **I am taking back dominion, my territory**. I'm getting ready for my territory to grow and prosper. Hallelujah! I come to bless Your Name! I am like a caterpillar in a cocoon; later, I will come out crawling. But now, Lord, Jesus, I am getting ready to move to my next level/growth. I am getting ready to fly, like a beautiful butterfly. The sky is the limit as I walk with You, Jesus Christ, my Savior. I have a right to bless and praise You. I leap for joy, celebrating Your birth. I'm pressing into...More of You God.
(Philippians 3:13-14, 2 Corinthians 5:17-18, Isaiah 65:16, Isaiah 43:18, Colossians 1:13-14, Ephesians 1:11, Psalm 30:5, Genesis 6:8, Psalm 90:17, 2 Peter 1:3-4, Psalm 84:11, Isaiah 61:1-2)

Year One:

_____
_____
_____
_____

Year Two:

_____
_____
_____

367

December 22

Hallelujah! The wise men knew there was **something special about the light of Jesus**. They knew **this new-star was a special-star**. Christ Jesus was born; they knew this star would lead them to Jesus. Today, Lord, Jesus, I look to Your light. I will open my eyes and ears to You, allowing You to direct my path. **First, I'm engulfing myself in Your Word every day, followed by praying and praising You.** After I have this special time with You, I will sit quietly, waiting on You, Lord. Give me a Word, Lord, Jesus. Speak to me! Speak to me! I'm waiting on You, Jesus. I do not want to take another step without Your lead or approval. I submit unto You, Lord. I surrender! I surrender! **This is a season I will follow the star; the star is You, Lord, Jesus**. Lord, You are the light of the world. I have been in darkness; but You, Jesus, are the way, the truth, and the life. **With You, Jesus, my world is bright; my future is limitless.** The glory of the Lord is here! I'm loving on...More of You God.
(Proverbs 1:5, Proverbs 21:20, Genesis 41:8, Matthew 2:1-12, John 8:12, Isaiah 42:6, John 12:46, John 1:4-9, John 12:35-36, 2 Corinthians 4-6, Acts 22:9)

Year One:

_____

_____

_____

_____

_____

_____

Year Two:

_____

_____

_____

_____

_____

_____

December 23

As I celebrate this Christmas season, today, I'm reminded of the task Jesus' parents, Joseph and Mary had, trying to find a room. They were preparing for baby Jesus' birth to take place. There were no rooms available for them, so they ended up staying in an outdoor dirty animal stable. **Is this the proper way to treat the King, who is entering into this world to save all of our lives? Today, God is speaking to me, asking me to make room in my heart for Him.** As I first love Jesus, God will do the rest, in and through me. It's not up to others to try to convict my soul, with what are the principles of God. God says, all I have to do is seek Him first, and He will add all things to me. It is not about others trying to judge my personal relationship with God. God knows my heart, and You, Lord, Jesus, will deal with me, as You choose. Lord, God, I have a special place in my heart, just for You. An intimate relationship with You, is what my heart desires. My heart is open and willing, to fill up with...More of You God.
(Luke 2:1-20, Matthew 6:21, Proverbs 3:5, Romans 12:2, Proverbs 23:26, Psalm 51:10, Psalm 73:26, John 14:27, Matthew 5:8, Mark 6:52, Psalm 19:14, Psalm 26:2)

Year One:

_____
_____
_____
_____
_____
_____

Year Two:

_____
_____
_____
_____
_____
_____

December 24

God, today, as I celebrate this Christmas season, **I look at the lineage of Your Son, Jesus Christ**. How amazing, Jesus, You came from an imperfect family; yet, everything about You, Lord, is perfect. **Jesus, You are the "Son of David"; David was an adulterer. Also, David's son Solomon, he worshiped idols**. I believe, Lord, You are speaking to me and to Your people through Your lineage. I am imperfect; but still, I am a child of the Most High King. You're showing me, I am royalty, no matter what the world tries to claim or speak. **Through looking at Your lineage, Jesus, I see Rahab who was a prostitute, becoming the mother of Boaz, who married Ruth. From whose son, Obed, was the father of Jesse. Jesse is the father of David whose lineage, Jesus was born**. I see You're showing me, it doesn't matter where I come from, You still love me. Moreover, it doesn't matter what I have done or what situation I'm in; because, **God, You have a way of taking the lowly people, using us to do great things**. You have a way of taking the ordinary folks to fulfill Your purpose. Hallelujah! I can't stop praising on and working for...More of You God.
(Matthew 1:1-17, Luke 3:23-38, Romans 4:16, 2 Samuel 11-12, 1 Kings 11:4-7, Joshua 6:25, Acts 10:38, Galatians 6:9, Colossians 3:17, James 4:17, 1 Corinthians 1:26-31)

Year One:

_____
_____
_____
_____
_____
_____

Year Two:

_____
_____
_____
_____

December 25

Merry Christmas! **A Savior is born!** Today, is a day, I give gifts to those I love in memory of, Jesus Christ, the King, being born. I'm not really sure of what day You were born; but this is the day we celebrate, as a nation. I rejoice, in song, in word, and in deed; **I'm loving on, More of You, God!** Hallelujah! Hallelujah! Hallelujah! Jesus, You came down to earth as a man. Bearing all of my grievances, You wiped out the serpent, and You wiped away all of my tears. Your birth is the reason why I am free. I bless You, Lord, Jesus, with all of my soul. I magnify Your Holy Name! Jesus! Jesus! Jesus! You are Emanuel! You are with me, and I'm mighty grateful. **Jesus, You were born to be the Savior, of all peoples, for all times, and places.** Hallelujah God! You loved me so much, You sent Your only begotten Son, for me to have, life everlasting, with You. I must bow down before the King, Jesus. You are Worthy to be praised! Just as the shepherds came, bowing down at Your manger; I come with great joy. Hallelujah! Hallelujah! Hallelujah! **My Savior is born!** I rejoice with gratitude. I can't stop, won't stop, loving on...More of You God.
(Isaiah 7:14, Matthew 1:22-23, Jeremiah 31:7, Luke 19:37-38, 1 Chronicles 16:23-31, John 4:21-24, Psalm 99, Luke 2:8-20)

Year One:

_____
_____
_____
_____
_____
_____

Year Two:

_____
_____
_____
_____
_____

December 26

"Do this in remembrance of me", thus says, the Lord. Today, I reference the reason why You came to earth. **I honor You, by taking part in Holy Communion (the Lord's Supper).** When I take part in **eating the bread, which represents Your body and the drink, representing Your blood, I know, this is an expression of the love You have for Your people.** During this Christmas season, I'm grateful; You came to give me life more abundantly. At the cross, You shed Your blood to remove all sicknesses and diseases. Jesus, You put all of this on Your perfect healthy body; so now, I can be free of illnesses and disease. I can now, walk in divine health and authority. **Before I take Communion, I repent and ask You to cleanse, renew, and restore me, from all of my sins. As I take Your communion, I remember what You came and did for me, (the greatest gift of all).** Your Word says, <u>**I should take it as often as I think of You and what You accomplished for me**</u>. This means I can take it every day, if it's what You put on my heart; I can take it by myself or with others. As I take it, I'm empowered each and every time, because You reside inside of me with Your holy power. Now, I'm accessing/activating my faith and tapping into You, my Savior. I celebrate You, Lord, Jesus. Because of Your sacrifice and love for me. I have more power as I have...More of You God.

(John 6:53-58, 1 Corinthians 11:24-29, Luke 22:19-20, Matthew 26:26-28, Acts 2:42, John 6:33, Isaiah 53:5, Luke 24:30)

Year One:

_____
_____
_____
_____

Year Two:

_____
_____
_____
_____

December 27

Now, a couple days have passed and Christmas is officially over**, but, I am declaring it's not over.** **I'm continually putting my eyes totally on You, Jesus.** I look to You with <u>new eyes</u>. I honor and praise You for who You are, Lord, Jesus. **What can I offer You, Lord, God? What can I give?** Lord, I want to offer unto You, all of **the treasures I have.** You, Jesus, are so special to me. Father, I want to offer **all of my life to You**, Lord. Remove all selfishness and self-control desires away from me. Lord, let my desires and heart embrace whatever it takes to please You, Lord, Jesus. Lord, I adore You! I have high admiration and respect for You. Jesus, I give You all of my praise. All my praise and worship, belongs to You. Everything I have, I give it to You, Lord. **My heart is on fire for You, my Savior**. You came on this earth to take my bad and turn to my good. Now, I am a new creature in You and Lord.......Lord........Lord........I am so grateful and thankful unto You, King, Jesus. Death could not hold You down. You rose on the third day. Now I have been set free. I live and breathe to have...More of You God.

(2 Corinthians 9:7-8, Luke 12:33-34, 1 Timothy 6:17-19, 2 Corinthians 8:7, Proverbs 3:9-10, Matthew 6:21, Proverbs 18:16, Psalm 37:4, Nehemiah 8:10)

Year One:

_____

_____

_____

_____

_____

_____

Year Two:

_____

_____

_____

_____

_____

_____

December 28

There is only one way to find peace with You, God; through Your Son, Jesus Christ. Today, Lord, God, I have so much gratitude and appreciation unto You, Father. You made a way for me. You sent Your Son, to pay for my sins. Now, I can have a life everlasting with You, my Creator. I thank You, Lord, God, You do not look at my outward appearance; You look at my heart. Jesus, I have a heart for You, Lord, God. I want to do what is of Your way and Your will. Cleanse me, Lord, and make me whole. I am a failure without You, Jesus. **Because of Your unmerited favor and love for me, God, You sent Your Son, Jesus, to rescue me**. Yes, Jesus, I know, You love me dearly. As this New Year approaches, I realize, **I'm walking into a season of more than enough**. A season of plenty. A season of joy, peace, and love. What the enemy meant for evil, You are taking it, and turning it into my good. My attentiveness unto You, Lord, Jesus, must stay focused. This is what makes life worth living, pressing into...More of You God.

(Philippians 4:13, Isaiah 40:29-31, Psalm 119:28, Ephesians 6:10, Mark 12:30, 2 Corinthians 12:9-10, Psalm 28:7-8, Psalm 118:14)

Year One:

_____

_____

_____

_____

_____

_____

Year Two:

_____

_____

_____

_____

_____

December 29

Jesus, **You are the bridge to life**. Lord, God, You are my refuge. You keep me from all harm and danger. Today, during this special sacred season, I'm looking over my life. While on my highway to heaven and during my storms, You keep me wrapped up in Your wings, in Your secret place. Jesus, now, **You are transforming me**; the way I act, the way I think, and even the way I look, is different. As I move and grow day-by-day, the world is seeing a new me. Now, I am a new creature in You. All can see I am a reflection of You. I'm moving into my destiny, boldly. This is my time for divine transitioning. **My upcoming year is a time, Lord, God, where You are shifting my assignment; You're giving me greater influence and higher authority in Your Kingdom.** Lord, Jesus, thank You for coming and advancing me, into Your purpose. I see You, preparing me to be used in a mighty way, all for Your glory and Your kingdom. Jesus! Jesus! Jesus! Thank You for doing a new thing in me. As I continue to move to the next level, You reveal to me all You have for me. Savior, as I patiently wait to hear from…More of You God.

(Psalm 46:1-3, Deuteronomy 33:27, Psalm 27:5, Psalm 31:20, Proverbs 18:10, , Psalm 18:2, Isaiah 43:19, Philippians 3:13-14, Psalm 51:10, Colossians 3:1-4)

Year One:

_____
_____
_____
_____
_____

Year Two:

_____
_____
_____
_____
_____

December 30

The oppositions I have faced this year, have not been easy. However, today, I speak to You, Lord, Jesus; **the God, who backs the devil up off of me**. The enemy knows I am a threat to him. He knows You are preparing to take me higher with You, to build Your kingdom. I have been under attack; I'm in battle with spiritual warfare. But, I win with You, Lord, Jesus. **I have on my full armor; the battle is not mine, it is Yours, Lord**. Father, as You move me forward, Lord, God, I will feel the discomfort of being stretched and reshaped. I'm entering into new very unfamiliar territory. This new season, I can feel Your grace and mercy. You are putting a new and fresh anointing on me. Lord, Jesus, I will be patience; my timing is not Your timing. Moreover, **Your timing is on time**. Lord, everything You do is perfect. You are perfect in all of Your ways. I accept this new challenge and new position. I will do what You say, Lord. I will go where You tell me to go, Father, God. Lord, You are not a man who will lie. **You will finish this work You have begun in me**. I will keep my eyes focused on You, Lord, Jesus. I am ready and waiting to walk with...More of You God.
(2 Corinthians 2:11, Ephesians 6:12, Revelation 12:11, Isaiah 54:2, Jeremiah 18:3-4, Isaiah 29:16, Isaiah 45:9, Psalm 32:8, Jeremiah 29:11, John 15:2-6, Isaiah 64:8)

Year One:

_____
_____
_____
_____
_____

Year Two:

_____
_____
_____
_____

December 31

Lamb of God, today, I'm preparing for great things to occur in my life. As I walk forward into this New Year, this new endeavor, this new life-changing season, I'm expecting great things to transpire. **I have a spirit of expectancy**; I am a child of the Most High God. **This will be a year of receiving what man calls, the impossible. "It can't be so." says man, but "Yes", it is so with God on my side.** Yes, greatness is occurring with You, Lord, Jesus; You're guiding and directing me to places, I have never been. I'm moving on and moving up; You, God, have gone before me, to pave the way. Doors will open up for me this year, no man will be able to shut. **This new season will not be easy; it will be hard work and take lots of commitment.** But, it is going to be phenomenal, incredible, magnificent, and indescribable. I'm convinced, **You are calling me to greatness, making Your Name great in crooked places.** I'm expecting to be changed, create changes, and see changes. This new season is all about You, Lord, Jesus. You are the reason for the season. I'm preparing to hang tight, grasp onto, and ride with...More of You God.

(Revelation 12:11, Acts 3:5, Psalm 62:5, Acts 1:8, John 10:10, 1 Peter 2:18-25, Matthew 24:13, James 1:1-27, Genesis 1:28)

Year One:

_____
_____
_____
_____
_____
_____

Year Two:

_____
_____
_____
_____
_____

Made in the USA
Lexington, KY
09 December 2019